CW00797996

GRETE WAITZ' GUIDE TO RUNNING

GRETE WAITZ' GUIDE TO RUNNING

Grete Waitz
and Gloria Averbuch

Stanley Paul
London Melbourne Auckland Johannesburg

Stanley Paul & Co. Ltd

An imprint of Century Hutchinson Ltd

62–65 Chandos Place, London WC2N 4NW

Century Hutchinson Australia (Pty) Ltd
PO Box 496, 16–22 Church Street, Hawthorn, Melbourne, Victoria
3122

Century Hutchinson New Zealand Limited
PO Box 40-086, Glenfield, Auckland 10

Century Hutchinson South Africa (Pty) Ltd
PO Box 337, Bergvlei 2012, South Africa

First published as *World Class* in USA by Warner Books 1986
First published in Great Britain 1987

© Grete Waitz and Gloria Averbuch 1986

Printed and bound in Great Britain by Anchor Brendan Ltd.,
Tiptree, Essex

ISBN 0 09 172683 2

This book is sold subject to the condition that it shall not by way of
trade or otherwise be lent, resold, hired out or otherwise circulated
without the publisher's prior consent in any form of binding other than
that in which it is published and without a similar condition including
this condition being imposed on the subsequent publisher.

to Jack,
for all the years and all the miles

Grete

Acknowledgments

Special thanks to Paul Friedman for invaluable contributions, research, and support; and to Kristen Damsgaard, our "Norwegian connection," for gathering information and contributing advice.

Special thanks from Grete: To my brothers, Jan and Arild Andersen, for their support and help in my career, especially by doing all those hard workouts with me! Also to my coaches Ragnar Nilsen (1965–69), Asbjørn Strandskog (1969–75), and Johan Kaggestad (since 1983).

More thanks to all our friends in the United States who've been so helpful and supportive over the years, and to everyone who worked as hard to make this book happen as I do to run races.

WORLD CLASS

Contents

Introduction (Grete Waitz) *1*
Introduction (Gloria Averbuch) *6*
1. *The Long and Winding Road—My Career from 1965 to 1978* *11*
2. *Life at the Top* *20*
3. *Fitness Norwegian Style* *41*
4. *For the Beginner—Basic Running and Fitness* *47*
5. *For the Intermediate—The Basics of Training and Racing* *66*
6. *For the Advanced—Training and Competitive Racing* *95*
7. *Mind Power* *120*
8. *The Marathon* *128*
9. *Balancing Your Sport and Your Life* *146*
10. *Coaching* *162*
11. *The Training Diary* *166*
12. *On Women* *182*
13. *Diet and Nutrition* *202*
14. *Restoration Therapy* *218*
Appendices *236*
Recommended Reading *249*
Index *253*

Introduction

Shortly after the 1984 Olympics, a proposal was made to me by a group of American acquaintances. It was the same proposal that Norwegian publishers had made many times before: to write a book. My initial response to the Americans was the same I had given to the Norwegians, the same response I had given to other types of endless offers, and the same answer I had given my husband, Jack, when he first mentioned my running a marathon: NO.

This is always my first reaction to anything that sounds unreasonable. When I first said no to the 26.2-mile marathon, it was because I'd never run farther than twelve miles. Now I was being asked to write an entire book, when I could barely be coaxed into being interviewed for a three-page magazine article! For a race, even a marathon, I could be persuaded more easily. That's something I understand; I know the language, so to speak. But a book—that was an unknown, out of my territory. I couldn't train for that as I do for a race. It wasn't tangible: in miles or meters, with a finish line. Who wouldn't be wary of something so foreign?

Actually, I had been part of one other book and knew just how much work it took—and that wasn't even my own book. Also, as a world-class athlete, the greatest portion of my time and energy must necessarily go to my running. So there were any number of reasons

1

to say no. But of all the people trying to convince me, there was one who seems to have a special talent for succeeding. "I'll help you," vowed Jack. "I'll do a lot of the work." That's what he always said, and he had used a similarly cunning approach to convince me to run the marathon.

This book was an idea that Gloria had held on to for two years, during the time I had put everything else off for the Olympics, and she obviously wasn't going to give it up easily. Now we sat over coffee: a group of literary people and Jack, intent on persuading me. "It's okay," I said, cutting short the well-prepared pleas. "I've decided to do it."

For years I have been approached in Norway to do an autobiography, an "inside-out," detailed life story. But I feel that Norwegians already know what's worth knowing about me. They have followed my life and career, dissecting every scrap, for the past sixteen years. Any other revelations would just be for the sake of gossip, and for that purpose I'm not willing to discuss the details of my private life.

But in America there are still things to tell. I was a track runner for ten years before I ever stepped up to a starting line in the United States, and although I have discussed my private life in the book as well as my running career, it is not for the sake of gossip. It is because I believe that part of my life, as difficult as it was to discuss, will enlighten the reader and contribute meaning and validity to my advice.

Why this book: neither solely autobiography nor solely training manual, but rather a bit of both? First of all, the bookstores are filled with either life stories or training programs. Second, running has become a lot more than just a sport; it's a total lifestyle. My book, I felt, had to discuss both the elements of training and lifestyle, and how to blend them successfully, sensibly, and permanently. For this reason, it had to be based on my personal experience, on how I have done those things through the many ups and downs I have experienced since I took my first run at age twelve.

Another important aspect of this book is its timing. I chose to write it at this point for a specific reason: to convey the reflections of my twenty-year career, yet to include the immediacy that can be communicated only while I am still competing. It is important to be able to express the emotions, the conflicts, and the aspirations while they are still so strongly with me. What you will read are not just memories, but the life I am still living.

One of the main goals of the book is to take the mystique out of the sport. After all, I got to be world-class without much scientific knowledge—no physiological studies of my heart, lungs, or muscles, or sophisticated professional coaching. I want to prove it doesn't have to be so complicated and to answer that one enduring question that will be asked as long as there are runners: what's the big secret to success? The bottom line, as far as I'm concerned, is simply hard work and enjoyment.

On the other hand, while I may have reached the top somewhat haphazardly, I haven't stayed there that way. I have learned a lot along the way, not only from my own experiences but from other people's as well. In the world of running and fitness, there is an art to consistency and longevity, and much of this book centers not just on the hows and whys of running, fitness, and competition, but also on making them part of a permanent, lifelong activity.

I have shunned the attention and rejected the title of "role model"— genuinely feeling that I did not fit the part and that I didn't want to, either. But I've changed. After twenty years I feel I *do* have something valuable to say. I see now that there are worthwhile contributions I can and want to make, and that I am qualified to make them. I've turned down numerous commercial offers throughout my career, to a large extent because they have compromised my beliefs or personality, or involved me in a superficial way: my name, my face, or a list of my running accomplishments. This book is a chance to do what I believe in, to reach people by speaking about my own views, in my own voice. And it was especially important to do it for runners and for those many people who have supported and inspired me throughout the years. Now I feel I can give them something back.

But life is practical, and so is getting words down on paper. There were some less philosophical reasons I agreed to do this particular book. Jack and I had discussed it and felt that, first of all, because Gloria knew me so well we would not have to start from scratch, to tell her everything. Also, as a serious runner, she shares with us a common understanding. She endured my nervousness under pressure, my need not to be pushed, and my daily priorities as a competitive athlete. There was a lot I knew I didn't have to explain or apologize for.

I doubt anything or anyone could have prepared me for what was to come once the writing process began. Blending my language and culture with an American approach was more difficult than I had imagined. Norwegians simply don't live and think in the same, or even similar, ways as Americans. Everything seemed so complicated. "Why, why, why?"—I thought I'd never hear the end of that question! Every race needed a feeling, every aspect of training a special rationale, every thought, habit, even morsel of food, a magic purpose. I had put myself through years of training, but never through such self-analysis! At first all I could focus on were the headaches I'd get after the long hours of examining my experiences. It was more tiring than my training runs!

Perhaps the most difficult aspect was explaining complicated ideas in English. People assume that because I can converse fairly well I am sufficiently fluent, but it's one thing to answer questions at a press conference and entirely another to do an in-depth evaluation of an entire career. Needless to say, it would have been difficult enough to do in Norwegian. At times the feelings and concepts, the shades of meaning, seemed impossible to express in my own language, let alone a foreign one.

But the work challenged me, and seeing the book take shape took my mind off the fatigue. Writing this book has been so much more illuminating than I had ever anticipated. It is as if the process had pulled out drawers in my mind, drawers that had been closed for many years. There was so much we had forgotten. Gloria made Jack and me think about things that likely would have stayed locked away in those drawers permanently. Going back to memories of my childhood and my first years in running, I could savor and appreciate my achievements in a way I never have. It seems there has never been time to reflect. Life has always been on to the next goal. Now I realize what it means to be an author: to reflect and examine, to see my experiences in a new light, to gain new understanding, to learn from my mistakes, and to take pride in my accomplishments.

I must say here how impressed both Jack and I are with what Gloria has found in me and my career. I honestly didn't see the entire story filling more than ten pages, and if it had been left to me, that's likely how long this book would have been. What also amazed me was how I could learn so much about myself through someone else's eyes. There were often times I would read new sections, not quite immediately recognizing in black and white a thought or an emotion. "Yes, that's me. That's how I feel, what I believe!" I would say aloud in surprise.

When you live and work with your body every day, physical expression becomes your language—not words, but time, pace, distance. Hard work, pain, joy, success, even failure, have always been expressed by medals and trophy cabinets, or by other people's words in newspapers and magazines. Yet looking at these pages is somewhat like looking at those symbols of my running career, and I feel the same positive anticipation for you to read them that I feel before a race for which I have trained hard and am confident I will run well.

For years, despite the cameras and the public attention, I have remained the same shy Grete, doubtful of having anything to say, reluctant to do so even if I have. No longer. Now, through the hours of self-examination—Jack, Gloria, and me sitting at more tables than United Nations negotiators—I have the words. In fact, after sixteen years as a world-class athlete, I have plenty of them!

What will success mean for me with this book? It obviously can't be breaking the tape as the first runner across the finish line or seeing a fast time on a clock. Success will mean that the book is well received, that it inspires and helps you in the way in which I intend it. This success has become just as important to me as any race, any medal.

—Grete Waitz
October 1985

Introduction

"Oh, I love it! It's great!" said Grete mockingly, throwing her arms out like a basketball guard for effect. "That's how you Americans talk," she teased with a laugh. I sat silently, unable to deny her accusations. Naked emotion is untypically Norwegian, yet Grete finds displays of it so common among Americans that she is never sure when, or if, it is genuine.

Contrary to her Norwegian manner—reticent and stoic—the private Grete has plenty of her own emotion. In fact, one wonders how she has withstood it all. For every race or hard workout, the intensity of her nervousness and will to succeed seems exhausting. People don't see this emotion when she crosses the finish line; but it's what drives her, makes her a winner. The emotions Grete doesn't hide are what sustain her beyond running: basic happiness, satisfaction, and an overwhelming love for her family and her life in Norway. She's too modest to take credit for making history as an athlete, but not too shy to show affection for Jack—lovingly teasing him, walking arm-in-arm—and to credit him endlessly and publicly for her success. And when Grete does show emotion, it is rare and serious—no idle gesture. You can believe it. One day, as she cheered loudly for her nephews in a race, she suddenly turned to me and said with feeling, "I love them as if they were my own."

I first heard of Grete Waitz when the rest of America did: on a warm day in October 1978, when she stunned the sports world by running a world record in her first marathon in New York. Like every runner and so many women, I was proud and inspired. I began writing about her in 1979, compiling a virtual library of notes and cassette tapes. Her European manner and background intrigued me. She had her own style, class, charisma. Her words had weight. She was not one to open up spontaneously, but over the years we would stray from the subject of running and, as two women of similar ages and interests, get to talking in general. I was always pleasantly surprised by her humor and increasingly impressed by her common sense and wisdom. Hers was, I realized, the unique experience and insight of a champion.

Grete provided the quote for the cover of my first book, *The Woman Runner*, and her endorsement of my work has meant a great deal to me. For several years I had hoped to write this book with her, capturing her qualities as a champion, embellished with the flashes of humor and emotion I had seen. When she finally agreed, she announced to the publisher that the book could be done only on one condition: that I be the writer. That honor has been worth a lot, both as a runner and as a writer.

Writing this book began with lunch in the kitchen of her home, a large, natural-wood dwelling located on a hill above the calm waters of the Oslo Fjord. Over a typical meal of Norwegian fish pâté on wholegrain bread, she did her parody of American emotion. "Okay, let's compromise," I finally offered. "In addition to the training advice, you throw in your experiences—all of them, since childhood, and no holds barred. I'll use your thoughts, in our joint voice, and add a bit of that 'American' you find so amusing: the emotion, the analysis, the language." Surely that naked emotion can't be all bad, I tried telling her with conviction (being especially careful to keep my hands from making those emphatic gestures!). By the time we got to dessert—biscuits with geitost, a naturally sweet goat cheese that is Grete's favorite food—it was agreed. Thus began the book — a collaboration between two women: a world-class runner who's been at the top of her sport for over twenty years, and a writer who has followed her as both a journalist and a runner.

So began the conversations and taping that would become the heart of a yearlong project. The difficult part was phrasing the personal questions gently, respectfully; the awkward part was trying to follow her around in a way that didn't seem to hint at hero worship. But Grete answered the questions candidly and made the trappings of her fame seem so simple. Could I possibly photograph her with one of the medals? I once asked shyly. She took them out from her kitchen cabinet, where they share a place with the cups and plates. I chose the Olympic silver, and putting it around her neck she held up the leek she was preparing to cook. There she stood, posing with that large green onion and her medal. "Is this okay?" she asked, laughing.

At worst, I feared she would close the door on those parts of her life that were understandably private, leaving me to construct part fiction. So I asked the hard questions first, wondering aloud how much she would be willing to put in print. To say it was not painful for her to speak about some things would mean her words meant less than they did. Often, she would answer difficult questions while distracted by driving, folding clothes, or washing dishes. It was easier than speaking face-to-face. Sometimes she blushed or shifted her weight uneasily as she spoke. But the answers came, remarkably detailed. "She has never talked about these things before," Jack confided one day. It was then I knew she had made the decision to give the book 100 percent of herself. Knowing what that meant for Grete the runner, I knew what it would mean for Grete the author. My previous doubts disappeared.

Jack and Kristen Damsgaard, one of Grete's first coaches and still a close friend, took me around Oslo to speak to her coaches, teachers, doctors, and Norwegian Olympic Committee colleagues. They extolled Grete with phrases like "ambassador for Norway" and "the best representative of our society." They spoke continually with that rare quality reserved for only the most serious Norwegian intentions: emotion— continually using words like "love" and "respect" to describe how Norway feels about its running star.

I had always admired Grete, but as the days and weeks went by I realized there is even more to respect than her greatness as a runner— in deed and in soul. Her quality as a person comes through in her well-chosen words, her ability to laugh at herself, her continual struggle for excellence, and her magnanimity. When she wasn't running or fulfilling obligatory endorsements, she was busy helping her brothers with their work in the printing business, meeting with the Olympic

Committee, or planning for the Grete Waitz Run for women. One day she and Jack drove seventy miles each way in order to spend a few hours talking and running with the talented teenage girls she supports through the Grete Waitz Foundation.

Grete, Jack, and I passed the hours in several states and countries. Often, they pondered and, like archaeologists, dug up and dusted the memories. Weaved into the English was the Norwegian that flew back and forth to express complicated thoughts and clarify every meaning. Eventually, they stopped excusing themselves to translate, and I learned a few words and phrases by osmosis. Although I constructed the topics, added ideas or research, and suggested some of the implications of Grete's experiences, the book had to be in her first-person voice. The life, feelings, opinions, and observations could be only hers. As Grete once said about being in a race, "It's a world you live in alone." The same is true of her experiences. Only Grete could have the memories and the visions; the words merely express them.

Layers of the past were uncovered, much in the way one might expect when intimate lives are shared. One day Jack took me around Oslo on his own, showing me the sights of early life in his and Grete's working-class families, and explaining the deep impact of Nazi occupation on the lives of Norwegians. He pointed to a dark prison on an Oslo hill where his father had spent two years as punishment for working with the Resistance. Grete took me to the patch of grass where she took her first run, showed me her scrapbooks, and shared the story of a tragic girlhood love.

Yet despite how well I often thought I knew her, Grete was still an enigma: reserved and serious at times, yet remarkably funny and flippant at others. Sometimes she seemed so unapproachable, and then she would startle me with her gestures of intimacy: turning up the collar of my coat against the cold, or bringing me the goat's cheese from Norway of which I had grown fond. During her warm-up before the Sentrumsløpet 10km (ten-kilometer) in Oslo, she appeared particularly aloof. I kept my distance, not daring to interrupt her race ritual. Suddenly she approached me. "Can you do me a favor?" she asked with a nervous gaze of urgency, her skin coated with sweat. Lifting her singlet in back and handing me a length of dental floss, she requested that I tie her bra straps together to keep them from slipping.

Her desire for privacy is still strong, part of the desperate need for solitude that most famous people have. She admits that her nervousness and preoccupation will be with her as long as she competes, as long as her thoughts must always be elsewhere—on the next workout or upcoming race. Yet even the most important thing in her life, her running, is always good for a laugh. At the mention of the day's hard workout, she would pose theatrically, lying on a chair with her limbs scattered, feigning death. How do you feel about the television broadcasts of your races? I once asked. To my surprise she shrugged and said she had never seen them. "What for?" she said, laughing. "I was there. I know what happened."

The best of times were those when we got off the subject. She would show me her clothes closet, and we would giggle like girls over our mutual timidity at being as stylish as we sometimes wish. "I wear powder," she confessed. "Otherwise, my nose shines like a light." "When this is over," I told her, still laughing about her nose and enjoying the departure from our usual conversations, "I swear I'll never ask you another question about running." I'm looking forward to being just friends.

In these pages I am sure you, too, will find the funny, intelligent, thoughtful Grete, as well as the Grete whose talent and grace have endeared her to millions of people everywhere. You will discover her skill as an athlete, her superior qualities as a person, and her wisdom as both a woman and a champion. You will learn from her so much about life and sport, as I have learned from knowing her and writing this book with her.

I hope Grete will smile when I say about our book — "Oh, I love it! It's great!" and when I express, in my oh-so-American way, the love and respect I have for two fine friends who made this book possible: Grete and Jack Waitz.

—Gloria Averbuch
October 1985

1

The Long and Winding Road—My Career from 1965 to 1978

I have always loved competition. As a little girl, I would pit myself against a bus or car and try to outrun it. Or when I was given chores to do, I would time myself, seeing how fast I could run to the grocery store and back. As children, we used to play cops and robbers, and it was from this game that I sensed for the first time that I had some running ability. When I was a robber, no one wanted to be the cop to chase me. Even the boys couldn't catch me, as I simply wore them down by continuing to run for such a long time.

My first training run was quite informal, to say the least. I was twelve years old when I laced up an old pair of spikes that were lying around the house. To this day I don't know who they belonged to, but I think they were from before the Second World War! Behind the house was a length of grass on which I ran back and forth, establishing my first regular training regimen.

Two months later, I decided I wanted something more organized than my solo sessions on the lawn. This meant I would have to join a sports club, as the schools had no organized running program. My older brother Jan already belonged to a track and field club in Oslo, but girls were not allowed. On my behalf, Jan spoke to our neighbor Terje Pedersen, the world-record holder in the javelin. Pedersen's club allowed girls, and just the fact he was in it—the neighborhood hero whom I greatly admired—was all the inspiration I needed. So I packed an athletic bag and together with a girl friend made the twenty-minute walk to the club, as we had no money for the bus. With that sense of excitement all children feel for a new adventure, I entered the locker room of the Vidar Sports Club, of which I am still a member today.

Running was just one of many hobbies and activities I had as a child. But of them all, piano lessons were most insisted upon by my parents. After two sons, they finally had a daughter, and they wanted a traditional model. Every Sunday I was dressed in my best and told to be dainty, not to dirty my finery. The piano was part of their little-girl image that included pink dresses and matching hair ribbons in my carefully curled blond hair.

But I hated the piano, which I had to suffer through for most of my childhood. When it came to practice, I would play and cry at the same time. I so disliked it that I would coerce my girl friends into pretending to be my mother, phoning to excuse me from piano and, later, acting lessons. The fact that these lessons were forced on me likely contributed to my loathing, but I think I also hated them so intensely because they frustrated me. Although I was a good student, I was an active child, with a lot of excess energy. I needed and enjoyed a physical activity, preferably one that involved competition.

I was thirteen years old when I won my first prize in competition, a type of ball-throwing event we do in Norway. It was exhilarating to have finally placed high enough to get a prize, as I had always finished in the back of the pack. It was also important to have proof for my parents: "I'm good," that prize seemed to announce. On the way home to show it to them, I dug my hand into my bag at least ten times, feeling for the award—a little silver spoon—to make sure it had not somehow disappeared.

This small success, and my ability to outrun my peers, had given me some confidence when I joined the club. However, I obviously had too high an opinion of my ability, because in my first races I was dead last. Of course, it didn't help that the longest distances we raced were 60 and 100 meters. I have never been a sprinter. It was only some years later when by coincidence I was put in a 300-meter cross-country race that I placed high enough to be noticed. But losing had never kept me from faithfully going to the club. In addition to my running (as well as high jump, long jump, shot put, and hurdles), I enjoyed the atmosphere. Somehow it enabled me to open up. The shy, quiet schoolgirl became chatty, fun-loving, and rowdy. I was even kicked out of the gym a few times for making a disturbance. The club was also part of my social life, and as a typical fourteen-year-old teenager, I'd fallen in love with one of the boys.

It was through the older boys in the club that I soon found my niche in running. The serious male runners, most of whom were about twenty years old, consented to let me come along on their longer runs (about six miles). It was tough for a teenage girl, but I kept up the 6:30-per-mile pace with considerable effort, determined to continue training with them. I went to their sessions regularly and doggedly put myself through that routine. It was then I realized I was a distance runner.

There is something about a challenge that has always brought out the fighter in me. Ironically, my first challenge in running was not a fellow competitor or a clock, but my parents. Initially, they weren't supportive of my efforts. To this day they don't recall an incident that I so clearly remember as it held such great significance for me. It is as vivid in my mind as if it had happened yesterday, rather than over twenty years ago. My parents wanted me to stay home from running practice to do chores. But skipping practice was where I drew the line; I refused to miss it. "Why bother with all this running?" my mother asked. "You're not going to be a running star, anyway." It hit me like a brick. As obedient as I usually was, this time I defied them. I grabbed my athletic bag and fled the house, vowing to myself that I would prove them wrong. When I became Norwegian Junior Champion, they finally realized I was serious. They even took me to buy an athletic bag and shoes. We made peace; there were no more protests. Most important, they let me drop piano lessons!

I won my first race when I was fourteen, a 400-meter cross-country event, considered a long distance at that time. Soon after, my brother Arild built me my first trophy case. At sixteen years old, I became the Norwegian Junior Champion in the 400 and 800 meters. It was with great pride that I was greeted by schoolmates who mentioned seeing my picture in the newspaper, which became one of the first clippings in the scrapbooks my parents have filled over the years. I made my first national senior team that year and went to Canada to compete. It was my first trip outside Scandinavia, and, quite simply, I was thrilled. Being chosen to make this trip, and the experience of it, motivated me to get serious about my running. I had come far, fast. I knew I was young and could develop my ability. I dropped my other hobbies and activities and concentrated on just running and school-work.

In 1971, when I was seventeen, I had my first experience in an international championship, the European Championships in Hel-sinki. It was a bitter one. Having to stand alone in the tunnel for a half hour waiting for my race was something for which I had not been prepared. I learned a lot more at this meet, and I got a lot older. In the summer of that year, I had set Norwegian records in the 800 and 1,500 meters. The Norwegian journalists, no doubt like press every-where, placed enormous pressure on me to succeed. They had over-rated me (or underrated the competition!), which proved to make things even more difficult. I ran terribly, but worse than my perfor-mance was the reaction of my countrymen. When I stepped off the track, the coach and team officials kept their distance. Perhaps they thought I wanted to be alone, but, on the contrary, what I desperately needed was support. I had lost before, but never had losing been so painful. Was this "big time" international athletics, I wondered, some-thing for which to work and dream? I escaped to the bathroom, where I cried for two hours. I was disappointed, perplexed, angry, and only seventeen years old.

Down but far from defeated, my bitterness fed my desire to excel. Just as with my parents, this denial of support strengthened my de-termination. It was not just coincidence that when, as a thirteen-year-old, I was assigned a school composition on "The Person I Most Ad-mire," I had chosen Wilma Rudolph, the woman who had overcome childhood polio to become the hero of the 1960 Olympics. One of my most enduring memories is of the day of the closing ceremonies at the Championships. As we marched through the pouring rain, the scoreboard flashed TO ROME IN 1974, the site of the next European Championships. "I'm going to do well there," I said to myself. "I'm going to show these people."

The greatest challenge in these years, however, was not on the track, but rather in my personal life. My boyfriend and coach of two years was the clubmate I'd had a crush on when I was fourteen. At eighteen, I was in love with and very dependent on this strong-willed twenty-four-year-old. In the winter of 1972 he became sick. But his strength and my youth were all the more reason that when he went into the hospital I simply assumed he would come out well, and we would live "happily ever after."

Soon I witnessed his once athletic body become appallingly thin. He was being consumed by cancer. I remember my mother telling me, "Surely you must realize he will not come out." I refused to believe it. I was young; he was young; what did we know of dying? "Of course he'll come out," I said. I spent every day in that hospital, doing my homework while my boyfriend slept. I made it through graduation and, despite it all, still managed to retain my first-place class ranking. In my boyfriend's last month, his mother asked the doctor to tell me what she could not bring herself to say: that I was watching him die.

After he died, my mother tried to console me. "Your suffering won't help anyone," she said, urging me to realize that my own world had not ended, that there was so much to look forward to in my life, and that I would get over it. But it was as if I were frozen, in shock. And from that time, something did change. I was left forever with a memory, and a pain and a sadness for him that such a young life had ended. To this day I still dream about him occasionally. The dreams are so real, it's as if I believe he is still alive. In one of them he walks into the room, and I wonder what to do with this apparent conflict: I am now married to Jack.

After my boyfriend had died, I lost the desire even to eat. My weight dropped, and I became ill. I felt devastated, empty. I saw no reason to do anything, let alone run, and could just as well have given it up for good. It was my boyfriend's group of friends from the Vidar Club who eventually pulled me out of my slump. They got me out of the house, kept me occupied, took me to dinner (my brother Arild even took me to discos), and brought me to the club to run. I used that running to help me forget, to help me begin to do other things, to try to live normally again. I had first been introduced to one of the older members of this group when I was twelve, and later my boyfriend and I had double-dated with him. His name was Jack Waitz.

* * *

The 1972 Olympics, in Munich, marked a turning point in my life. Slowly I was learning to live with what had happened. After my boyfriend died, I had thought, "No Olympics for me." I had dropped out of one qualifying race, too physically weak and depressed to finish. But fortuitously, on one of the last opportunities to qualify I just made the team.

Simply being at the Olympics was the important thing. Running was secondary. Although I ran a personal best of 4:16 in the 1,500 meters, I didn't place well. What I did gain, however, was the experience. Just to jog around in the tunnel, waiting to come out on the track in the stadium, was overwhelming for an eighteen-year-old. Then there was the atmosphere: the opening ceremony, life in the Olympic Village, and seeing the athletes from around the world. I was so young and so swept away, especially by the unlimited supply of food! Paradise was a twenty-four-hour cafeteria and all the soda and candy bars we could eat supplied to our rooms. Like many novice Olympians whose regimented lifestyle suddenly crumbles, I gained five pounds. I left Munich three weeks after I had arrived, the heaviest I have ever been. But I left feeling it was worth it to be a runner. I'm glad I realized that, even if it meant getting fat!

At this age, I was still too young to fully comprehend some things, and terrorism was among them. The murder of the Israeli athletes in Munich left me perplexed, sad, and frightened. It happened only 200 yards from where I was staying, and I called home to Jack for reassurance. Yet despite how close I was to it, in another sense I felt very far away. Even though I attended the memorial service in the stadium, I didn't grasp the magnitude of what had happened. Years later, when security became such an integral feature of the 1984 Olympics, I was struck by what a horrible tragedy Munich really was.

Politics was again the focus of the Games in 1976, when the African countries boycotted. I identified with the disappointment of the athletes, as I knew how hard I had worked to be there and could imagine how I would feel if the government of Norway were to call me home. When I spoke to Mike Boit of Kenya, a leading contender for a gold medal, I understood the tears that accompanied his words. By now I realized how easy it was to use sports as a political background. It doesn't cost anything. It's only the athletes' careers that are sacrificed. So it was no great surprise when the Moscow Olympics, in 1980, and Los Angeles, in 1984, became more of the same.

In 1972 I began a winning streak in Norway that was to last twelve years. The following year, 1973, was a good one in both my personal and my running life, which I was learning go hand in hand. I moved in with Jack, now my steady boyfriend and training partner. We weren't ready to get married, but living together certainly saved on commuting time. My parents weren't exactly thrilled with the idea, but I sold it to them with a speech on how much time I was saving and swore the arrangement would last only for the summer. However, by fall I had spent all summer slowly moving my things into Jack's apartment. I was studying hard in teacher's college, which I felt lucky to be attending as it is extremely difficult to gain entry. I rode to school every day on my Vespa motor scooter, trying to keep a straight face when I would overhear the neighbors gossip. "There's the runner. She's living with the old man," they would whisper. Jack was all of twenty-five, six years older than I.

I was the Athlete of the Year in Norway after an unexpected bronze medal in the 1,500 meters in the 1974 European Championships, in Rome. No one had anticipated my success, but it was no surprise to me. I had not forgotten the vow I made on that rainy day in Helsinki four years before.

In the summer of 1975 Jack and I were married. We made our arrangement legal with hardly a disruption in our lives. Running was there, as always, to make things interesting. The morning of the wedding we got lost on a long run, and I barely made it to the hairdresser. The day after the wedding it was back to the track for a hard interval workout—such a romantic honeymoon!

I had finally fully recovered from a nagging knee injury caused when I crashed with the Vespa in 1974. With the help of Jack's coaching advice, I was ranked number one in the world in 1975 for the 1,500 and 3,000 meters, and ran my first world record in the 3,000. All this made me a hot news item in the Norwegian press before the 1976 Olympics, in Montreal. Again, with their lack of understanding, the press believed that my warning not to talk medals was mere modesty, despite the fact I assured them it was actually sheer realism. The

Russian women were running sub-four minutes for 1,500 meters, and I would practically have to fly to beat them all. My goal in Montreal, a more realistic one, was to reach the final.

I was in a tough semifinal, one that was later protested for being too heavily weighted with the favorites. I didn't make the final, as just having made it to the semifinal was an accomplishment in itself. My heat turned out to be a history-maker. In fact, it made *The Guinness Book of World Records*. There we are in a finish-line photo, five girls abreast, all finishing within two tenths of a second of one another!

These Olympics were a bitter disappointment to me. I had trained longer and harder than I ever had—undoubtedly too much it turned out—and had juggled that twice-a-day running around two hours of commuting on buses and trains every day to my new job as a teacher, at which I also worked hard, determined to make a good name for myself. The press, as always, added to this already enormous pressure, creating a weight that threatened to crush me. Despite my warnings, the Norwegian people were led to simply assume I would win. I became a victim of the Norwegian expression "a silver medal is defeat"—if you don't win, you lose. Although I had never run faster in my life (setting a Scandinavian 1,500m record in the process), it wasn't enough. Overwhelmed not so much by the failure to meet my own expectations as by the reaction of the press, I walked back to my room in tears— first from disappointment, then from anger.

As at so many other times in my running career, my defiance surfaced. I was tired from training and leading such a busy life, tired of having to bear the pressure and come through for others. I decided to run on my own, without the support of the Norwegian Federation scholarship, responsible only to myself. Next time, if I was going to do the hard work, I was going to do it for myself. If I were to succeed, I would do it for myself as well.

After a season of cutting back my running, competing in cross-country skiing, and playing some team handball, I felt good again. I was rested, enjoyed my running, and got back my confidence and my hunger to compete. My move had been the right one. My times that year were personal bests, and in the inaugural World Cup, in 1977, I won the gold medal in the 3,000 meters in one of the best races of my life.

The press was at it again, however, for the 1978 European Championships, in Prague. Their interviews and my answers were beginning to sound like people trying to communicate in different languages. "Is the silver medal okay if you don't get the gold?" they wanted to know. "Hey, wait a minute," I told them. "I have to run first!" The Eastern Europeans would bring their famous finishing kicks to the race, and I knew if they were still with me with 200 meters to go, I would be in trouble. Sure enough, I got "only" the bronze medal. The Norwegian paper ran a big headline the following day: SORRY NORWAY it read, above a picture of me pointing thumbs down.*

At this point I already had a relatively long and successful career. Through running I had grown up, seen some of the world, and experienced my share of ups and downs. I could have just as well retired, and I strongly considered it. Track had been a wonderful career, but an erratic one as well. There were months and years I trained so hard—at one point running as many as 125 miles in one week—that I'd cry from fatigue. From 1974 to 1976 I didn't miss one day of training. At this time I felt that no matter how much I trained I wasn't going to get any faster on the track, nor was I going to avoid getting outkicked by the Eastern Europeans.

But Jack had been reading too many running magazines and started trying to talk me into running a marathon. Craziness, I told him— it's too long. I'd never run more than even twelve miles. But he kept at it. It would be our first and only chance to see America, he said enticingly. Although I was fairly prominent in Europe, when I came to the United States for the first time, in 1978, I was an unknown. It was no wonder. Who had ever heard of a track runner lining up for the start of the New York City Marathon?

---

*I think it gives some insight into the pressure and difficulty I felt in dealing with the press by illustrating its significance in Norway. Oslo alone has seven daily papers, and, according to the 1985 World Almanac, daily newspaper circulation in Norway is 479 per 1,000 population. By contrast, in the United States it is 279 per 1,000 population.

2

Life at the Top

WORLD RECORDS

"How far is twenty-six miles?" my fourteen-year-old students asked on my return to school after the New York City Marathon in 1978. It is the distance from Oslo to another Norwegian town, I told them. "How many times did you stop?" they asked in amazement. They understood as much about the event as I had when I lined up at the start. After all, since the farthest I had ever run was twelve miles, I wasn't even sure I could finish a marathon. So my world record was almost as much of a surprise to me as it was to everyone else. The real surprise, though, was how much that day changed our lives.

Despite my setting a world record, after all, it was only a race. I had won races before and set plenty of records, including a world record. It certainly wasn't as if a record had suddenly changed my life. After my first world record in the 3,000 meters, I had realized how little difference it made, at least to me. I came home and thought, "Well, the house is still the same." Then I looked in the mirror and said, "I'm still the same. What's different? It's only that yesterday I wasn't a record holder, but today I am." It wasn't earthshaking. It didn't really change my life or who I was.

After the marathon, life went back to normal, or so it seemed at first. I didn't realize the importance attached to that race until a few months later when I received an invitation to attend a *Runner's World* road race and clinic in California. It wasn't the invitation that seemed so extraordinary; it was what happened when I explained to Bob Anderson, then publisher of the magazine, that I was unable to come because I couldn't cancel a family vacation. He responded by offering to bring all six of us from Norway! I couldn't believe the organizers would pay so much money. It struck me just how much they really wanted me, and all because of that marathon.

Offers, opportunities, travel—a whole new world opened up from road racing. I had been a world-class track runner for years, but the popularity and exposure of big road races put my achievements in a new category. Victories and records: I couldn't believe the doors those minutes and seconds suddenly opened. Although it was both surprising and flattering that Americans saw it otherwise, the marathon record didn't mean much to me, as the tough competition was still on the track.

The *Runner's World* race was the first in a series of invitations and offers that attached an importance to these records I have never fully been able to appreciate. Records have always seemed so much more glamorous to others than to me, because I know what they cost— and it's a high price. Besides, I've never been a runner motivated by breaking records. I'm probably different in that respect from many runners who set time goals. My goal is to win and to improve.

The joy of breaking a record seems forever overshadowed by the pressure, the nerves, and the effort. In fact, sometimes when I break a record or win an important race, it's as if I had lost. Of course I'm happy, but I also feel a kind of emptiness. I plan and train and dream for so long, and then suddenly it's over. Instead of an addition, it's as if something has been taken away. It's like getting the pot of gold at the end of the rainbow only to discover there's nothing to spend it on.

I'll never forget how strong this feeling was after one of the highlight victories in my career, a victory I had worked and hoped for long and hard after a year of ups and downs in 1981–82. Jack and I were walking through the tunnel, away from the track in Helsinki after the World Championship marathon in 1983. The bike on which he had ridden to various spots of the course to cheer me on was slung over his shoulder, and I was carrying the flowers and the medal I'd been awarded. We turned to each other at the same moment with that vacant feeling, as hollow and empty as the tunnel. "Well, what's next?" I asked.

The subject of breaking records is part of an unbridgeable gap between me and the public. Sometimes I'm pulled two ways, between what I want—to run my best and to win—and what the public usually expects: a race against the clock and a record. Sometimes even when I win the race—which is what *I* care about—all I hear is "that time was such and such off the world record." I wish people would understand that we athletes aren't machines; we're human beings. We're happy enough for the victory. Some days we come up with just the right combination of circumstances to achieve a record-setting performance, but it can't be made to order to suit the press, the race organizers, and the public.

I've had some remarkable winning streaks and records. I have set four world marathon records, more than any woman or man in history. In my entire career I never lost a cross-country race until 1982 or a road race until 1983, and I was unbeaten in Norway from 1972 to May 1984. To be honest, I don't regret the losses that broke these winning streaks. It took an enormous amount of pressure off me. As I told the press after the European Championships in 1978, "I must have the right to lose."

THE PRESSURE

One thing that never leaves me is the pressure. In fact, I can't remember what life is like without it. Coupled with the pressure I feel to live up to people's expectations is the fear of what I have to go through as a runner—the intense physical and mental effort in the race. The conflict over pleasing people was especially hard when I was younger. "Fear of failure is my biggest problem," I said in a 1974 newspaper article. "I'm very vulnerable. If negative things are written about me in the paper, I feel hurt." The fear of the effort isn't so bad now but will probably always be with me to a degree as long as I compete. For years I was so overwhelmed by nervousness that I'd have to tell myself before a race, "I'm not going to die. I know it will hurt for a minute or two, but then it's over." In 1976, my high-pressure year, I was so nervous I used to go to Jack's office during lunch just to have him help to calm me down. "Why am I doing this?" I kept asking myself about living with this pressure.

At times failure has brought me pain, and at other times anger. "Everyone loves a winner": I can personally testify to that, but the love fades when you're not wearing the laurel wreath. I had a bad year in 1982 because of injuries. I had dropped out of the New York City Marathon several months before and Boston in April 1982, and could not run the first European Championship marathon. It was also the first year I didn't win the World Cross Country Championships— placing "only third." This was when I overheard the talk that I was finished, "washed up." What is especially tough for an athlete, or anyone in the spotlight for that matter, is the fickle attention and loyalty of the media and the public. Nothing makes a person angrier than a rumor that isn't true, and nothing tests one's patience more than having to wait her time to prove it. Did they really think one off year out of twelve outstanding years meant the end? Frankly, though, no matter what I believed and was determined to prove, their negativity still ate at my confidence. After dropping out of two marathons, I was a bit shaky when I lined up for my next one. When I won it—New York in 1982—my first feeling was a tremendous sense of relief. I had always known I would come back; now I didn't have to feel any doubts. "You don't have to be a quitter," I told myself.

My performances are not the only things that have created dissonance between who I really am and how I am perceived by others. Like most people in the public eye, I have been misquoted, misunderstood, misrepresented, and the source of much unwanted interest and speculation. So difficult is it to make people understand what I do that even those closest to me can sometimes seem miles away. Each time I raced the Russian Svyetlana Ulmasova, I gave it everything I had, but each time she beat me. After one such race against her, Jack and a Norwegian sports journalist who had followed my career thought they had it all figured out. "You didn't run as fast as you could have," they said. "You weren't aggressive enough." "I ran as fast as my legs would carry me!" I shot back. There they were, judging and dissecting my effort. That's easy to do from the sidelines, but I'm the one doing the running. One thing every runner ultimately learns is that when you're out there no one else ever truly knows what you're going through. No one can be in your body or your mind, feeling your effort and your breaking point. Yours is a world you live in alone.

When I look back, everything seems so different. While I'm competing, it's like being in battle, yet it seems as if I never take a moment to savor my success after I've "won the war." I take so much for granted in terms of my performance. Occasionally, when I have seen videotapes of my races or analyzed my times, I am struck by how much better they are than I realized at the time. For example, it's hard to believe Jack and I discussed that race against Ulmasova as a "failure" when I ran 8:38, one of the five fastest times in the world that year! In 1979 and 1980 I set four world records, including a 30:59.8 for 10km on the roads, which I ran unchallenged and on a hilly course. It's probably the best race of my life, yet I hardly paused to give myself even a small pat on the back. The same is true of the Los Angeles Olympics, where I was so emotionally wound up that it didn't strike me until months later: when I stood on that stand with the medal around my neck, my eyes were filled with tears.

Although I speak with some bitterness about the pressure of life at the top, I don't want to seem ungrateful. I gripe about the demands and the lack of privacy, about the tough training regimen and the limits it puts on my life. But it's not so much a complaint as it is the need to give some perspective to the myth that life at the top is all glamour and triumph. For every finish-line tape a runner breaks— complete with the cheers of the crowd and the clicking of hundreds of cameras—there are all the hours of hard and often lonely work that rarely get talked about.

For the most part, though, it's been a wonderful life, one that has given me all the best. I've made more than a good living. I love to travel, and I've been to thirty-nine countries, including such exotic cities as Tunis and Abu Dhabi. I've run under the Eiffel Tower, around the Colosseum in Rome, and through Hyde Park in London—even through the corridors of the White House.

Twice I have been the guest of Ronald Reagan—in 1983 and 1984, after my New York City Marathon victories. For some reason we were late one of those years, and you just don't miss an appointment with a president. So we ran down the hall, barely slowing to a jog, right into the Oval Office at the exact moment I was scheduled to shake

Reagan's hand. In fact, the entire visit was quite memorable. After the Oval Office, it was off to the Rose Garden and more journalists than I had ever seen in one place. When the aggressive television reporter Sam Donaldson began throwing out political questions, I froze. This was during the crisis in Grenada, and, obviously, the nation's attention was not on marathons. In fact, I was surprised Reagan still wanted to meet with us during this time. "She's here on behalf of women's sports," the president told Donaldson, saving me from what would surely have been mere babbling. At the end of the visit, I gave Reagan a replica of the statue made of me in Oslo, and he gave me a jar of jelly beans.

Another notable meeting was in California with the cast of the television show *Dynasty*, a show that was also big in Norway but that I had never seen in my life. "Who's that?" I asked when I heard I was to be introduced to Joan Collins. Thank goodness she doesn't understand Norwegian!

Other illustrious events included an invitation to a reception with the queen of England on the yacht *Britannia*. But true to form, training comes first. (I don't think I can ever change.) We didn't go because it was held too late at night! Oh, yes, and Jack and I didn't have the "proper attire." "Don't you regret not meeting the queen?" friends have asked. Sorry, can't say that I do.

FAME

My strongest memory of the New York City Marathon is not of the records, the cheering, or the adulation, but of the day I lost my anonymity forever. "Who is number 1173?" people all around me asked in panic after I crossed the finish line. I could even hear it being asked over the loudspeaker. That was my race number, and I laugh now when I recall how I had to go from one to the other telling them who I was, and where I was from. That was the first and last time I ever wore that number or heard that question.

After the race, suddenly there was all this attention I wasn't used to. Of course, I had won races before, but that was mainly on the track, where I shared the focus with other winners. It was quite entertaining to watch the people in New York. They were more excited than I was! I suppose I should have been more enthusiastic, but we didn't realize at the time what it meant. My success was taken for granted in Norway, where I had already established myself. Winning New York was like getting a fresh start. The attention was exciting, but it was also very tiring. First of all, I'd just run 26.2 miles. Second, my English wasn't that good, certainly not up to the pace of the New York media, so I had to summon all my powers of concentration just to understand what people were saying. Soon I just wanted everyone to leave so I could go back to my room and relax.

Americans really love famous people. Being famous in the United States sets you apart. In Norway, there's an unwritten law, which is actually based on the theme of a thirties novel, that governs our society: you shall not think yourself better than anyone else. If you do, you're looked down on. But in America you're respected and admired for standing out. Suddenly I was in a world where people strive to be better than everyone else and where they are encouraged to do so. In the streets of American cities I was stopped by people expressing admiration, and while I was very shy about my commercial endorsements, they were openly praised as well-deserved rewards. This open discussion of something commercial or financial would never happen in Norway.

When I was younger, it was exciting to be famous. When people recognized me or asked for my autograph, I was flattered. I got a kick out of the fact that my picture was on chewing-gum cards in Belgium. But about ten years ago, the attention started to become burdensome. Even the symbols of fame have become fleeting pleasures. The medals have lost their shine. In fact, people are surprised I don't display them, that I keep my Olympic and championship medals in the kitchen cabinet with the dishes and silverware. Because my rewards are within me, intangible, usually the tangible rewards mean much more to other people. One year one of the restaurant waitresses who served me regularly so admired one of the four or five New York City Marathon awards I had received that I gave it to her. When someone in Norway kept calling and asking to photograph me with the award, I couldn't dare tell him I had given it away, so I had to come up with some pretty creative excuses to get out of it.

I have aspired to greatness as an athlete, but that doesn't mean I aspired to the fame that came with it. On the whole, I don't really like the position I'm in. I don't like being recognized or considered "a star." I'd rather be anonymous. Maybe it's everyone's dream to be famous, but it's never been mine. Perhaps most famous people deny that they truly enjoy the fame, but that's not my disguise. What of all the opportunity fame has given me? Despite it all, the truth is, I could live without it.

For one thing, nothing about my personality or my background is harmonious with being famous. Fame often puts people into a world not of their own choosing. Sometimes I feel life would have been so much easier being a normal person, without the fame. When you're famous, people expect you to be special, different, and to have an opinion on everything. But I don't have an opinion on everything, especially on things I know nothing about. That's what I would have liked to have told Sam Donaldson! "What, are you going shopping?" people in stores ask me. "Yes," I answer. "And I wash clothes and clean house, too." I haven't changed since that day in 1978. I'm the same person. It's just that a lot of things around me have changed.

Walking through Oslo is like being onstage. I've got to be on my best behavior, a good actress, never missing a line. I don't even dare go to a restaurant past a certain hour to talk business with a man, as I'm sure it would cause a wave of stories and rumors. My life is very restricted in Norway. It's a small country, which limits my privacy. Coming to America is a pleasant escape, a chance to be anonymous. I'm still recognized, but not so much that I can't go down the street and disappear into the crowd.

There are some great risks, sacrifices, and pressures that come with being famous. It's a constant intrusion that can put a terrible strain on one's personal life. There's been farfetched gossip about me that runs the gamut from a pregnancy to an impending divorce. Some runners get to the top only to find they've jumped on the carousel of fame and attention too soon. Their subsequent marital troubles become full-page newspaper stories. Luckily, this has never been my problem, but I've seen it happen enough to know what the pressures of fame can do to people.

I miss a normal life sometimes: getting out of the house, going to work from nine to five, being spontaneous once in a while, not having to think about my afternoon workout. Running, and the time it requires, is a singular effort. My life is fairly isolated. Sometimes I miss being around people, being social. There are days when I look out the car window on the way to the physical therapist, watching a woman walk down the street and wishing with my whole heart that I were her. Or I'll go to the bank and look across at the teller, imagining her life were mine. I guess it's only natural to want to change your life. At the same moment I long to be in her place, that bank teller probably wishes she were in mine.

Fame is only meaningful if it makes you happy and if you can use it to do something worthwhile. It hasn't always meant the former for me, but at least I can say it has meant the latter. It has given me financial security and the opportunity to expand my career in health and fitness, which ensures my involvement in the sport after I stop competing. My fame makes my family proud and allows me to bring them on trips, and that makes me feel good. And there are moments of deep personal satisfaction when runners tell me I'm an inspiration.

The long-term value of fame is that it has allowed me to do something I feel is truly meaningful, especially with children, who often listen to people like me more than they do to their coaches or even their parents. The Grete Waitz Foundation, which supports teenage female running talent, the Grete Waitz Run for women, and my position on the Norwegian Olympic Committee are some examples. Beyond the sport, there are the charities I have begun to work with: Save the Children and the Cystic Fibrosis Foundation.

CAREER

Although invitations steadily increased after my marathon wins and records, I could accept them only during school vacations. I was enjoying road racing, and I've always loved to travel. With training and all these opportunities, teaching was becoming a burden. Increasingly, I was forced to take time off to travel to races, yet I felt bad being away from my students. It was a classic case of mixed emotions. In 1980 I took a one-year leave from my job teaching high school

English and physical education. Then I took another year leave. I didn't quit outright because I didn't want to burn any bridges. What if I broke my leg and couldn't run? I thought. Finally, after the two-year leave, the headmaster told me I had to make a permanent decision. I enjoyed teaching, but the world of running was enticing. The choice became obvious: I could always teach, but I couldn't always compete.

It's very hard to have a job and be an elite runner. It's difficult—some say impossible—to be the best or compete with the best, while working full time. Although I did it for many years in the past, I don't know of any top runner who does it today. It isn't just the time and energy needed for the training; it's all the things that surround that training: the necessary rest and medical treatment (regular massage and physical therapy in my case), the travel to races, and the promotional work that is part of endorsement contracts. There was a time that when I said I was a runner, people asked what my job was, what I did for a living. But I don't think people expect world-class runners to have another job anymore. They better understand what it requires for us to be on top.

I stopped teaching because I realized I could make a living from running. In the beginning it felt nice not to go to work. Eventually, though, I realized that my running was now a job, not a hobby. When I went out for a training run, I would sometimes leave a note that said, "I've gone to work. Be back in an hour." Actually, I consider it a privilege to run for a living. First of all, the money in road races has enabled us runners to stay in the sport longer. Until fairly recently, most top runners couldn't truly reach their peak because they couldn't afford to put time into training and competition, but now they can make a living and support a family. In addition to prize money in races, there are product endorsements and commercial possibilities, including opportunities to build future careers in media or business.

My endorsements include a long-term contract with Adidas (through 1988), for whom I wear shoes and clothing and also serve as a spokesperson and technical advisor, and Team Xerox in the United States, for whom I run and do clinics. Most major races I run also include a clinic or an exposition in which I agree to participate, especially as an Adidas athlete if the company is a race sponsor. I currently advertise only one product, which I have been doing since 1979, XL-1, a Norwegian electrolyte-replacement drink. In addition to this book, my other major project is an hour-long home video, *Running Great with Grete Waitz*. Jack serves as my agent, and for contract negotiations and general business advice in the United States we use our New York lawyer and friend, Michael Frankfurt.

What does a company expect in return if it sponsors me? With Adidas, for example, there are no specific boundaries or definitions in my contract that describe exactly what I must do, yet it is understood by both parties. Basically, I should continue to produce good results as an athlete, make appearances, and do advertising. Years ago I was reluctant to sign my very first contract, which was with Adidas, wondering what I would have to do to be worthwhile to the company. There came a day, however, when I realized I was valuable and that the company benefits from the arrangement just as much as I do. Since the beginning, my relationship with Adidas has always been excellent. When necessary because of foot problems, they have made special alterations of my shoes and brought me to training camps in Germany and France. Jack enjoys the same good relationship in his job as Adidas promotion coordinator for Norway.

What I choose to do commercially has always been one of my biggest conflicts. I've been offered endorsements for everything from fountain pens, leisure shoes, and milk to cars—with several offers of free models in the bargain. Recently I have allowed my picture to be used on the front of Norwegian flatbread crackers (the Wheaties of Norway in terms of popularity), as I am considering doing more promotional work for Norway. I care about my country and have, therefore, recently agreed to become a member of a group of 100 prominent Norwegians seeking to increase Norway's image abroad. I believe it's time our country learns to promote itself the way American business does.

Generally, I've been very slow to agree to do anything commercial. First of all, while I'm still competing, anything else besides running must always compromise my training to a degree. This became clear to me the week before the 1985 New York City Marathon. My media schedule for my home video was a product promoter's dream—network television, a gala reception, endless interviews—but I curtailed it all midweek as it was exhausting and distracting me from my race. In addition, it only reminded me of the pressure I felt to win the race. Second, I have to believe it is a quality product that I would feel completely comfortable endorsing, which is why, so far, I have never endorsed a product I don't personally use. I even turned down milk advertising in Norway because I don't drink it. If I believe a product is good and that I can be associated with it without compromising my beliefs or my personality, then I consider it, even though I still don't like to see my picture in magazine advertisements. Advertising makeup, for example, would be out of the question. Actually, even the thought of it is ridiculous: "Grete Waitz always runs her marathons in Brand X eye shadow!"

My attitude has changed somewhat since about 1980, when I still refused to be involved in most endorsements or commercials. Jack and I still argue about it, though—what and how much I should do. He thinks I should get more involved, and it's because of his powers of persuasion that I am. The fact that running has developed to the point where other athletes are also used commercially has helped make me feel more comfortable about doing it myself, and I accept that making a living from running involves some endorsements. I can't run competitively forever, so to be able to branch out and still remain involved in the sport gives me more security and adds more substance to my career. Actually, once I'm involved in a good project, I end up getting a lot of satisfaction from it. That doesn't mean, however, that I'm looking for a lot of things to endorse. My feeling is that it's better to take on only a few projects and do them well.

If I weren't still competing, and didn't have to do all the training, I think I would enjoy undertaking more projects and endorsements, but it's very draining work, and as it is now I don't have the time and energy to devote to it. So I do as much as I feel I can do well, though I can always find some extra energy for something more meaningful, which uses me as a person rather than just using my picture. Then I'm willing to get more involved. Believe me, I would rather write a book than sell something with my face or my name.

MONEY

On my level, a runner would be foolish not to make money from the sport. That doesn't mean I aspire to be a millionaire; it's one thing to be greedy and another to be foolish. My goal is not to get rich but to enjoy the extras that afford me a nice lifestyle. Nor am I interested in being able to retire; I always want to work. I don't have ambitious financial goals. What I've already achieved financially is beyond anything I ever dreamed. If someone had told me ten years ago that we could buy a house, for example, I would have said that person was beyond dreaming, too! Both Jack and I come from working-class families. Our lives were very simple, very average. We have always lived in apartments, and I just assumed when I grew up that I'd live in an apartment, that I'd lead the same kind of life I always had.

It isn't as if I have always been deluged with offers, either. As unbelievable as it seems by today's standards, it wasn't that long ago that we runners did it for nothing. I didn't even get a free pair of shoes until 1976, after I had made two Olympic teams! My first contract with Adidas wasn't until 1978, and even then it seemed strange. Such a big responsibility I felt, and I certainly didn't need or want the added pressure. What if I didn't run well and win races so they could get the publicity they had paid for? Although I was reluctant to accept it, Jack never was. "Why not? They're using your name," he told me. "It's natural they pay for it."

I can't say I've actually ever signed a contract myself, as I'm not allowed. The Norwegian Track and Field Federation signs in my name, in keeping with the rules to maintain my amateur status. Running is not recognized as a professional sport, so a system of athletes' trust funds has been established in the last several years. All my money goes into the fund, from which an athlete can draw to use for living and training expenses. This International Amateur Athletics Federation (IAAF) rule protects the athlete for competitions such as the Olympics. I am glad there is now this system of trust funds because it sets clear guidelines. It was always difficult to know how to react to all the illegal payments, to make sure to keep myself "clean."

Until 1980, my only prizes were trophies or products. Track was different from road races and cross-country; there was money in track, but only for the big stars who drew the crowds. Even then, you had to be more than just a good athlete—you had to have an image. This has never been fair, in my opinion, but, of course, many things in life aren't fair. In a road race, on the other hand, anyone can win money. A good but not outstanding runner can have his or her day and win a thousand dollars—while in track, this person can't even get into the race. Most road races currently offer only prize money, not just appearance money to show up (as in most big track races), although now road races are beginning to offer big appearance fees in addition to prize money. In 1985 there was a great deal of publicity over appearance fees in the rival New York and Chicago marathons. One article attributed a highly inflated appearance fee for me of $30,000.

Of course, it seems fair to be compensated for doing press conferences and promotions, but I still prefer the prize money, as it is fairer: equal pay for equal work, so to speak. My prize money for winning races has varied from $2,500 for a 5km Terry Fox Memorial race, in Canada, to $10,000 for the Cascade Run Off, in Oregon, to $25,000 plus a Mercedes-Benz in both the 1984 and 1985 New York City marathons (I sold the car each year. I would have liked to keep them, but it was too complicated to bring them back to Norway). Some races also offer a bonus system for setting records, but I don't choose races for the money, but rather for the quality of the competition, and the races I run in Norway don't even have any money.

What about "under the table" money and the days when athletes were secretly and illegally paid so as not to jeopardize their amateur status? There was so much talk going on about it that the supposed secret was common knowledge for years. As we say in Norwegian, "It's so secret, it's no secret." When I ran my first marathon, New York City in 1978, I knew there was under-the-table money in track, but I didn't know there was in road racing. As a matter of fact, the only cash I saw after that race was twenty dollars, which was given to us for a cab to the airport when I told the race organizers we had no way to get there. At the time of that race, I felt it was more than enough that my expenses were covered and that Jack had also been given a plane ticket. Frankly, I am probably history's last world-record holder who didn't get paid.

I think the system of prize money is fair, if a bit glamorized. After all, only a handful of runners really make a living from the sport, and the money in running is a drop in the bucket compared with tennis or golf. I don't think the money in running will ever get as big as in those sports, but then there are other sports, like swimming and gymnastics, that don't have any money at all.

I absolutely believe that we runners should be able to make a living from what we do. The Association of Road Racing Athletes (ARRA), headed by former Olympian Don Kardong, really helped in this regard by being the first to establish open-prize-money races. In the 1981 Cascade Run Off, top road runners defied the rules by openly taking money to protest the hypocrisy of the system. Athletes such as Anne Audain, Lorraine Moller, Allison Roe, and Patti Catalano ran a big risk in taking that money, for which they were temporarily banned from all competition except for a few open-prize-money road races (which are not sanctioned by the IAAF). Although I had to stay away from that race because I was still running track and would have become ineligible, I appreciated their struggle and agreed with what they did.

In the last few years there have been more questions about the money in road races than about the competition itself. When people get more concerned about the financial end of the sport, the athlete's performance often gets lost. When "over the table" prize money was first announced for the New York City Marathon, in 1984, it got more coverage in Norway than I did for winning the race. Maybe the attention is understandable because open prize money is new, and people have to get used to it. I just wish it weren't so overwhelming. Sometimes it seems as if the event is part of a Las Vegas casino rather than a foot race.

DRUGS

Although drug testing for illegal substances has been done for years at major track meets in Europe, the first time I was ever tested for drugs in the United States was in a track meet in San Jose in 1985. Now all international championship track meets, as well as other meets of international caliber, administer drug tests. Testing is generally conducted for the first three finishers per event and for a number of other athletes chosen at random, who are required to produce a urine sample immediately following their event. One of the most common and controversial illegal drugs is anabolic steroids, a synthetic male hormone believed to increase strength and endurance. But steroids are not the only substance the use of which can result in disqualification. The number of banned substances fills an entire page and includes everything from amphetamines to large doses of caffeine. According to IAAF rules, discovery of illegal substances results in immediate disqualification from the event and a minimum suspension of eighteen months.

Athletes have to check carefully even the ingredients of common cold and asthma medications, as it's easy to use a banned substance accidentally. Before the World Cross Country Championships in 1978, I took some over-the-counter nose drops for a cold. It turned out they contained ephedrine, which is on the list of banned substances. Fortunately, I had used the medication several days before the competition, so my doping test was negative. Subsequently, I found out that almost every type of nose drops except one has some banned substance.

Putting the seriousness of the subject aside for a moment, this testing can be pretty amusing. First of all, like most nervous runners before a race, I've already gone to the toilet at least a dozen times, and on top of that, I'm dehydrated from the race. The rules require we go to be tested immediately after the event, but what's left to give for a urine test? Usually, there we sit, a roomful of athletes who simply can't go on cue—drinking and drinking and drinking... trying to summon the ability to take the test. In San Jose I sat with the Olympic gold-medal sprinter Valerie Brisco-Hooks. It took me an hour and a half, and it took her two hours. Once we've done this test, if we were ever shy, believe me, we aren't anymore. This is no private visit to the WC. We have to pull down our pants and go into our little cups right in front of an "official spectator."

Sex testing is also done for every woman who competes in an international event. As far as I know, since 1973 this has been a one-time test, and after I passed it that year, I got something like a passport, a "license" stating that I'm a woman! At the World Championships in 1983, for example, they asked to see my "license." They now do this test by taking cells from the mouth, but, imagine, in the 1960s the women used to have to parade naked before a committee to verify their legitimacy.

The first time I had undergone sex testing was at the Munich Olympics, in 1972. At the time they plucked a piece of hair that they looked at under a microscope. When it came my turn, my hair became the source of great discussion; it seemed as if they were having a committee meeting over it. The woman in charge started to shake her head. I started to sweat. The line behind me was growing. I was nervous before the test—having heard stories of women who weren't really women—and the images in my eighteen-year-old mind were vivid. As the group held its discussion over my hair, I seriously began to think that maybe I wasn't really a woman after all. Then one of my eyebrows was plucked and examined, and finally I was given the okay. It turned out the hair on my head was so fine, they couldn't find what they were looking for. As I walked out, I remarked to a teammate, "Whew, it's okay. I'm a woman."

At my first running clinic in California, in 1979, someone boldly asked, "Are you using steroids?" I almost fell off my chair! I couldn't believe this would be asked so openly and that anyone could think a long-distance runner would use steroids. I've never even considered taking them. To this day, the only drugs I've ever taken are naprosyn, like a stronger form of aspirin, and a cortisone shot in my knee, which I had in 1983 as a drastic measure in order to treat an injury before the London Marathon. The questioners in the clinic persisted. "Why don't you use steroids, if they could make you run faster?" The way these runners talked about drugs, I got the feeling that if they believed they could improve from a three-hour marathon to a 2:50 they would take them, despite the consequences. This, to me, is absurd.

Do top runners take drugs? I'm sure they probably do. Like most people in the athletic community, I have always assumed that some track runners use them; it's common knowledge. From about the time of the 1976 Olympics, more rumors about drugs began to circulate, especially about women taking them. At that time the talk was only about the Eastern Europeans; now the gossip is about anyone, regardless of country. With all this drug talk, there were times I felt I was up against an unbeatable force when I raced the Eastern Europeans. In fact, Jack believed that some of my losses were caused not by my lack of talent but by the unfair advantage my competitors had.

But a private assumption is a far cry from a public confirmation. In 1979, when the *The New York Times* called to ask my opinion on the incident, I found out that seven of the Eastern European women, three of whom were my competitors, were tested positive for anabolic steroids after the Balkan Games, in Athens. At first I couldn't answer, I was in such shock. Suddenly it wasn't just a rumor or suspicion; it was fact. My first feeling was terrible disappointment because they were cheating. I also feared for the future of the sport. Surely these women weren't the only ones taking the drugs, merely the unlucky ones who got caught. Deep inside I had always wanted to believe it wasn't true. How could I have kept pushing myself through double workouts if I had believed my competitors were cheating? For my own motivation, for the sake of the sport, and for the sake of those women, I had wanted to believe they were clean. "These are not the only girls who are not clean," I was quoted in *The Times.* "This is one of the reasons I wasn't interested in the Olympics. You know Russia and other East European countries will do anything to win the gold medal. The only thing I can do is train and run."

For days after I got the news, I still felt depressed, flat in my training. What can I do, I thought, when training isn't enough? Yet as time passed, I developed a different attitude. "I'll show that a person can run fast without drugs," I told myself. I had beaten those women before; I could do it again. It turned out I didn't have to worry about those three particular women, as these former world champions and record holders never produced quite the same results. One of them, Tonka Petrova, of Bulgaria, doesn't even appear on the list of Olympic finalists in 1980—the year after they were caught—and Natalia Maracescu, of Romania, finished only an unimpressive ninth place in the 1,500m.

Other than these women and several other track runners who have been caught, I do not know personally of any long-distance runners, including road runners and marathoners, who take steroids. However, after the 1984 Olympics in which Finnish long-distance runner Martti Vainio lost his silver medal in the 10,000 meters for positive steroid tests, he proclaimed, "I think there are others. I am just the only one who was found guilty. It is right that I am punished, but many other athletes should be in the same boat." So if Vainio took them, who else does? A September 1985 article in *The Runner* magazine estimates that one million people may be trying steroids in the United States alone, and world-class runner Dr. Tony Sandoval thinks that between 25 percent and 60 percent of top runners are using some kind of performance drug—from human growth hormones to caffeine.

Why would a long-distance runner take steroids? These drugs are usually associated with body builders or athletes who want to add bulk and strength. But taken in small doses, steroids have been shown to increase endurance, speed healing from injury, and reduce the amount of body fat. Greater training loads are possible as the recovery time is also shortened and the energy level is increased. So for the short term, they probably do help a runner. But the dangerous side effects of these drugs are well known. Immediate side effects include acne, aggressive behavior, and growth of facial hair in women. Long-term side effects of continued use include everything from kidney and heart problems to cancer, and in women they can cause birth defects. Taking steroids is risky at best, and dangerous and shortsighted at worst. Besides, they are illegal!

It is my opinion, as well as the opinion of many experts, that drugs are going to become more prevalent in the running world. Officials are working harder to catch people as it is becoming such a serious problem. The United States Olympic Committee (USOC) plans random testing at Olympic training centers, and American colleges are considering instituting this testing as well. Since the advent of international championship road races, I'm sure there eventually will be drug testing in road races. Despite the documented evidence of the dangers, there's still a lot of talk that to be the best in the world you have to take steroids. It must be especially frustrating for young people to hear you have to use dangerous and illegal substances to be the best in running. Well, it just isn't true. I'm here to prove you can be the best in the world without them.

RETIREMENT

There are few races and medals left that I truly hunger to win. I've lived all my dreams. Throughout all the years of training and racing, I have always known what those dreams were, what I wanted. So it's strange I should forever be so unsure about one thing: retirement. After all these years, my feelings are still mixed about quitting. One part of me wants to stop, and the other wants to go on—but neither of these things can be done halfway. The part of me that wants to quit is tired of training, tired of always having to be so organized and structured, with every thought revolving around running. And it never ends; there's always another training session. If I were free of it, what would I do? Be more flexible, maybe have a job, go visiting friends at random hours, run for fun—but surely not get up at 5:00 A.M. every day!

But if it were gone—the training, the races—I'd miss it. There are times when I love it, especially when the weather is fine or the victory is sweet. These are the times I can't imagine living without it, when even the pressure of racing and the focus and attention aren't outweighed by my enjoyment. It's the atmosphere at the races and the fact I've always been a part of it. I simply know no other way of life. Maybe that's what keeps me at it.

Jack and I talk about my quitting all the time, and we always come to the same conclusion. As long as I can still enjoy my running and still be competitive, I'll stay with it. I don't want to have the feeling in ten years' time that I should have kept going for another few years. As goals are always important, mine are to keep winning and eventually run a personal best in the marathon.

As I went through my scrapbook of newspaper clippings for the book, I laughed when I realized there has been one thing I talked about *every year* since I began: retirement. "I don't want sports as an occupation," I said in the spring of 1976. "After the Olympics I'm definitely going to quit—just be a jogger." It was always some variation of the same sentence, until 1979 and the beginnings of my road racing when I finally announced that I enjoyed running as an occupation. My present plan is to race through 1986, but as of now I don't want to be running competitively by 1988 and the next Olympics. I will always run, though, maintaining about forty miles per week, and racing for fun and to measure my fitness.

Throughout all my ambivalence it's been Jack who's kept me steady. He's let me have things my way, accommodating my needs and the mood swings I experience when I'm under pressure. He's been very patient and understanding. I used to train alone, but the last few years I've started to tire from summoning my lone motivation, and so Jack has joined me in my morning runs and my brothers, Jan and Arild, frequently join me in the afternoons. Their companionship has renewed my pleasure, and so has their own success. Jack recently ran a personal best for 10km of 33:40, and Jan has begun to win or place well in major races in the over-forty category.

When I retire, I'd like to have another goal. Through 1988 I know I'll be working for Adidas and with the Norwegian Olympic Committee. In addition, I recently began working part-time as a consultant at Akti-Med, a preventive health care clinic in Oslo. I think I can find just as much excitement working for the sport as competing. And there are so many other things I haven't done. I'd like to travel—to *see* places. That's not what most serious athletes do when they travel to a race. All I see is a hotel room and a starting line. I've never been to Asia, and I'd love to see Japan. When I'm at home, I'd like to take up cross-country skiing again for fun and try some other sports (anything but miniature golf, the most boring game I have ever played in my life, and which I'm terrible at, besides!).

What do you do when the main thing in your life disappears? Pleasure/dread, love/hate—I feel them all for this sport, this life. And I've always lived with them both. In one way I look forward to retiring because it's tough to go out and train every day, twice a day. But in another way I'm afraid of that day, because it will be like a house in which the fourth wall just falls down. Competitive running has been my life for over fifteen years. What will my life be like without it?

3

Fitness Norwegian Style

The definition of fitness, according to the President's Council on Physical Fitness and Sports, in the United States, is "the ability to carry out daily tasks with vigor and alertness, without undue fatigue and with ample energy to enjoy leisure-time pursuits and to meet unforeseen emergencies." The Norwegian Sports Federation defines sport as "any recreational or competitive activities where bodily positions and movements are primary, and where the performer's own physical exertion is decisive for the result."

My definition of running and fitness is a combination of these two. Running is both a lifestyle and a sport. Being fit is the ability to run for the benefits of health, participation, and enjoyment. Fitness is also the necessary basis for running as a sport, providing the ability to train for enhanced conditioning or competition.

Fitness has come to describe not only a physical condition, however, but a social movement. It is part of how we live—what we think, what we eat, the way we spend our time. Whether one does it or not, everybody talks about exercise and lives under its influence. Although the trend toward living fit is fairly new in the United States and some other countries, we are fortunate that it has always been a part of life in Norway. The American running boom developed almost overnight. In 1968 there were only an estimated 100,000 runners in the United

States; in 1984 there were 34 million. The roots of Norwegian sport, however, go back to its first organized phase in the late 1800s. For this reason, I will often refer to the Norwegian lifestyle throughout this book. I believe the unique and valuable fitness habits we have developed in Norway can be instructive to those involved in fitness in other countries.

From early childhood we are involved in sports, which are an integral part of Norwegian society. According to a 1983 survey, 49.5 percent of our population over the age of fifteen usually participates in physical activity. In addition, over 25 percent belong to one of the country's 11,000 sports clubs (1,300 of which are for track and field). That's the number of clubs for a population of only four million! Jogging/running has been the fastest-growing sport in Norway since 1979, and it is third in popularity only to hiking/walking and skiing. With the lowest population density in Europe, much of the country is mountains and forest, where no cars are allowed. Norway is sports heaven. My hometown of Oslo has 2,300 kilometers of skiing and running trails, all of which are lit at night in winter.

In Norway we take a healthy way of life for granted. We take it for granted that we get reasonably priced, fresh, whole-grain bread every day, that we don't have to worry about preservatives in our food, and that exercise and sports are a lifelong priority. Ours is a very wholesome, very natural way of life, based on the farm society from which we originate.

There are no McDonald's or pizza parlors on every corner in Norway, and almost everything closes at 5:00 P.M., making late-night binges nearly impossible. Very few Norwegians go to restaurants, except to celebrate special occasions, and alcohol is extremely expensive and its use discouraged. This doesn't mean we're not slipping, though. The younger generation is beginning to aspire to be like its American peers, right down to the hamburgers and french fries. But it's not nearly the way of life it is in America. I realize the Norwegian lifestyle is not as easy to adopt in the United States, where it takes a conscious effort to make the right choices. One needs an iron will to resist the many temptations: the hundred varieties of ice cream and chocolate-chip cookies, the double and triple fast-food burgers. I know this from my frequent visits there, during which I am often a victim of the enticing multiflavored ice cream.

In response to the ill effects of this fast-food lifestyle, an increasing number of Americans are engaging in regular exercise—100 million of them, according to recent statistics. It is important that this growing fitness movement become permanent, the mainstream of American life. My experience from years of speaking at running clinics is that there are still endless questions about exercise and diet, and a widespread lack of basic sensible information. I suppose this is understandable in the States, where the fitness movement is so new and the advice often contradictory. As a result of this endless enthusiasm to learn and understand, I often feel that some clinic participants know more about nutrition than I do!

To help make fitness a way of life, several of Norway's programs could be beneficial in the United States. One is health education at an early age, which should be as basic a requirement as the ABCs. Nutrition is a perfect example. Instead of cookies and candy for snacks and rewards, it should be something healthy like bread and cheese. That's what we were given.

I learned the basics of nutrition as a child in the Oslo Breakfast Program, part of a post–World World II plan to provide good nourishment. This breakfast, which we were given in school, included the Norwegian staples: whole-grain bread, cheese, and milk. One of my strongest childhood memories is of sitting at the long table and asking for seconds—raising one finger for white cheese and two fingers for geitost (*yayt*-oost), a naturally sweet brown goat's milk cheese. It was from this early education that I developed my present eating habits. In fact, one of the few endorsements I have done is for geitost, one of my favorite foods. Although I now cringe at the memory of lining up for the cod liver oil we were also given, I'd probably do it more willingly now that I realize it was healthy.

In addition to our sports club system, we have a newer national program called K-jog, which includes thousands of runners. ("K" stands for condition in Norwegian, as well as the name of the bank that sponsors the program.) Groups of runners, numbering anywhere from 25 to 400, are formed in neighborhoods throughout the country. Each group is comprised of eight levels, determined by ability and goals, and includes a volunteer group leader who sets the pace and directs the workout. To keep the training both sensible and not overly competitive, no one is allowed to run in front of the leader. After the run, the eight levels join for an organized stretching session, conducted by one of the group leaders. Booklets on how to start and conduct K-jog are provided by the Norwegian Track & Field Federation. This program helps spread the running and fitness habit, and it is a good blend of the serious and informal, with the social and athletic benefits of our club system.

K-jog has also been adapted for use in the schools as part of physical education class. The weekly program for students is printed in the newspaper, and an instruction booklet for both teacher and pupil is provided for the primary, junior high, and high school levels. I know of both formal and informal running groups in the United States, but too often they represent the extremes: too competitive on the one hand or too informal on the other. The K-jog structure provides an important balance of seriousness and sensibility, with groups that vary from beginning joggers to marathoners. Local clubs, schools, or groups in the United States could easily adapt the K-jog system, or new groups could be modeled on this system.

As in other Scandinavian countries, Norway has its problems with alcohol consumption, so a great deal of our national education and many of our races, too, stress the motto: No Alcohol. This campaign includes drugs as well, and its logo is printed on all the race material and T-shirts. It would be difficult, I realize, to institute a campaign like this in the United States, where the alcohol industry is formidable and beer drinking for some runners is a way of life. Some American race organizers already refuse any alcohol and, surely, cigarette sponsors because they are not in keeping with the image of the event. In Norway it is illegal to advertise cigarettes and alcohol in any form, and statistics show that at least cigarette use is declining.

I think health and social issues and running can be an important affiliation. A relevant social message expands the influence and significance of running and fitness. For example, the antidrug campaign has been very successful in Norway, especially among the youth. In addition to alcohol and drugs, there are other options for race-education campaigns. What about an eat-right program, like "junk-food busters," or races to benefit worthy causes, in which steps are taken simultaneously to educate the participants?

As our habits can influence Americans, we are learning a great deal from them as well. For example, K-jog is actually an outgrowth of the American jogging movement. Not long ago Norwegians would never have considered jogging unless they were lean and fit athletes, until American visitors of all shapes and sizes began running in the streets of our country. I, too, am affected by this influence. It was American road racing that kept my interest in running alive and inspired me to set new goals, and I am always learning something new and valuable every time I attend a clinic in the States or speak with other runners there.

It may be easier for us to live the fitness lifestyle, as it comes automatically with being Norwegian, but that's no guarantee. We, too, must make a conscious choice to live fit. Every runner should make the same choice. As you develop new exercise and dietary habits, you must be prepared to undergo psychological changes. Your priorities will likely change: your leisure activities, the way you budget your time, the way you relate to other people. Your social life will likely change as you are drawn to a supportive group of people who share your interest in fitness.

This is true in my life, which is dictated by my running. I have a very regular routine. Up at 5:15 A.M., in bed by 9:30 P.M.—I obviously don't keep late hours, nor would I be much fun at late-night parties. I have a simple but sound diet, and I tend to gravitate toward other runners, or at least those who understand what I do. In fact, my closest friends are my training partners and those people with whom I run in races. I guess my daily life might sound unadventurous or boring to some, but it has always made me feel healthy and happy. As you read on, I'm sure you'll agree that my lifestyle gives me plenty of rewards in terms of my running.

One of the main differences I notice between Americans and Norwegians is that people who exercise are more passionate about fitness in the United States. That enthusiasm is great, but I also know that it has created a trend toward the "fast and furious" approach. Enthusiasm is one thing, but devoting oneself to a sport as to a religion is something else. In my experience, runners who can't think about anything else but running usually don't last in the sport. "Hurry slowly," as we say in Norwegian: work hard, but be patient and take time to build. That's a major theme throughout this book.

I have enjoyed my sport for twenty years, but I haven't stuck to it by rushing or by letting it consume all my thoughts and my time. I am a runner, but that's not all I am. I have always tried to live a normal, ordered life, filled with as many other activities as possible. One needs the right perspective; and with the proper blend of enthusiasm and this perspective, running and fitness can last a lifetime.

"Why do you run?" I've been asked in clinics. It seems such a simple question, but where I come from no one would ever ask it. As I said, we Norwegians take a lot for granted. It's almost impossible to answer that question, to give words to my experience as a runner. Running makes me feel strong and healthy and gives me a sense of accomplishment, but I think to truly understand why anyone runs you must have firsthand experience. If I can share my experience by getting you to run, or helping to improve your running, I think the question will be best answered. This book, therefore, is my way of answering that question. It will tell you how and why I run and live my lifestyle, and detail the best way for you to apply my experience to your own life.

Among the runners I meet, there's certainly no lack of desire. In fact, as devoted to the sport as I am, sometimes I feel the average American runner is more dedicated than I. I'll never forget the first time I saw someone running in place while waiting for a red light. "Only in the States," I thought, laughing to myself. I, for one, have always stopped at the light, thankful for the chance to rest!

4

For the Beginner— Basic Running and Fitness

Who are you, the runner? The beauty of the sport is that you can be anyone, in any condition, from under age six to over sixty, regardless of athletic ability, or lack of it! No matter how great our differences, as runners we share a basic commonality. Running is the great equalizer—we all put one foot in front of the other toward our goal of fitness and athletic achievement.

I have seen all types of people take up running, and just when I think participation has reached its peak, I come to a race to find the crowds have swelled. The growth in the variety of runners is what I find most amazing. It isn't just those in the twenty- to forty-year-old age group joining in. Consider these examples: running programs that emphasize fun and participation are springing up for children, including "peewee" runs for those under six. A *Newsweek* Gallup Poll shows that a record 78 percent of college students now exercise at least once a week outside of gym class, and running is their most popular activity. The greatest percentage of members joining the New York Road Runners Club—the world's largest running club, with over 25,000 members—has been those over fifty. In fact, from 1981 to 1985 the club's record growth was in the sixty to sixty-nine age group, with an astounding increase of 93 percent.

Perhaps no group of runners better illustrates the sport's unlimited potential than the Achilles Track Club in New York. This team of over one hundred disabled runners includes people with all kinds of disabilities, such as blindness, cerebral palsy, paralysis, or amputation. They meet regularly for coaching, group workouts, and races. Twenty-four of the club's members completed the 1985 New York City Marathon, and two of them have been invited with me as honored guests to the White House. Achilles members are a source of tremendous inspiration for everyone in the running community. The participation of these runners shows the unlimited possibilities of the sport and best defines who runners are. They are truly everyone!

In addition to the well-known benefits of health and well-being derived from exercise, there are other unique advantages to being a runner. You are more attuned not only to your body but also to the world around you. The outdoor life you lead as a runner gives you a special relationship with your surroundings: nature, the climate, the seasons. As you depend on these things to accommodate your activity, you grow to understand and appreciate them. The weather, for example, is a runner's constant companion. I am always aware of it, always interested. Checking the temperature is the first thing I do when I get up every morning. In Norway, with its severe winters, the weather often dictates my plans, including the type of workouts I do.

You have undoubtedly heard how easy running is and about the great benefits it provides. It is important to understand not only the physical gains of health and fitness but also how running can become an overall lifestyle. True and lasting fitness goes hand in hand with the rest of life, and it must do so harmoniously. Experts say the future trend is toward *total* fitness, which includes a combination of exercise, diet, and motivation. Today's health clubs, with an estimated dropout rate of 90 percent, clearly are not working. Experts in sports medicine, training, and weight control will likely staff the more scientific facilities of the future.

Experts also emphasize that future fitness will stress the thorough, gradual approach. This is the result of statistics that show a high injury and dropout rate among beginning exercisers. Many enthusiastic exercisers push too hard, too soon. For every one person who finds a sport for life, there are dozens more whose failed efforts result in closets overflowing with unused exercise gear.

CONSISTENCY

Consistency is the key to any successful fitness or athletic program, on any level, and has been the primary strength of my career for over twenty years. Consistency is achieved by a combination of methodical training, experience, patience, and common sense. I have seen plenty of runners come and go—victims of overzealous training, injury, burnout. My aim has been to remain consistent at the top level in what is notoriously a high-risk sport.

In order to achieve consistency, you will have to make a conscious effort to ignore the false promises of instant results: thin thighs and a flat stomach in mere days, weekend weight loss. We're fed these promises as if they are the goal of what we do, rather than just some of the many positive results. Spot reducing isn't total fitness; it isn't the real reason most of us run, nor is it enough of a motivation to keep us running. Besides, "quick fitness" is a contradiction in terms. Becoming a runner and getting fit isn't like placing an order at a fast-food restaurant. The reason we value it so highly is precisely because we work hard for it.

It took me several years to become a decent runner. I finished dead last in my first races. It took even longer to become a serious contender, and I was an international competitor and a veteran of two Olympic Games before I ran my first 26.2-mile marathon—a feat that is often undertaken these days by those who've been running for less than a year. You certainly don't have to run as long as I have to get good results, but you do have to be willing to give it a minimum time commitment.

It is all too easy to become one of the many people who expect to see progress immediately. After two or three training runs, they hope to lose five pounds and run five miles. Obviously, this sounds unreasonable, but it's hard not to hope for with all the hype over instant fitness. The motto of my program, therefore, and my recommendation throughout the book, is best described by the Norwegian expression I mentioned in Chapter 3: Hurry slowly. Be dedicated and disciplined and work hard, but take your time. Move ahead, but be patient. If you want to enjoy and succeed at running, it's important to keep this rule in mind. This doesn't mean you won't see dramatic results fairly quickly. It's simply a recognition that each phase of your program requires full attention and development, and that each of these phases has its own rewards. Every day of running should be both a means and an end in itself.

I don't want to create the impression that you have to look like Father Time before you get anywhere! Running is remarkably simple and provides some very basic and immediate results, which is one of the reasons I have always enjoyed it. It has given me countless pleasures, and even in the high-pressure world of competition my top priority is always to run for enjoyment. Without that enjoyment, I couldn't stay with it. Of course, I have many professional opportunities through running, but that isn't what got me started, nor is it what has kept me at it since childhood. I have always enjoyed being active: to feel my body move, to breathe hard, and to work up a sweat. From the beginning, running has given me what it still gives me today: a time to let loose, be free of daily burdens, or socialize with friends. And I have always been driven to test myself, to set a goal and achieve it: to be stronger, to run farther, faster.

Running was not my first sport, however, nor was it my only sport. In the beginning I never ran every day or in an organized fashion. My athletic career began as a young girl with gymnastics, team handball (a European sport that resembles a physically rougher form of soccer and basketball), and cross-country skiing. This variety of sports builds endurance, agility, and muscle, bone, and joint strength. So although I did so unconsciously, by combining a variety of physical activities, I developed an overall fitness. My beginning running program, therefore, is based on achieving this balanced conditioning by using walking, jogging, stretching, and strengthening exercises.

Developing overall fitness is essential, but it's not acquired as casually or as easily by adults as it is by children. From the day they can walk, most children are constantly active, exercising and getting fit in almost everything they do. The beginning program for adults must achieve the same result with a similar sense of enjoyment, but do so sensibly, methodically, and gradually.

In my case, my club coach kept me on a slow and sensible program. I ran for five years before I even began to get interested in formal training, which I started at age seventeen. Even then my attitude was very easygoing. If the coach said, "Today, intervals," I shrugged and said, "Okay. Today, intervals." It was no big deal, and I was in no hurry to get anywhere. Fortunately, I was not influenced by an ambitious, competitive society. No one was talking about how great or important it was to run a marathon.

GOAL SETTING

The aim of your beginning program is fitness, which is also the basis of any intermediate or advanced program. So the first step is to make this fitness your goal. To achieve this goal, it helps to personalize it. A personal goal is more meaningful and will, therefore, keep you more motivated. Don't take the medical profession's word for it that fitness is important, or the testimony of friends or exercise buffs. Make your goal important to you for your own specific reasons, whatever they may be.

Make what you do important to *you*. I don't think it's enough to begin running to become thin or fit for your spouse or because everybody else is doing it. I have learned this only too well from my own career. My first major realization in terms of goals was that above all else I must run for myself, not to please or impress anyone else. I spent my early years running to impress coaches, my peers, or the public, until I realized I would never truly enjoy what I was doing, or be successful, until I ran to please the one person for whom it most mattered: me.

A concrete goal helps maximize the chances of attaining it. Vague plans or promises are not a good foundation for success. Don't try out running by just chasing after the bus. Make your goal specific. For example, it might be to run three miles after ten weeks. To strengthen this goal, verbalize it—tell it to yourself and to family and friends. Make it visual by putting up a sign to remind you. Make it a top priority. This is what I do when I focus on an important goal. I decide that preparing for and achieving the goal come first and foremost.

Write down your goal in what will become your running and exercise diary, as keeping track of your progress can be a good inspiration. It need not be formal and detailed, just a record of what you do and when you do it. A diary will also help you learn about what works best for you by allowing you to look back and get perspective on what you have done. Seeing your progress will also help educate and motivate you for future training. (For more on a diary, see Chapter 11.)

Always be flexible about goals. If you realize your goals are unrealistic, don't let a rigid commitment keep you from changing your plans. Adaptability is another important key to my success. My entire career has been full of changes and new goals. These changes have kept my interest alive, kept my training fresh, and helped me to continue learning about myself and my sport. If you tend to be stubborn like me, however, and stick solidly to a plan, it takes a conscious effort to make yourself bend and adapt. As long as two years after my first marathon, despite my achievements on the roads, I refused to consider myself a road runner, to adapt my training to a new event. I insisted on remaining a track runner, not straying from what had been my career for thirteen years. Finally, I realized I could be both a track and road runner. That worked for a while, until the competition got too tough to be successful in both and it became clear I was spreading myself too thin. Track is my first love, and although it was hard to let go, I changed again and became only a road racer. Now I think of how much I would have missed if I had not been willing to change my goals.

Before you try running for one day and hang up your shoes in exasperation, you should realize that your initial goal to get fit requires a commitment of at least ten weeks. Consider the strength of your commitment. In order to get any benefit from running, you must train at least three times a week. I meet so many people who sigh and say, "I'd like to run, but I don't have the time." I don't have to remind you that if you want to do something, there's always time. I'm great at organizing my time, especially to *avoid* what I'm not eager to do. I've got a list of great excuses. Be honest and firm with yourself, and you will, if you'll excuse the pun, start off with the right foot forward!

After you have established a goal, made a commitment, and decided to be methodical and sensible, you can best utilize the how-to advice. I have always considered the proper attitude in running a necessary foundation to lay before building anything else. Through my experience in working with runners in clinics and camps, I have seen time and again that a sensible goal and the proper motivation are essential from the moment you take your first running steps.

GUIDELINES

On to the practical advice: it is recommended for people who have been inactive for over a year—especially those over forty or with a personal or family history of health problems—to get a physical checkup before beginning any exercise program. Though it's not mandatory, you can seek out a qualified expert at a fitness or sports medicine center to determine your present level of fitness. To start running, all you really need in terms of equipment is shoes, but the proper pair is a must. (Check the Appendices for shoe guidelines.)

My ten-week beginning running program at the end of this chapter is designed for you to achieve and maintain the maximum benefits of fitness. By the end of this program, you should be able to run 3¼ miles continuously, which will put you above the national average. This program is basically the same as a Norwegian version that has been tested by 15,000 people and subsequently refined and improved with the help of fitness experts and coaches. I will outline some of the basic principles of a beginning program, many of which I feel need special emphasis or are my personal recommendations.

Studies have shown that the ideal amount of exercise for optimum fitness (done at a moderate level of intensity, which can be determined by target heart rate)* is no more than twenty to thirty minutes three times a week. Those who run more than this are doing so for reasons beyond fitness. After ten weeks, you may vow to stay on the level you have reached, or you may want to increase. Then the next chapter,

---

*To calculate your estimated target heart rate, first determine your maximum heart rate (subtract your age from 220). Your training heart rate ranges from 70 percent to 85 percent of that number, but gauge it by getting to know your body as well. However, as numbers may vary, keep this rate over a period of time to find your own average, and make sure also to use the "talk test," described on page 55.

for the intermediate level, will be relevant to you. Meanwhile, after you have reached this fitness level, you need not do more to maintain the benefits; simply stay with thirty minutes of running three times a week.

I should call this a jogging program because that is what you should do as a beginner: jog. Running comes later. Although these words are used interchangeably, you must jog before you can run. Both are enjoyable and beneficial, but one precedes the other. In fact, every runner's program, no matter what level, includes some jogging.

Give yourself time to get used to the exercise movements and to develop good overall fitness. Beginners often feel that this recommended program is too slow, that they have the strength and energy to do more. However, although the heart and lungs are quick to respond favorably to exercise, muscles and joints take much longer. You must equalize this discrepancy by taking it easy at first, even beyond what seems necessary. If you immediately run as far and as fast as you feel you can, you risk injury. Especially if you've been sedentary, your body isn't ready for it. Common beginners' complaints of breathlessness or pain in the knees, legs, or feet are usually due to the fact they have done too much, too fast, too soon.

Use the first four weeks to get a general education. Pay close attention to your body; learn to read its signals of fatigue and stress, or when you can push beyond them. It's like learning another language. It may seem foreign at first, but, eventually, you will begin to understand the meaning of various physical sensations.

You must be particularly careful if you have been previously inactive. It's important not to test yourself by going out and running as long and as fast as you can in the very beginning, even if you feel great. Everyone knows at least one person who felt like Rocky one day and was a walking wounded the next, ready to retire permanently. Don't use your running at this stage to prove you're tough, that you can keep up with a friend, or that you can push just a little bit extra. It has to be enough to know from within that you're tough. With time and training, you will achieve this inner confidence.

Your program should take into account these factors: the distance or amount of time you run, pace, terrain, warm-up, cool-down, and supplementary exercises, like stretching and strengthening. (Just as with your running, you must progress slowly with these exercises.)

The principles of training frequency and intensity basically apply to all levels and are the foundation of the ten-week program. For an explanation of these principles, the next chapter might interest you.

Use the "talk test" to determine proper pace. You should be able to hold a conversation while running, without becoming breathless. If you can't, you're going too fast. Another indicator of proper pace is target heart rate. Inexperienced runners sometimes think that if they aren't breathing hard they aren't benefiting, but this isn't the case. As I have explained, the legs often suffer most from a breathless pace. If you are running properly at this stage, you should finish feeling enthusiastic, as if you could do more. One of the basic running commandments for all levels is, when in doubt, do less, not more. Few runners do too little; many runners do too much. Don't be one of the latter.

A proper warm-up is essential. One study has shown that those who exercised without warming up had irregular EKG tests, although they had no heart problems. A slow version of your activity will do the trick—a brisk walk or jog for five to ten minutes, which could get your blood pumping and bring on a slight sweat. No one is too good not to need a warm-up; even world-class marathoner Rob de Castella warms up by doing his first mile of a training run at a relative snail's pace of about nine minutes, although he can run a marathon in under five minutes per mile. A cool-down is equally important. Don't suddenly end your run by plopping down like a rag doll. End with a brisk walk or jog, followed by stretching.

Don't hesitate to use walking in your program. You needn't feel you must run without stopping. In fact, some people begin with a walking program if they need preliminary conditioning. If you feel you are one of them, work up to a mile at a time of brisk walking, three days a week. When this is comfortable, you can begin the running program. Brisk walking is also good supplementary or alternative exercise, and a good habit in general. Healthwalking, which can be done by anyone, employs the style and form of racewalking, which is also a competitive sport. For more information on healthwalking or racewalking, you can contact the Walkers Club of America, 445 East 86th Street, New York, New York 10028.

Practice good running form. With proper form, you'll be more efficient, you'll look good, and that will make you feel good. Proper form also helps prevent injury and establishes good habits for the future, when form is especially important as you start running faster and going up and down hills.

Run tall, with proper posture, and always stay loose and relaxed. Imagine yourself connected to a helium balloon, being lifted upward. Keep your toes, knees, and arms pointing straight ahead as much as possible. Keep your arms bent at the elbows at about a 90-degree angle, and swing them close to your body, letting them naturally cross in front. Keep your hands slightly cupped.

DON'T shuffle your feet; DON'T run up on your toes: DON'T make fists with your hands; DON'T swing your arms and body from side to side; DON'T let your arms hang at your sides or bring them close to your chest as if you're holding something.

It's not easy to know if your form is good, as you can't see what you look like when you run. However, you can get a good idea of your posture and arm swing by practicing in front of a mirror. If you swing until your arms are tired, you will notice what begins to happen as your form falls apart. Do your elbows move away from your body? Do your shoulders begin to rise? Do you tense your neck and face or grit your teeth? Now you'll know what happens on the run when you fatigue or lose concentration, and seeing these weaknesses will help make you aware of what to work on. More informally, you can also check your form from top to bottom by catching a glimpse as you run past plate glass windows.

TEN-WEEK BEGINNING RUNNING PROGRAM

This program is designed to bring you from your armchair to running 3¼ miles (5 kilometers plus) continuously. The program employs all the same principles as running on every other level and is the necessary base for moving on to the intermediate section in Chapter 5. However, you need not move ahead or increase. To maintain basic fitness, simply continue doing the schedule in Week 10.

Many beginners who feel this program is too easy are tempted to increase or jump ahead. I recommend, however, that you start as I did: gradually and conservatively. Remember: Hurry slowly. Following this program builds a better foundation and helps you to avoid injury. You have plenty of time to "press the pace."

On the other hand, if the program is too strenuous, take your time, even longer than the ten weeks if necessary. Stay with a given session as long as you feel you must, and move ahead when you feel you are ready.

Each session of this three-day-a-week ten-week program takes about forty-five to sixty minutes and should also include a five-to-ten-minute warm-up and a cool-down, followed by stretching and strengthening exercises (see Chapter 14). Allow at least one day off between each session. Don't worry about exact time or distance. All guidelines are approximate.

Week 1

Alternately jog/walk (8 of each) 100-yard segments, for a total of one mile.
Same workout for all three days.

Week 2

Alternately jog/walk (5 of each) 200-yard segments, for a total of 1¼ miles.
Same workout for all three days.

Week 3

Alternately jog/walk, vary the segments between 200 and 400 yards, for a total of 1½ miles.
Same workout for all three days.

Week 4

Alternately jog/walk, but walk only half the distance of each jog. Vary the segments between ¼ to ½ mile, for a total of 1¾ miles.
Same workout for all three days.

Week 5

Day 1: ½-mile jog, ¼-mile walk, ½-mile jog, ¼-mile walk, ½-mile jog, for 2 miles total.
Day 2: ¾-mile jog, ½-mile walk, ¾-mile jog, for 2 miles total.
Day 3: jog 2 miles, no walk.

Week 6

Day 1: ½-mile jog, ¼-mile walk, ¾-mile jog, ¼-mile walk, ½-mile jog, for 2¼ miles total.
Day 2: 1-mile jog, ¼-mile walk, 1-mile jog, for 2¼ miles total.
Day 3: 2¼-mile jog, no walk.

Week 7

(Only jogging, no walking from this point on; however, you can vary the pace of the jog.)
2½-mile jog.
Same workout all three days.

Week 8

2¾-mile jog.
Same workout all three days.

Week 9

3-mile jog.
Same workout all three days.

Week 10

3¼ miles total (5 kilometers plus).

Congratulations: Graduation Day!

THE RUNNER'S LIFESTYLE

Obviously, I believe running is satisfying and enjoyable, but with all the hype over "runner's high," people sometimes feel disappointed when they come back from a run tired and sweaty, wondering where the high is. "Runner's high" implies that a person transcends the body and experiences sensations of floating, flying, or dreaming. However, serious runners don't use running to get out of the body, rather the opposite is true: we deliberately focus on the body, as I have advised you to do by monitoring your physical response to training. I can't be sure whether such a thing as a runner's high even exists, as I've never had it, and most top runners say the same thing. The closest I can come to an equivalent experience is the feeling of total control and mastery that I have felt in two major victories in my career, the World Cup 3,000 meters in 1977 and the World Championship marathon in 1983, which is why you will often read about these races throughout the book. These were no "magic" experiences; I got them not through dreaming but through hard training—here on Earth.

Some people feel "transformed" from the first day they begin running; others feel that it's just plain hard work. Most of us realize it is both. I know how great running can feel, but I also know it can feel not so great, even downright awful! It can be fun, but it takes work to have that fun. Part of the challenge is to find satisfaction in both elements: both are important, and both can be satisfying. Here are some tips to help you get the maximum benefits and enjoyment from the sport.

The main objective in the beginning of your running program is to get out there and move. Don't worry about what you look like, your outfit, or if anyone is watching you. Do it joyfully, and if you feel self-conscious, that's the first thing to eliminate. You'll never enjoy the pleasure and sense of freedom running gives until you rid yourself of any and all psychological constraints. It may help to remember you're hardly alone out there. Fortunately, the days are over when we runners, like criminals, waited until after dark to venture out.

Make your running a group experience, rather than a lonely one. Find running partners, or engage your family in your activity. I enjoy my running much more since it has become a family affair, which also helps get me more motivated for my workouts. I run with Jack in the morning, and I often do my second training session in the afternoon with my brother Jan. Sometimes I run with my two brothers, my nephews, or occasionally some of the other Norwegian women runners. We're often a big group at a race, cheering and encouraging one another.

Keep your running consistent but interesting. Vary the terrain, the course, and the location. Beginners have a tendency to do the same thing on the same course every day, which is often why they feel running is boring. For example, I'm a lot happier running in the miles of woods in Oslo. Of course, time and weather do not always permit running in the most ideal location, but a change of scenery as often as possible will keep your interest alive. Even small changes help. After tiring of running one route in New York's Central Park, it took a mere change of direction to wake me up. In order to introduce you to variation, my ten-week program employs different distances and patterns, and in time you will naturally vary the pace.

As in any endeavor, you will likely experience a cycle of hurdles and breakthroughs in your running, which obviously will greatly affect your enthusiasm and energy. One day the thought of getting out of bed to run gives you a headache; the next day you're up early, eager to go. One day you'd like to burn your running shoes; the next day you're ready to buy another pair.

If you sometimes feel discouraged, bored, or apathetic, don't let it get you down. Mood swings in running are as natural as they are in anything else. It's normal, and I, for one, get these feelings often, especially when I'm tired. A certain level of fatigue is part of getting in shape, and you have to expect it and learn to cope. Some of it may be physical, but if you're training properly, a lot of it is likely psychological. Usually, if I'm feeling tired, I won't make any decisions about my workout until I do a fifteen-minute warm-up run; by then I'll know how I feel physically, rather than just what my mind thinks my body feels.

Your general enthusiasm depends on your goals, what kind of person you are, and how you meet challenges. If you have negative feelings, try to translate them into positive ones. Think of your experience not as a struggle to get into shape but as a new way of feeling and a new way of life. It may help to remember a positive experience on the job or a task or hobby that you enjoy and at which you excel. Then transfer these feelings of mastery and confidence to your running.

If you train sensibly, you can avoid any physical problems or injuries. However, sometimes muscle soreness or other minor aches and pains are inevitable, especially as you're using muscles you probably didn't even know you had. This is a hurdle you have to overcome in any exercise program, anytime you use your body. You know the feeling of "brain drain" when you're learning something new; well, it's the same with your body. In time, the tired muscles will become strong. However, if you feel severe fatigue or a persistent ache or pain, cut back, rest, or consult a medical expert. It may also help to refer to the alternative training methods in the Chapter 6 section, Supplementary Training, and the advice on caring for your body in Chapter 14.

A breakthrough takes you not only over a hurdle but often a step beyond. It means you have reached a new level of training or ability, and likely gained important self-confidence. A breakthrough may mean making it through three miles of running or going the distance feeling refreshed instead of washed up. You should be aware of, and expect, both hurdles and breakthroughs, and deal with both patiently. Don't quit at the first sign of fatigue. On the other hand, don't sign up for a marathon the first time you can jog a few miles without stopping.

Now that you are joining the ranks of the active, you will have to consider your daily life as a runner. Organization, discipline, and proper perspective are key elements to accommodating your activity and adapting to your new lifestyle. I can't stress these points enough.

They have been an essential foundation of my running career and my life. The more serious you become about your running, the more important they will become for you as well.

Determine a running schedule. To do so, consider all the variables: first, your "body clock." The time of day you feel at your best is probably when you will feel best running. Some people like to run first thing in the morning; others feel only half alive in the early hours but wake up in the late afternoon or evening. Devising a schedule, however, isn't always as simple as running when the mood strikes. Your schedule must also take into consideration your responsibilities. When are you most likely to make time, and keep time, for your running? Do you have flexible hours, a nearby changing facility (like a gym or a health club), or a training partner or group? If you do run in the dark, as I am frequently forced to do in Norway, make the necessary adjustments. Watch your footing, and take essential safety measures, like wearing a reflective vest or other clothing and not going into deserted or unlit areas alone.

I grew up in a family of early risers, so I have always been one myself. I am what is commonly called an "A" person, one who functions better during the day, as opposed to a "B," or night, person. I'm up before sunrise but usually sound asleep by 9:30 P.M. Because I get up so early and start my running soon after, Jack calls me an "AA" person! Although you may not be a morning person, I highly recommend you consider running at the start of your day.

If you are like most people—busy throughout the day with work, plans, and responsibilities—you know how easy it is to get caught up. The time slips away, something unexpected comes up, you're tired—all reasons to skip your run. If you haven't done it, you're likely thinking about doing it, and this preoccupation, usually accompanied by guilt, is a waste of time and energy. That's why I think it's better to get your run done in the morning if you can. I realize some people have trouble even getting out of bed in the morning, let alone doing exercise, but I believe that can be changed. After all, Jack was a classic "B" person—a real night owl—until he got used to running with me at 5:30 in the morning. I may have to tell him fifteen times to get up so we can get going, but at least his busy schedule and unexpected meetings don't keep him from running. By getting it done in the morning, you have no excuse not to run (except sleep of course!).

My morning run is usually one of two training sessions a day, and it starts my day off right. Without it, I feel edgy and thrown off. I get up between 5:00 and 5:15, usually before the alarm goes off (I hate surprises and a racing heart). First, I wash my face to wake myself up, and then I check the weather. Walking up and down the stairs to consult the thermometer and to dress helps get me warmed up. After I choose the appropriate training gear, I do a few small chores around the house to further awaken myself, and my body. I'm constantly doing something: putting away newspapers, setting the breakfast table, or folding dry clothes. I'm the type who can't sit down; I need to move.

I drink a glass of water before I run—more water if it's a very warm day. However, a cup of coffee or tea if you're accustomed to it may help, especially if you're not inclined to go straight from the bed to the road. I never eat before a run. Food immediately before rigorous exercise is not recommended. You'll learn by experience what's best for you, but if you have special nutritional needs or specific questions on pre-exercise diet, it may be best to consult with a nutritionist or your doctor.

Remember to start slowly, as the body is often a bit stiffer in the morning. (Never stretch cold. A modified version of the run acts as a sufficient warm-up.) I know that even though I'm used to a morning run, part of me is still in bed. If it's very cold out and you're inclined to start too fast in order to get warm, try an indoor warm-up like jogging in place, jumping rope, or walking up stairs. You'll likely always feel a little chilly when you start any run. If you don't, you're probably overdressed and will soon be overheated. If this tends to happen, wear layered clothing so you can take off a layer and tie it around your waist.

After a cool-down, it's a good idea to change into dry clothes and spend at least ten to fifteen minutes stretching and perhaps doing some strengthening exercises. One of my failings, I admit, is not doing enough strengthening exercises, like sit-ups or push-ups. The longer I'm away from it, the harder it is to get back in the habit. Don't make the same mistake; devote sufficient time to these exercises, especially if you have upper-body weakness that might affect your back or your posture.

After a shower and breakfast, I'm ready to start the rest of my day. If you run from a gym, or are in a hurry to get to work, why not pack a nutritious breakfast from home rather than relying on fast food? See Chapter 13 to learn how we Norwegians prepare our own "carry-out" meals. It's important to remember that among your dietary needs as an exerciser is plenty of water. Especially in warm weather, you should drink before, during, and after exercise, not necessarily just when thirsty. Check that your water consumption is sufficient by weighing yourself before and after exercise. At most, you shouldn't lose more than a pound.

Speaking of food, I'd be remiss if I didn't acknowledge one of the major motivations for beginning runners: weight loss. Millions of people have discovered that running is perhaps the cheapest, fastest, and most effective exercise for weight control. Running is at the top of the list for calorie burning among the most popular forms of exercise. It uses anywhere from eight to eleven calories per minute. That's about 300 calories for a half hour, the size of an average breakfast. In addition, research has shown that physical activity leads to increased metabolism (thus, higher calorie burning), even up to twenty-four hours after training. Running and a good diet virtually guarantee you will lose weight. But even more important, it tones your body as well.

I am 5 feet 8 inches tall, 115 pounds, but I haven't always been this size. I have never been heavy, but I was beefier before my years of intensive running (see photo section). I lost seven pounds, a significant amount for my build, from 1974 to 1976, when I increased my training. And the more I did, the more the shape of my body became honed. Quite simply, I think nothing works off the weight and adds tone like picking up your own body weight step after step.

Weight loss is a constant obsession. It's no wonder, as 34 million Americans risk a health hazard from obesity. However, of the 50 million Americans who are dieting, only 5 percent will maintain that weight loss. That's why the recommended weight-loss prescription is a combination of diet and exercise. My advice is to use the two creatively, according to your best personal advantage. Don't necessarily follow a strict or special diet and exercise plan if you sense it won't work for you. Do the same for diet as I recommend for training: find what works best for you. If necessary, select from several plans and create your own program according to what fits your psychological profile and capitalizes on your strengths.

For example, some people can't entirely give up sweets or find doing so too restrictive. I never crave cake or desserts but feel no hesitation about having a few small pieces a day of the caramel candy I like or an occasional ice-cream bar. That doesn't mean I eat the whole bag of candy or container of ice cream every day. My motto has always been "If I want it, I eat it." But I balance that with a degree of inner discipline about what I know is good for me and my training. I make sure my diet is well balanced and healthy. Running also inspires you to eat right. You won't want to undo all your good work by loading up on empty calories, and it feels better to run light. It helps to know that the tempting dessert you see at lunchtime could come back to haunt you on your afternoon run!

Don't feel you have to have a certain body type to be a runner, even to become a good runner. If you look at world-class runners, for example, you notice all kinds of shapes and sizes. For every thin runner like Bill Rodgers or Mary Decker Slaney, there's a stocky Rob de Castella or a Joan Benoit Samuelson. In fact, I think the variety of runners is favorably changing the image of the sport. The point is not to be thin but to be strong—whatever your build. This is something I want to emphasize, especially to all the women who try not to eat merely to get thin. What you think you may gain in looks, you may likely lose in strength.

In addition to finding your own successful dieting techniques, look for creative ways to get more exercise. You'll get in better shape, burn more calories, and help make fitness a way of life. Take the stairs instead of the elevator, or head for your appointment early so you can walk. Play tag with the kids—good for their fitness as well as yours. Bend, reach, carry. Use housework or gardening as exercise. Do things the hard way when you can; avoid all those energy-saving electrical devices like power lawn mowers or electric mixers. Use a hand lawn mower, and beat your batter or knead your bread by hand.

Your first strides and your new lifestyle are only the beginning of what can become as essential and natural an activity as eating and sleeping. Running can give you health and joy, a sense of well-being, challenge, and endless discovery—about yourself and your abilities. I know it can do this for you, because it has done it for me.

5

For the Intermediate— The Basics of Training and Racing

Congratulations, you're a runner now! Exactly what does this mean? What separates the intermediate, or even the advanced, from the beginner? What is the difference between a jogger and a runner? This is a question that is asked so often that I feel it deserves some special attention. "Jogger" and "runner" are arbitrary terms for which there are no standard definitions; even I am asked at times if I'm a jogger (I just smile). What's in a name? you may ask. For the purpose of the various training programs, it may be useful to give these names meanings.

I define jogger and runner not by pace or ability but by goals. Quite simply: a jogger runs for fitness, which means about thirty minutes, three times a week. This fitness is an excellent goal in itself and is the essential foundation for any intermediate running program. However, running more than the amount necessary for fitness implies other goals, such as additional weight loss, conditioning, or to participate in a fun run or race.

The move from beginner to intermediate is often made quite casually. Most people start out running for fitness and go on to the next stage without even realizing. One day they're jogging, the next they're running a race. In the interest of proper training, however, I recommend a more deliberate increase. This chapter is for those who have achieved a basic level of fitness and who are now "hooked" on running with the rest of us. You are ready to increase your distance and develop your endurance, speed, and conditioning. For this purpose, I will discuss some of the fundamentals of training, with an emphasis on how they apply to my own running program.

If you follow the beginning training principles, you can't go too wrong. The basic formula for fitness is fairly simple. That's why so many millions of people choose to run. The complications arise when you want to become a better runner. Experience, knowledge, ability, and discipline all become more important variables. If running initially attracts people for its simplicity, it keeps them at it for the challenge of developing these variables.

Before I lay down the laws of a training program, you should know that there aren't any laws or, rather, there are many. How's that for the first complication? Training is highly variable. I have always said first and foremost about training that what is good for one runner might be disastrous for another. For this reason, there are almost as many running programs as there are runners. The trick is to find one, or create one, that suits you.

Training is very individual. This is why I don't necessarily recommend my program for anyone else and why you should be careful with any program you choose to follow. What I do recommend are the *elements* of my program, which also include the fundamentals of any sound exercise program. The samples I give employ these elements and are the building blocks from which you can construct your own program. To a degree, the best way to build a successful program is by experimenting, but this should always be done carefully and by following the basic fundamentals. This is why the beginner's program is designed to provide not only a base of fitness but a foundation in proper training. One basic law should be stressed. Simplified, it says: When something works, don't change it. When something doesn't work, it's probably not for you. Follow this law and you'll be on your way toward developing important consistency.

Once you have achieved basic fitness, established a goal, and evaluated your strengths and weaknesses, you are ready to create your own intermediate program. One of your greatest resources is other runners. We can all learn and profit from each other. Some of my training has evolved from comparing notes with other top runners and coaches, and I usually find something good in all runners' programs. Over the years, I have built my training based on my goals, my physical and psychological profile, and the guidance of coaches and advisors. In addition, I have gained great insight by evaluating the training of other runners.

I am at the point where I know when I see another person's training whether it has something I can use. For instance, I have adapted some interval training from Alberto Salazar and his coach, Bill Dellinger, specifically mile repeats, or "in and out" miles (a cycle of running a fast mile, followed by a moderate or slower mile). On the other hand, some top runners' programs make me tremble: 120 miles a week of pounding the roads, much of it at a fast pace. I know I'd collapse after two weeks! Other programs employ too much long, slow distance, which I am too impatient to do and feel is a waste of time. My training falls someplace in the middle of these extremes. I run fewer miles than most of my peers but do more intense, quality training—which is an extension of my track background. Although I respect runners like Joan Benoit Samuelson and Ingrid Kristiansen, I could never run the megamileage they do to be world-class runners. Some runners log unbelievable mileage. I have read that Japanese marathoner Toshihiko Seko runs up to thirty-seven miles in one run! To me that sounds crazy but as you, too, will soon discover, many roads lead to Rome.

If there were only one road to Rome—if training were an exact science, as easy as "time plus distance equals progress"—my task in advising you would be simple. But training is both a science and an art—a blend of physical, mental, and environmental factors, and well-developed self-knowledge. Despite the many established "dos and don'ts," you have to learn most things through your own experience. You can't always go by the book; my own experience has proved it.

In 1980 I was trying to decide what to do with my career. Would it be track or road racing or both? How would cross-country fit in? This indecision was reflected in my training; I was tired and bored with it. So I changed it. I began a regimen of intense training specifically designed to improve my track running, but at the same time I didn't give up road racing. I added strength training to my running: exercises and drills. I did bounding and jumping—usually sprinter's drills—and changed my running form with the aim of gaining greater efficiency of movement on the track. According to "the book," I should have improved, but I only got injured. I got plantar fascitis (pain in the arches) and sore Achilles tendons, both from extensive running in spikes. This forced me to take three weeks off from running.

When you learn from other runners, remember that you can also learn from their mistakes. My mistakes in this case could have been avoided by taking some of my own advice, most of which is detailed in the chapter for beginners.

1. Have a definite goal. I was sitting on the fence between track and roads, restless and undecided.
2. Set realistic goals, and be flexible. I realized the competition was becoming too tough to be both a top track runner *and* a road racer; I was spread too thin. It was unreasonable to try to do everything, so I had to change my plans.
3. Don't add to or change a running program too quickly; the body needs time to adapt. I suddenly began running a lot in spikes, in addition to adding another new element: bounding and jumping. Failing to follow this rule is probably the reason I was injured.
4. When something works for you, don't change it. My form had gotten me pretty far up to that point; it would likely go on serving me just as well.

Obviously, not every rule applies in the same way for every runner, but there are some basic laws that apply to us all. Here they are.

Hard/Easy

The cardinal rule of running, and of any exercise program, is the hard/easy system. For every hard session of exercise, there should follow the proper amount of easy training or rest, both to help your body recover and to absorb the benefits of the training. This applies to single sessions as well as to cumulative weeks, months, and seasons. Alternating hard/easy isn't always as clear-cut as running one day hard, followed by one day easy. Hard/easy is a relative principle, and how it applies depends on experience and ability. For some, one hard day a week is plenty; others can handle three or even four, while still others incorporate moderately difficult training interspersed with hard/easy. Some people need much more rest between hard efforts than others. I notice that in the last few years I need more recovery time between hard workouts. After so many years of hard training, whether it's physical or psychological or some of both, I feel as if my body is wearing down.

The hard/easy system applies to the distance of the run as well as to the intensity. Some intermediate runners work their way up to thirty or thirty-five miles a week, but they run the same five miles at the same effort each day. To alternate hard/easy, this type of runner might try the following schedule:

> *Day 1* (Sunday): seven miles; *Day 2*: three miles; *Day 3*: eight miles; *Day 4*: two miles; *Day 5*: six miles; *Day 6*: four miles; *Day 7*: five miles (or a day off).

Maintain the hard/easy system while increasing your mileage as well; remember to increase no more than the recommended 10 percent per week. Contrary to the hard/easy system is the error some people make when they compress a large part of their weekly mileage into the weekend, because they have more time then. That may fit the clock's cycle, but it doesn't fit the body's cycle. For this reason, such weekend running may do more harm than good.

Here is an example of how I use the hard/easy system in my program:

> *Saturday*: two sessions as usual, but both easy, for a total of 12–15 miles. *Sunday*: a long, hard run of 18 miles. *Monday*: same as Saturday. Saturday and Monday may not seem like easy days, but when compared to my average double session of 15 miles done at a strong to all-out pace, they are, in fact, recovery days.

Don't worry about resting too much. Resting can't harm you. Remember, it is an essential part of the training cycle. That doesn't mean you should follow the advice of the old joke "When I feel the need to exercise, I lie down until it passes." However, often by this level it takes just as much discipline to rest as it does to run. I judge what to do by how I feel, and I'm not afraid to cut out a session or two if I'm tired. That's why my running varies between eleven and thirteen sessions a week. To this day I often recall the words of Ron Clarke at my first running clinic in California back in 1979. Clarke, the famous Australian runner, once held world records for events between two miles and 10,000 meters, but he never won an Olympic gold medal. When he was asked if he would have done anything differently in his career, he answered, "I would have rested more."

QUALITY TRAINING

With a base of fitness, there is no reason an intermediate runner cannot do quality training. The purpose of this training is to educate the body to run comfortably at a faster pace. My purpose in this chapter is to give a basic definition of this type of training so you can utilize it on the intermediate level and understand how it is used throughout the rest of the book. I think a basic grasp of this training is sufficient at this point; however, to understand the detailed reasons of how and why quality training works, and for detailed training programs, refer to the books in Recommended Reading (page 249).

Most of my running is done at a steady pace, which means it is not a jog, but neither is it a speed that leaves me breathless. It's not exactly conversation pace, either, as I use my energy to run, not talk. On my long runs, however, I purposely converse to keep the pace slower. Although mine is a strong but comfortable pace, some runners get better results with a slower, recovery pace. Technically, both types of running can be said to follow the "continuity principle,"* which means a constant or nearly constant work load of longer duration in order to increase general endurance capability. This type of running

*From Sigmund B. Strømme, Harold Frey, Ole K. Harlem, Oddvar Stokke, Odd D. Vellar, Leif Edvard Aarø, and Jon Eric Johnsen, "Physical Activity and Health," *The Scandinavian Journal of Social Medicine*, 29 (1982).

on your own relative level constitutes the bulk of your training.

In addition to this endurance running, I do quality training, commonly called speedwork, in the form of intervals and *fartlek*, Swedish for "speed play." Interval training* is running with periodic changes between exertion and rest, or between a high and a low work load. Intervals are a structured system of speedwork usually done on a track or other measured area. Fartlek* is a less structured version of interval training, but employing the same principles. Fartlek usually consists of segments of exertion and rest for random distances or times, and it is done off the track.

My weekly program consists of a long interval session (repeats of 1,000 meters to one mile) or a short interval session (300 to 500 meters), a fartlek run of between eight and ten miles, and one long run (from fourteen to eighteen miles, sometimes as much as twenty). The exact layout depends on my racing schedule. The remaining eight to ten weekly sessions are steady-pace runs of between six and ten miles. This program is what I do year-round and is more or less what I have always done (except for the long run, which I began after starting to do marathons).

• The purpose of my long intervals is to do some quality running faster than my race pace. This is the only occasion in which I time myself on the track. Mentally, it is my most difficult workout, which helps toughen my mind as well as my body.
• The purpose of my short intervals is to maintain leg speed and efficiency.
• The purpose of my fartlek is to simulate a race situation as best as possible. This varied-pace running on the roads also helps my body, especially my legs, to be prepared to handle any change in pace or terrain that may occur in the race.

The key to successful training is to match your goals with the proper program. Adequate recovery and improvement in times are good indications of a successful program, as are cumulative results in a series of races. I also happen to know that my training is correct

---

*From Sigmund B. Strømme *et al.*, "Physical Activity and Health," *The Scandinavian Journal of Social Medicine*, 29 (1982).

according to an evaluation, including a treadmill test, done by noted sports physiologist Dr. David Costill in 1981. He affirmed that my training program is well suited to my goals.

HOW MUCH IS ENOUGH; HOW MUCH IS TOO MUCH?

This is a difficult question, especially as most serious runners don't lack the desire to train. If anything, they are often overambitious. If you have taken your running this far, you are likely fairly ambitious. As you improve, there is a logical tendency to think that more is better. From my experience, I think advanced distance runners (especially on the world-class level) are always balanced on a narrow line between top shape and a state of overtraining. The closer you approach your ultimate ability, the easier it is to tip that balance to the wrong side. Again, you learn to find your own balance by experience; however, there are some signs to guide you.

If you are training properly, you should progress steadily. This doesn't necessarily mean a personal best every time you race, but don't get into what I call the "one step forward, two steps back" cycle: a few spectacular results, followed by an injury or a slump. In the beginner's section I discussed the natural cycle of hurdles and breakthroughs. A series of progressive breakthroughs lets you know you are training properly. Each training session should be like putting money in the bank. If your training works, you continue to deposit into your "strength" account, using the same formula that results in improvement. You might slowly add intensity or mileage, but the formula remains the same. I've run farther and faster using the same basic system since 1971.

Too much training has the opposite effect. Rather than build, it tears down. Your body will tell when you have begun to tip the balance. Just be sure to listen to it. Both physical and emotional symptoms should warn you. There are the obvious signs of chronic fatigue, heavy legs, apathy toward training, and lack of appetite; and a classic indication is also an elevated resting pulse. My resting pulse before getting out of bed in the morning has been as low as thirty-eight beats per minute. Although I don't measure mine regularly, I would know if I were in the danger zone if it were consistently five to ten beats higher.

Actually, I judge my fatigue more by my moods, because for me heavy legs can sometimes be a false sign—caused by something psychological—a temporary feeling that for some reason disappears after I begin running. However, I know it's time to rest when my legs are so heavy that the skin feels too tight for the muscles. If it's hard to sleep or I'm cranky, impatient, or annoyed, I'm probably overtraining. In my case, family and friends often know when I'm overtrained even before I do. When I begin to snap at Jack, he knows it's time to analyze my training and probably cut back.

However, you need not be completely sidelined. In the case of overtraining or injury, you can maintain "active rest," a system of light or alternative exercises that allows your body to rest from specific kinds of stress. You might do a week of running only easy days. Or if it's your legs that are weary, try swimming, walking, or light cycling.

Here are some questions to ask yourself if you suspect you are overdoing it. If you answer yes to three or more of them, it's probably time to cut back.

- Does your normally comfortable pace leave you breathless?
- Are your legs heavy for far longer than the usual recovery period after hard workouts or races?
- Do you find it especially hard to climb steps?
- Do you dread the thought of training?
- Do you find it exceptionally hard to get out of bed in the morning?
- Do you have an extended loss of appetite?
- Are you more susceptible to colds, flu, headache, or infections?
- Is your resting pulse five to ten beats higher than usual?
- Is your target heart rate (see footnote, page 53, Chapter 4) higher than usual?

The Race

Why run a race? You can do it just for fun or for a new experience. That's why I ran my first road race, in 1978. I had a chance to come to America and see what the road-running scene was all about. But the ultimate reason to run a race is to test yourself: both your preparation and your ability. I equate running a race with taking an exam. Your training is the studies, and the race tells you what kind of student you've been. It shows you if your training is correct and, if so, inspires you to continue with it. After all, you put so much into it, it's important to know that it's worthwhile.

How serious you consider the race, and for what reasons you run it, will vary with your goals and preparation. There can be a different goal or motivation for each race. It's perfectly reasonable that some races will be more serious than others. Not every exam need be a final exam. Although I give most of my races an all-out effort, I enjoy some of them just to be part of the event; and others I use as hard workouts.

The race appeals to me for a variety of reasons. In addition to a test of my ability and improvement, I enjoy the sense of support I feel running with thousands of others and chatting with my competitors afterward. Sometimes I compare notes with them: where we felt tired, where we got a second wind and picked up the pace. This atmosphere may be something other runners take for granted, but when you've always run track, where a handful of separate egos often never so much as exchange greetings, a road race is a real pleasure.

There is something about the ritual of the race—pinning on the number, lining up, being timed—that brings out the best in us. In this way, we are all alike. We all share the same experience: the same clock, the same distance, the same determination. The race is run by you, for you, and it's all your own. Just as no one else can do it for you, no one but you can feel the same challenge and personal satisfaction from your effort. Another aspect of the race is universal: the runner's enjoyment of performing. There's a little bit of the actor in us all. We like being watched. We may run the race for ourselves, but it's significant that we do it in front of spectators. Without being on that stage, it just isn't the same—not for me, anyway.

When I ran the 1984 World Cross Country Championships, at the Meadowlands, in New Jersey, I never saw a spectator or heard a cheer. I later discovered there was a crowd of 17,000 in attendance, but they were inside a building that overlooks the horse-race track where we ran. Without those spectators, I felt like I was running a low-key race instead of a world championship; I just didn't get the same rush of adrenaline. I had won this event five times, but in this race I came in third, outkicked in the final stretch. Who knows, maybe those crowds would have helped me to push just that extra bit harder. On the other hand, when I come off the Queensboro Bridge in the New York City Marathon, where the crowd is famous for its size and cheering, it gives me goose bumps. How can I help but feel inspired to pick up the pace? If I had been put on the starting line alone in this race with just a pace car, I could not have set those world records.

Even in training we runners are motivated by being watched. When I run with Jack and there's no one around, he's inclined to fall off the pace, to lag behind. But when there are people around, he works hard to keep up. We would all probably be that much better if there were spectators for all our training runs!

RACE PREPARATION

There are many details that go into preparing for a race, and it's these details that can make or break a perfect day. You've already done the training, so to be able to put it to good use it's essential you consider the other aspects of preparation.

One of the most important is tapering off in training, which should begin days before the race. I cut back to one easy run several days before an event and do even less the day before, and some runners like a day of complete rest before the event. How much tapering you do depends on your personal needs as well as the type of race. For example, some people feel sluggish or insecure taking a day off and do even a twenty-minute jog just to keep their rhythm; others enjoy the feeling of being rested to the point of edginess, so they're hungry to race. The more serious you are and the longer the event, the more you will likely taper in order to make sure you're very well rested. More tapering is obviously necessary for a marathon than for ten kilometers, as both physically and mentally it's easier to run six miles than twenty-six. A diary will help teach you if you're tapering properly. This is how I learned. When I look back on the preparation for good races, it's clear that I obviously did something right, and so I follow that same preparation.

If the race is at a time of day you don't usually train, it may help to do some running at that time. The week before a race I try to do my training runs at the hour of the event. If you're running a race far from home, try to make the trip in sufficient time to rest from a long drive or plane ride. If there is a time or weather change, allow several days to a week to acclimatize. During those days, try running at the same time as the event, even if your body is on a different time clock.

LOGISTICS

If I'm running a morning race, 8:30 or 9:00 A.M., for example, I get up between 5:00 and 5:30 to make sure my body is fully awake before I ask it to race. There's nothing worse than trying to run a race an hour after waking up; it's just too much shock for a sleepy system. After I get up, I go out for a walk, which serves as my wake-up and warm-up. If it's a warm day, I'll begin drinking fluids from the time I get up. If the race is midmorning or at noon, I'll have tea and toast (no butter, just jam). I know what I eat doesn't help me in the race, but it does get rid of my hunger and that empty feeling in my stomach, so for this reason I always have something small.

The most important rule for every aspect of the race applies to food as well: do not try anything new. No matter how well runners know this, there is always that temptation to experiment before the race, to try to get that winning edge. If you don't usually drink coffee, don't do it before a race because you've heard it gives you a good jolt. If you're used to having something to eat, do so, as long as it's easily digestible and eaten at least two to three hours before the event. (More details on prerace diet are in Chapter 13.)

In terms of practical considerations, I make sure I know where my racing gear is and that it's clean and ready. It saves me time and aggravation to have all my gear out the night before the race, especially if it's an early-morning event. I pin my number on my singlet and drape it on a chair, as seeing it also gets me motivated. I pack a bag with petroleum jelly, hair pins, toilet paper, extra safety pins, and a snack for after the race. A change of clothes to get out of my wet gear and alternative clothes, in case the weather changes before the race, are also included. In case of rain, I bring extra socks and shoes. I also bring a plastic bottle of water if I'm not sure there's water at the start. In terms of these provisions, my theory is that it's better to bring too much than too little. How and when to pack a bag may seem elementary, but nothing becomes more complicated or nerve-wracking than hunting for things the morning of a race when you're nervous or realizing you've forgotten them when you arrive.

Know the course. I always make sure I know the basic layout of the course, either by looking at a map, driving it, or running it. I know where the start and finish are, the up- and downhills, and the water stations. The 1985 L'eggs Mini Marathon taught me just how important it is to thoroughly know the route, and it was a costly lesson. By not taking the time to inquire about exactly how to run the tangents (the shortest allowable distance), I added about fifty extra feet by running wide around curves, which cost me five to ten seconds, obviously critical in a race I lost by only three seconds. It had never mattered before how I ran this race—so when Jack had brought it up, I was too nervous and distracted to pay attention. It just proves that after all these years I'm still learning, and, believe me, in this case it was one tough lesson!

Read the race entry blank thoroughly for special instructions. If I don't understand something, I ask the race organizers or officials for clarification. Know the travel route, and arrange transportation so you know you'll arrive at the race with plenty of time. Doing these things puts you in a state of greater readiness. The more well informed and prepared you are, the more confident you feel. The more confident you feel, the better you race.

These details may seem obvious, but you'd be surprised what you miss when you're nervous. There are hundreds of runners who wait anxiously for their precious New York City Marathon applications, only to read the instructions hastily and make any number of careless errors in their rush to send them back—forgetting to sign their names, for example. This may prevent them from getting into the race, but how about the kind of nervous disorganization that prevents people from running at all? I know of runners who have warmed up and been all ready to race, only to discover while beginning to take off their sweats that they had forgotten their shorts! "Novices," you may say. Hardly. Carl Lewis is one of them.

Mental Rehearsal

I also prepare for a race by going through a mental rehearsal; that is, I run the race in my mind. I create a scenario—imagining how the race will develop, who will set the pace, and how I will perform. (For details on developing your mental powers, see Chapter 7.) As race day comes closer, it's natural to think about the event; but at the same time I'm thinking positive thoughts, I'm also a little nervous. However, the race shouldn't become a constant, nerve-wracking preoccupation, rather an awareness that the event is approaching and a positive feeling of anticipation.

Nervousness is a good sign, if you have it under control. There's an important difference between nervousness that comes from excitement and that which comes from fear. If you're too nervous, it will hurt your effort. If it's to the point where you can't sleep or eat— you feel like a wreck—that's too much. This kind of nervousness is tiring. It wears you down and detracts from your effort. Nervous excitement, on the other hand, is that funny feeling you get in your stomach, that surge of adrenaline that tells your body, "Let's get running." Some people have asked me, "Are you still nervous after so many years?" Sure I'm nervous, all the time. It's part of "race readiness," and if I didn't have this nervousness, it would be time for me to retire.

Keeping the race in mental focus can be a mixed blessing. I'm the type who needs to think about the event, to plan and discuss, to get myself psyched up. No matter what I'm doing, I keep the race in the back of my mind. I don't necessarily recommend this for everyone, especially those who can't differentiate between anticipation and dread. If you feel destructive nervousness, if the race is too much in the forefront of your mind, it's best to try to distract yourself: visit with friends (preferably nonrunners in this case!), go out to dinner or to a movie.

Although I like to contemplate my race, I need distraction as well. Since my mind sometimes strays from a movie back to the race, I do crossword puzzles instead, which require concentration. In the States I might pass the time shopping for items that in Norway are unavailable (like toothpaste in a pump) or expensive (like underwear). I've even gone dancing, although I usually reserve this for after the race. I haven't given up coaxing Jack to teach me some of the dances he did as the Norwegian Latin-American Dance champion. He always tells me he is too old now (he was champion at age seventeen), but I think he's just taken too much teasing from my brothers about his accomplishment.

At times I just have to go out and be a little spontaneous—such as before the 1980 New York City Marathon. I had spent a long time gazing at the ice skaters at Rockefeller Center when suddenly I turned to Jack and asked, "Would you like to try it?" "No thanks!" he wisely answered the woman who was about to run a marathon. No matter. I turned to my brother Jan and asked the same question. "Sure," he said. (Sometimes siblings are on exactly your wave length!) So while Jack and Jan's wife stood on the sidelines in a state of anxiety, Jan and I skated. To this day, I don't know why I chose to do something so risky before a race, but I certainly had a good time!

Nervousness often causes runners to feel and behave rather oddly before a race, so you have to be prepared, and also prepare others around you, for this possibility. Although I am a fairly even-tempered person, I get easily irritated before a big race. I remember going for a jog the morning before the 1984 New York City Marathon. I was with my two brothers, who were also going to run the race, and Jack, who wasn't racing. Jack was making a lot of clever chat, but no matter what he said we weren't answering. We were in that stage of mental rehearsal, in our own world of concentration and nervousness. Finally, I thought to myself, "This is too much; he must quit talking." I stopped dead in my tracks and snapped, "Please, stop talking; we're concentrating!" Fortunately, Jack understood, as he was a competitive runner for years.

Sometimes I dream strange things before a big race. They are never dreams of winning or of success, but rather classic dreams of anxiety. I dream I come to the start and I don't have my shoes or I've forgotten to put on my shorts. Another version of the dream is that I come too late to start or I get lost on the course. These dreams are so real that when I first wake up, I'm not quite sure if the race has been run or if I still have another chance.

Like many runners, I have a love/hate relationship with the race. This is illustrated by my race-day fantasies, the most vivid of which involve the New York City Marathon. I often laugh about these fantasies, except on that particular October day when I am tortured by them. As I sit on the bus that crawls through heavy traffic toward the start, I wish with my whole heart that we would stay in that traffic jam for hours, never making it to the start. The other fantasy involves the Verrazano Bridge, on which the race starts. I imagine the bridge collapsing, preventing the race from beginning. I realize, of course, how upset I would be if these fantasies became reality. I truly want to get to the start. I want to run the race. You may likely have similar fantasies due to nervousness: the race is canceled, it will snow, no one will show up. You know that you've prepared for competition, but a little part of you doesn't want to "face the music." We're all that way to a degree; it's a natural feeling.

When you have a lot at stake, when you have trained hard and the success of your training and preparation is connected to the outcome of the race, these fantasies are the most vivid. Elite runners know the feeling well. One race can sometimes change a runner's life. I understood just how Joan Benoit Samuelson felt when she discussed her thoughts near the end of the Olympic marathon. Coming through the tunnel that leads to the track and the last lap of the race, she said to herself, "This is the dream. This could change my life. It's not too late. I can still hide in here and not come out."

Moods, dreams, and fantasies prove that there is a lot involved emotionally with the race. You should expect these emotions—not fight them—learn to deal with them. After all, they are part of the total experience of the race. For me, they are an important part. If I do not experience at least some of these emotions, I know I am not totally ready to race.

PRERACE WARM-UP

The principles of the warm-up are included in the beginners' section and apply to the race warm-up as well. If you do not already have a warm-up routine, you should establish one. The warm-up you use in training can be modified for the race. It should be very thorough in colder weather, and especially if you intend to start the race at a fairly brisk pace.

If I'm running a race in the 10km range, I start my warm-up forty minutes before the start. Your warm-up need not be as long as mine, but it should serve the same purpose of getting you physically and mentally prepared, and keeping you loose and relaxed. I jog for twenty minutes, stretch for five to ten minutes, and then do some pick-ups: short, easy sprints that get me into high gear. Pick-ups get me loosened up and raise my heart rate, preparing me to take off at high speed from the start. I warm up much less for a marathon, as it's a long race and a slower start. However, I still do pick-ups to relieve my nerves, feel geared up, and stay loose. You'll also see runners before a race shake out their limbs or roll their heads to relax.

Don't be dismayed if you feel dead-legged and generally terrible during your warm-up. When runners in clinics are asked if they ever feel this way, most of them emphatically say yes. This is a common feeling both right before the race and in the days prior, and it is usually just nerves. From my experience, I can tell you that how you feel may have little to do with the race. Frankly, most of the time I don't feel very good in my warm-up, especially before a big race in which I end up doing well. In fact, sometimes I feel good in my warm-up—fast and light—and end up bombing in the race. If you don't feel great, don't take it as a sign of things to come; just work on convincing yourself that you'll do fine once the gun goes off.

POSTRACE RECOVERY

Don't end the race by finding the nearest bench and parking your body on it. After taking a reasonable amount of time to catch your breath, take a brisk walk or jog, and then stretch. I do the same forty-minute routine (minus the pick-ups) to cool down as I do to warm up. Recovery extends to the several days following a race as well, during which you should remain active. Remember, active rest—what you do the days following the race—has a direct effect on how quickly you recover. I do easier runs, take warm baths, and get a massage.

Take a sufficient rest from hard training after a race. Don't make a classic mistake. If you have run well, you feel invincible and resume hard training immediately. If you run poorly, you're determined to train harder to improve, and you make the same mistake. Often the day after a race or hard run, you're not especially sore, but two days later you feel it. Some people call it the two-day lag, and it's almost universal.

I get very hyper when I win a race or perform well, so I've had to be very careful to control myself in training. The fatigue always hits me two or three days later. In 1979 I ran a world road record in the L'eggs Mini Marathon and with little recovery resumed hard training. I paid the price with a lingering fatigue that lasted for over a month. Even experienced runners have a hard time learning. I did the same thing, after the same race, with the same result, in 1980.

After a hard race, take the first two days easy. Then work up to your normal training distance, but run it at a slower pace. Build back up over five or six days. Remember, this is very individual. Be careful during these days: listen to your body. Be flexible. During my planned recovery, if I find it's too much, I cut back or stop running, even in the middle of a session. Be conservative. Feel yourself holding back during recovery, as if you could do more.

The race is a mental as well as a physical stress, so you need to recover mentally as well. Mental fatigue or burnout is just as real as the physical version. If I feel mentally tired, I'm apathetic, not motivated to race. I know I won't perform well. This is especially true after a marathon, which requires tremendous concentration and mental energy. I don't even want to think about another marathon after New York in October until at least the following spring, and I usually run only one marathon a year, at most two. When I lined up for New York in 1983, it was my third marathon that year. My body ran the race, but my heart and mind were asleep. I had overraced—three marathons in seven months, and I wasn't inspired. All I saw ahead of me was a 26.2-mile training run.

POTENTIAL RACE PROBLEMS

You should be prepared for a number of potential problems in a race. Training prepares you for some of them; however, there are some complications that can occur only in the race and can come as somewhat of a shock if you have not experienced them before.

Since the growth of the sport, it is not uncommon to find yourself positioned among a sea of runners in a mass start, with all those anxious bodies like a bomb about to explode. Sometimes people get pushed around right after the race starts, and sometimes a runner falls. I fell at the 1983 Peachtree 10km, in Atlanta (a race with 25,000 runners), where the same thing happened the year before to Mary Decker Slaney. It was both an upsetting and a frightening experience. People tripped on my legs and I was badly shaken. I still don't know how I managed to get up and run 32:01. Despite the fall and the extreme heat and humidity, it was one of my best races. I still have the scars to remind me.

Now when I wait for the start of a mass race, I am always on my guard. If I feel the wave of pushing, I repeat to those around me, "Take it easy; don't push," for my sake and theirs. If there is still a crowd of people around you after the start and through the early stages of a mass race, take it easy, jog until the pack thins out, and hold out your arms for balance and protection. The time you lose waiting for the pack to thin out is insignificant compared with the energy you waste trying to push through or dodge and pass other runners. Besides, you can also trip and fall running this way, or trip someone else. Most mass races are well organized so that runners rarely fall, but if you do, get up and out of the way as quickly as possible. If someone falls near you, although your first instinct may be to stop and help, don't do it if you risk causing a pileup by others running into you.

Always line up early for a large race. I will never forget the nightmare of trying to get to the starting line of the 1983 New York City Marathon at the last minute. Somehow, I ended up in the back, 17,000 runners away from where I was supposed to be. Of course, they were just as nervous as I was, so it made my task especially difficult. "Who's pushing through?" people angrily asked. In tears of panic, I had to ask runner after runner to let me by. It was quite upsetting (no one likes being snapped at by thousands of people) and a waste of energy that detracted from my race effort. A situation such as this can be avoided by more careful planning. Know where the start is, wear a watch so you know when to line up, and, most important, listen to the announcements by the race officials. If you don't hear them, or are confused about what's going on, don't hesitate to ask questions.

Line up honestly according to the pace signs. Often, bib numbers are coded to correspond to your best time, so the officials and the other runners will know if you aren't standing in the proper place. This is unfair to others and could be dangerous for you. I have seen more than a few tennis-shoe-clad entrants on the front line stubbornly nodding in the affirmative when asked by officials if they can run a five-minute-mile pace. Within several hundred yards they are being plowed into by a steady stream of faster competitors.

POTENTIAL PHYSICAL PROBLEMS

Tying up, also called "rigging" (short for rigor mortis), the "bear on your back" in sprinters' lingo, and a variety of other descriptive names, is the feeling that all of your muscles have locked. It's as if your body is closing down, out of service. Tying up naturally occurs at the very end of the race, when you have put in a hard physical effort. But if you tie up so early that it drastically slows your pace, you've gone out too fast. A hard effort in a distance race does not mean an all-out sprint from the start; rather it's a strong, steady effort that builds toward an all-out finish. If you tie up early repeatedly, you are consistently trying to run beyond your ability.

When you tie up, you are forced to relax your muscles in order to continue, which means you must slow down. The runners who speed off from the start and who are later seen walking are victims of serious tying up. The energy expended in tying up and slowing down will greatly undermine your rhythm in the race, and it's highly unlikely you will regain your momentum. Once your muscles have filled with lactic acid, a substance produced by an oxygen depletion that causes muscles to tighten, you have a problem that is to some degree irrevocable.

Don't do battle with your body when you run. Find a balance between pushing at a pace for which you are trained and struggling or forcing yourself. When I put too much pressure on myself, tell myself I should be going faster, I tend to tie up. It's a "panic and push" syndrome. I get tense when I try to push the pace too far beyond what my body can handle, and the more I force it, the more my pace and technique suffer. I experienced this most dramatically during track training. Now when I begin to tire, rather than gritting my teeth in angry determination in an effort to speed up, I tell myself simply to relax and maintain the pace. When I tell myself to relax, my times get better.

Pace yourself. As you get more experience, you'll learn to use split times (the pace often called out at mile points or read from your own watch) to determine what your body can handle. Some of those new to racing get carried away with a too-quick early pace and are just determined to hang in there. That's no way to run a race. A race should be a test of ability, not survival.

If you try to force yourself, try to push through the feeling of tying up, you probably won't run faster. Tense muscles are not as efficient as relaxed muscles, and by forcing the effort you tighten up even more. You just dig yourself into a hole. To be able to run fast, you must do quality training, which accustoms you to running relaxed and efficient at a faster pace, prolonging the amount of time you can run without tying up. This relaxation is essential. The reason that great athletic efforts often look so easy is because in one way they are; they must be.

Other common physical problems that may arise in a race include blisters, chafing, cramps, dehydration, and a troublesome stomach or intestines. Blisters and chafing are not considered major injuries but can be just as debilitating. To avoid them, I rub petroleum jelly on blister-prone areas on my feet, especially before a marathon. If you feel "hot spots" develop from friction—red, warm areas of the skin— try putting petroleum jelly on them as a preventive measure, before they blister. Properly fitting socks that won't wrinkle or bunch help prevent blisters, as do properly fitting shoes. Contrary to popular belief, shoes that are too large rather than too small can cause problems, including the black toenails that runners sometimes get. Tight socks, short shoes, and downhill running can also contribute to black toe-nails. In addition, if you are plagued by sweaty feet, try corn starch or talcum powder to absorb perspiration. Decreasing caffeine consumption also reduces sweating. Damp socks can be troublesome, so especially in warm-weather races, I change my socks after a warm-up and before the race.

You can also use petroleum jelly or Band-Aids to prevent chafing. Common trouble spots are the backs of the underarms if you are running in a singlet, between the thighs, the nipples for men or for women who run without bras, and under bra edges, seams, or straps. Avoid these problems by not wearing any new or unfamiliar clothing; certainly never race with new shoes. Everything should be tested and well worn.

I am fortunate to seldom get cramps, side or stomach stitches, in a race. My brother Arild, on the other hand, gets them constantly, and we are still trying to figure out why. The problem can arise from having eaten too soon before the race or from sucking in too much breath without expelling it. If a side or stomach stitch occurs, try bending over and applying pressure to where it originates, or raise your arm to try to stretch it out. If it is a recurring problem, practice deliberately expelling air every fourth breath or controlling your breathing. Concentrate on deep, even breathing from the diaphragm when you get tired, rather than rapid, shallow puffing. It's impossible to be in complete control of your breathing when you're running hard, but loud panting won't help you run faster. I may make a few random sounds with intense effort, but I'm not a loud breather.

To avoid dehydration, which is especially common in warm-weather races, you must remember to drink before, during, and after the race—something people often forget while caught up in their effort. Your thirst is not a good indicator of your need for water; you should drink even if you don't feel particularly thirsty. Practice drinking during training to get used to running with water in your stomach, and slow down or stop in the race to drink at the water stations if you must. I'm sure that the leg cramps I experienced in my first marathon were due to the dehydration I suffered when I couldn't get enough water. There was plenty of water available, but I didn't know how important it was to drink, and it was hard to get it down as I wasn't used to drinking out of a cup on the run.

In terms of toilet needs, you can expect your prerace nerves to make you go more times than you probably have in the last month! I must go at least a dozen times before a race. Don't worry, though; once you begin the race, your need to urinate will usually disappear as your kidneys shut down during intense exercise. If you've had a lot of fluid, however, don't be surprised if you have to make a pit stop midrace. Be prepared for everything. One of my more serious emergencies occurred in the 1974 European Championships. While I was waiting in the tunnel before the race, "the need" struck. In order not to miss my race, I had to go practically out in the open. Racing often forces you to lose all inhibitions!

Occasionally, the problem becomes more complicated. If your intestines are not empty, you may have trouble. Eating too much or too soon before the race (even a large meal late the night before), or foods containing roughage, should be avoided. Don't eat spicy or greasy foods, either, or eat or drink anything you're not used to having. If you should need to relieve yourself during the race, you will obviously be in a difficult situation. Always know if and where there are toilets on the course or, as a last resort, where you can find a bush. Despite following all the rules, trouble sometimes strikes. My problems have been only in races longer than an hour, like the marathon. One year in New York I ducked between two parked cars, and in 1984 and 1985 I just kept running, despite the fact my diarrhea was apparent for all the world to see on network television. Fortunately, I was too focused on my running to worry about being embarrassed.

SCHEDULING RACES

If you've run your first race, you may be wondering: what next? Or perhaps you race regularly and need to determine how best to choose your races systematically. This task used to be much simpler in the days before the road racing boom, when racing was more seasonal. Now there are road races all year long of virtually every distance on every weekend; it's overwhelming. Therefore, you must be selective and learn to pick and choose wisely. One of the biggest problems for runners on all levels is the risk of overracing, which is especially the case in the United States. In Norway, by contrast, we don't have many races during our extremely rough winters, and certainly no road races.

How much you race should also depend on how seriously you race. If you take it easy in a race—just do it to participate and run well within your limits—obviously, you can recover faster and race again sooner than if you push to your limit. If you run hard, an average of one race a month is a sensible schedule, which is about my average. When you race again also depends on the race. The general rule is to allow *at least* one day for every mile of the race before you race again—that's the minimum. After a hard 10km, I usually wait a minimum of four weeks. If it's an easy race, three weeks—but not before. This is my schedule for warm-weather racing, which takes more out of me.

You don't have to race regularly, though. You can run one or two races a year if your aim is only to participate. You should still be in good enough shape even if your objective is just to complete any race you enter. Expecting a great performance with no race practice is very risky, though, as you are banking on putting it all together on one given day. Racing takes practice. It usually requires a few races to synchronize all the aspects of training and iron out any problems. Deciding on which and how many races to run goes back to one of my first recommendations for beginners: decide on goals. If you're running your first race, then your goal should be just to finish. If you're a new racer, set reasonable short-range goals: one race at a time. You can set your next goal after you have experienced the satisfaction of achieving your first.

If you are planning to race with any regularity, it's helpful to establish both long- and short-term goals. Short-term goals give you something more immediate on which to focus and are stepping-stones to a major race. This is how I establish my program. Since 1980, my short-term goals have been races in the ten- to fifteen-kilometer range. My long-term goals have been the marathons in the World Championships, the Olympics, and New York. In a typical year, I aim to be in good shape for such races as the L'eggs Mini Marathon 10km in June, the Gasparilla 15km, and the Miami Orange Bowl 10km, with an eye toward the New York City Marathon, in October.

The hard/easy, stress/rest principle holds true for racing as well as training. I have low-key months in March and September, during which I cut back on serious racing. This period precedes my serious races in spring and late fall. The races I do run during this time are more like hard training runs, for which I do not extensively taper or give a maximum effort. For example, I do races like these in February, and unlike with other events, I don't choose them for the competition.

Some runners can't race without going all out. These are usually intense, achievement-oriented–type people. Once the gun goes off, despite their decision to take it easy, the adrenaline just takes over. They may also be the type who always race hard because they feel a psychological setback if they are passed or beaten by others of lesser ability, and they fear—sometimes legitimately—that a half effort sets a pattern they cannot break when it comes time to run all out. There's nothing wrong with these runners; in fact, they are usually very tough competitors. They just can't turn that competitive instinct on and off. They must recognize that for them it probably isn't a good idea to try to use a race for practice or as a workout.

How much to race is one consideration; when to race is another. If you live in an environment with severe seasons—cold winters and hot summers—it's best to do your serious racing in the spring and fall. If I lived under these conditions, I would plan for peak efforts during the milder seasons. If you do plan to race in difficult weather, especially heat, adjust your pace and goal to the conditions. Don't stick to your plan, thinking you can defeat hot and humid weather, and find yourself slowing to a crawl halfway through the race. Always check the weather forecast before the event so you can be physically and mentally prepared to make any necessary adjustments.

Racing must also be planned around your life. Periods of heavy work or stress are obviously not the best time to race. It's like putting stress on top of stress. It's true that some running is a release from stress, but not racing. Your mind and body do not differentiate between certain types of stress. According to one study, in fact, those who focused on competitive thinking in workouts more than doubled their levels of norepinephrine, the hormone that soars in stressful situations. Going for a jog may relieve the tension of a busy day, but training for a race is part of a busy day. If I have too many stressful promotional obligations surrounding a race, I can't run well. So I don't race in those events for which I must work hard, or I limit the obligations for my serious races.

If you have planned to race seriously and a sudden crisis or other stressful situation arises, it is usually best to postpone your plan to race or drastically lower your expectations. When my brother wanted a PR (personal record) in the marathon and the race coincided with his first year in a hectic job, I tried to warn him I thought it was impossible. He didn't get his PR. Of course, it's often easier to see someone else's mistakes, but try to learn from them for yourself as well. I often wish I could skip races during stressful periods in my life, because when I have had to race during these times I didn't perform very well. In fact, my losses in road races have almost always been during periods of either illness or stress. After too much travel, too much hard training, and too many business dealings, I'm done in. Unfortunately, however, I can't just tell an organizer who has counted on me that I'm too tired to race. This is why I have become so careful in planning my schedule.

Set a reasonable racing schedule, and be prepared to change it as you go along. Jack and I set my schedule for the year, but after a couple of months, we usually find it's too busy, too difficult. It always looks easy when we see it on paper, but when I have to do it—that's another story! So we reschedule races as the year progresses. I plan at least one race a month, but sometimes even that's too ambitious. If I plan a marathon, however, I am especially careful. I decide on it six to nine months in advance and work carefully around that plan.

THE RACE EXPERIENCE

I have said that training is a science and an art. This is even truer of racing. There is logic to it, but there are also many intangibles that make a good racer: the ability to focus, natural talent, and sometimes just plain luck. You can follow all the rules, do all the right preparation, and still go wrong. On the other hand, you can take a few risks, break a few rules, cut corners on preparation, and pull off what seems like a miracle. Of course, the chances of succeeding are obviously greater if you follow the rules.

When the race works, when you feel you have mastered it, there's nothing like it. But when it doesn't come together, when you feel like you're running in quicksand instead of with wings, it can be frustrating beyond belief. "What went wrong?!" you ask yourself in frustration.

Successful racing is a combination of many factors. The mistakes you'll make are part of your progress, so don't torture yourself over them. If I dwelled on all the mistakes I've made in running, I would have quit from frustration long ago. And even though I've been at it for fifteen years, I still make mistakes. Sometimes they're subtle; other times they're embarrassingly obvious. I often think it's the best runners who don't follow the rules. In the 10km race in Miami in 1984, for example, I passed the halfway point in 15:30, world-record pace, but the temperature was 86 degrees and the humidity 80 percent. Needless to say, I wilted.

Then there are those times when you haven't made any obvious mistakes and the race still doesn't go well. According to my training for a 1,500-meter race in Sweden, I calculated a reasonable time of 4:05–6 (four minutes and five or six seconds). In order to be sure, I did a mile time trial on the Bislett track, in Oslo, which went fine. In the race, I felt fine—for the first lap, anyway. By the second of the four laps my legs tightened, and I finished the race in 4:16, way off. I was incredibly frustrated. I couldn't understand why I didn't run faster, as I knew I had done all the right preparation. I analyzed the training in my diary, and I still didn't find any mistakes. To this day I don't know what went wrong in that race, but as the saying goes—

and you hear it all the time in the sports world—it just wasn't my day.

When the race is going well, though, it's a rare feeling. It's like magic. You feel great, powerful—and it's clear why you've worked so hard. You don't have negative thoughts; you don't question anything; you don't torture yourself or remember your fear or nervousness. In a good race, everything is right. The crowds are great in New York, where I have run well, but they were stifling in Boston, where I didn't.

I wish I could bottle the formula for those once-in-a-lifetime–type races. I will never forget my victory in the 3,000-meter race in the 1977 World Cup. It was one of those races. I felt great the entire way, with everything under control. Whatever moves the other runners made, I knew I could respond. If I had to, I could run faster. I felt if I had to, I could fly! The World Championship Marathon in Helsinki was also one of those races. That feeling of mastery was with me from the gun. I remember thinking that if I had to I could have run six miles beyond the 26.2 for that gold medal.*

Being in good shape isn't always a guarantee of success. It doesn't necessarily mean you will have your day. This is probably most clearly illustrated in the Olympic Games. I doubt there is a single athlete who comes to the Olympics in anything less than top shape, but if that magic isn't there—the set of intangible circumstances which make it that certain day—an athlete won't take a medal home.

Having a great race is what keeps us running, and though that perfect race often seems just beyond reach, we continually try to grasp it. Being the master of your race is largely a question of control. Obviously, you can't be in control of things like the weather and your competition. However, you can do a lot to be in control by being prepared and by being confident. Make a plan, and stick to it. Run your own race. Don't let what others do or say sway you. When your competitors take off in a sprint at the start, don't automatically follow them in panic. You'll likely see them soon enough, when they've slowed

---

*I will often refer to these races because they were major victories and they had that "magic." The New York City Marathon is also frequently mentioned, as I have run seven of my ten marathons there.

down and you pass them. Running your own race takes confidence, the kind of confidence you get from good training. I ran my own race in the 1983 World Cup Marathon, in Helsinki, and went home with the gold medal; Joan Benoit Samuelson did the same in the 1984 Olympics.

6

For the Advanced—Training and Competitive Racing

As with the other levels, I define an advanced runner by intent rather than ability or achievement. For example, the effort one runner invests to do a 2:30 marathon may be the same as the runner who does it in three hours. Therefore, I consider you on the advanced level when you are serious about your running. This means it is a high priority, possibly even your main priority after job and family. As an advanced runner, you train daily and usually will not skip a run unless forced to by fatigue or injury, and almost never for social reasons.

This chapter is based not necessarily on where you finish in the race but on your motive for being there. You may race to better your time or your place or to win trophies. The great thing about the race is that although there can be only one person to finish first, there are many victories in the pack. In fact, I consider the motto of the road race also one of the themes of this book: Everyone is a winner.

Because running is a top priority, you must be skilled at organizing your time. You will have to be a good planner to accommodate your training. At this level, organization, discipline, and sacrifice become even more important; and the higher your aspirations, the more this is the case.

In order to run on the world-class level, I must put my running at the center of my life. Although I worked as a teacher through two

Olympic Games, it would be difficult to do that now with the present trend in full-time running. My priority is my training, and every other activity is secondary. Some advanced runners try to squeeze training in around their other activities, which I think is a mistake. I squeeze in other activities around my running. Again, the level of your commitment and the strength of your focus are something you must decide before you set your goals. If you want to be a good runner, you will have to make sacrifices. My strength is not just from training but from having developed a strong will.

What is your goal as an advanced runner? It is no longer fitness; that you already have. It is not primarily to run for fun or for relaxation; that you can do already. As I see it, your goal is to become the best runner you can be. That is what this chapter, and the rest of this book, are designed to help you do.

How good can you become? Don't worry about getting a late start in your running. Never mind your age. "Have you reached your prime?" I am often asked. There is no prime as far as I'm concerned. Look at Joyce Smith, consistently running under 2:35 in the marathon at age forty-six, and Priscilla Welch, who ran a 2:28 marathon just before her fortieth birthday, only a few years after taking up running. Carlos Lopes, who leads the world in the marathon and keeps getting better, broke the world marathon record at age thirty-eight. Just as I know I can still improve in my thirties, you, too, can become a better runner no matter what your age.

My goal, as well as yours, is to continue to improve. I run not to burn calories or to relieve anxiety but to prepare my body and mind for a test of my ability: the race. By doing what I can to become a better competitor, I am improving my ability as a runner. This doesn't mean you can't have a good time while you're doing it. I continue to run primarily because I enjoy it; that's always at the top of my list of motivating factors.

TRAINING

The Norwegian training system differs fundamentally from the typical American system in several ways, according to Kristen Damsgaard, former Norwegian national coach and my coach from age seventeen to twenty. Because we are a nation of only 4 million people, and European in our approach, our system has been influenced by a number of other countries, including those in Eastern Europe, West Germany, Finland, and New Zealand. Since the foundation of our system is track, the basic approach to running in Norway has always been quality training (versus endurance training), which has only recently become popular among most advanced road runners in the States. This is due in large part to the influence of the increased number of track runners who are taking to the roads.

The size and resources of the United States have been both a benefit and a drawback in the development of training technique. On the one hand, road racing has made enormous contributions to the sport of running, and Norway has also been positively influenced by the jogging and running boom. On the other hand, such factors as inexperience and the system of college competition (racing week in and week out, sometimes two or even three events per meet) have tended to make an athlete's career short-lived. According to many Norwegian coaches and exercise experts, one of the biggest problems in the States is the desire to progress too soon. Unlike the American college athletes, who are usually programmed to last for only four years, our athletes in Norway train with the long term in mind.

Keep this in mind as an advanced runner. A beginner and even an intermediate may initially see rapid progress, but if you want to reach the top of your ability, you have to give it time. You may reach plateaus and level off for a while before you progress further, so be patient. If you introduce something new into your program, like hill workouts, for example, give it six months for full benefit. The analysis of my training in Chapter 11 shows that I have made changes or added intensity very slowly. Although I may have trained hard my entire career, any *adaptation* of training has always been gradual. Further analysis of my training shows that significant breakthroughs were often a result of training that took several years, as consistent training has a cumulative effect. For example, I started doing longer distance training in 1975, and although I wasn't training specifically for a marathon, I built a base that allowed me to set a world record in that event three years later.

An advanced training program is based on the motive that you are training to race, not training for the sake of training, to accumulate megamiles. Quality running rather than quantity is what will make you a better runner, no matter what your level of ability. Since running a race is a test of speed, speed training is the most important aspect of any advanced program. This has always been my approach. The workouts must duplicate the demands of the race in order to prepare the body for the effort. In other words, you have to run faster in practice in order to run faster in races. Don't neglect to develop your basic speed no matter what distance you plan to race or how fast you hope to do it. I was an Olympic 1,500-meter runner for over a decade before I was an Olympic marathoner. Take a lesson from most world-class runners, for whom basic speed is an important foundation.

These days even marathoners realize they need quality work. This is what I was saying when I came to the United States in 1978. I had never run farther than twelve miles at one time before I did my first marathon, but as a track runner, I did all that running hard. It amazed people that I ran a world record, but I told them, "Just wait until the other track runners get on the roads!" At that time, long, slow distance training was popular, but I have never been a fan of this type of training, although I know many runners have had great success with it. Of course, you need to do some long runs for a marathon, but you also have to put in the quality.

The better you get, the closer you come to the limit of training you can do to improve. The trick is to develop a balanced program, which is based not only on what you do but on how and when you do it. In the section on training for intermediate runners, I defined the systems important in my training. Here I will explain how I apply them to achieve maximum effect for the advanced level. Their application is, once again, very individual.

Workouts: at least two, often three, of my training sessions per week are quality workouts. Usually I do one workout of long repetitions, either fartlek or intervals. Like many advanced runners, I do my speedwork in the afternoon, in racing shoes. This is when and how I feel looser and lighter, which is important both physically and psychologically. Fit your training in when you can and when it feels right. Some runners do morning intervals for reasons just as good as mine for doing them in the afternoon.

Some runners feel fartlek is easier than intervals because it's less structured and less monotonous, but it's all the same for me—I run just as hard for both. Both intervals and fartlek serve the same basic function, so mixing them is dependent on convenience and the desire for variety in workouts. A sample interval workout I do on the track is six times a half mile, run under 10km-race pace, with a quarter-mile recovery jog between each. When I'm away from a track or other measured distance, I substitute this workout for six times two and a half minutes hard, with a two-minute rest between each. As a long-distance runner, I concentrate on doing a greater number of repeats at a strong pace, rather than fewer repeats done all out. The point of this type of session is to build the strength and endurance necessary to maintain your desired 10km-race pace. To progress I don't try to run a faster interval; instead, I try to shorten the recovery time between hard efforts. I know that if I can do long repeats in training at my race pace with very little rest between them, I can likely run this pace for the entire distance in a race.

My other weekly quality workout consists of short repetitions, like twelve times 200 meters (half a lap of the track),* with an equal-distance recovery jog between each. The purpose of this workout is to develop speed and efficiency. Unlike in the long intervals, I run these repeats at well below 10km-race pace, closer to 800-meter- (half-mile) race pace. Because the purpose of this workout is to develop speed as opposed to endurance, adequate recovery is needed between intervals. Unlike with the long intervals, as I progress I maintain the recovery time and distance, but I aim for faster interval times.

A *time trial* is a form of quality work in which you run a portion of an upcoming race—no more than two-thirds of the distance— usually at about ten- to fifteen-seconds-per-mile slower than your race pace. This serves a dual function: as a good way to simulate the race

*All track workouts given in the book are geared to a standard outdoor quarter-mile track.

effort and as a method to assess your race pace. If you can run near your goal 10km-race pace in a three- to four-mile time trial feeling under control, you should be able to do it in a race.

A time trial can give you essential confidence. In 1975, when Jack told me I could break the world record in only my second 3,000-meter race, my first reaction was "No way!" To convince myself I had a chance, he had me run a 2,000-meter time trial. When I realized I had only to keep up that trial pace for another 1,000 meters, and that I could even drop ten or fifteen seconds, I was convinced. I did, in fact, set that record (with a time of 8:46.6). As marathon training requires passing up a lot of other races and I am anxious to assess my conditioning, I have run a time trial before Helsinki and again before the Olympic marathon on a measured five-kilometer portion of the road. My time trial before Helsinki was 15:20, with which I was very pleased, and before the Olympics it was 15:09, only one second from my personal best on the track. This is how I knew I was in great shape on both occasions.

I race frequently, so I use time trials only occasionally. But for those who have gaps in their racing schedule (or gaps in confidence!), a time trial is a good way to simulate the race effort. However, do not expect a time trial to duplicate the race. You will likely disappoint yourself. Usually, only the race itself can provide the atmosphere to bring out your best.

The time and place of your quality workouts can be very important, as they simulate the race in both physical and mental effort. For example, I don't do interval workouts in the morning because I'm not physically or mentally prepared. There's a big difference between going out for an easy hour's run and doing an interval session of six times one mile. To give this kind of workout my best effort takes all-day preparation. When I wake up on the day of a quality workout, I begin my mental preparation by rehearsing the workout in my mind, thinking about where and how I will do it. This way I begin to feel more geared up. By midafternoon, I have already put the kind of extra energy into that workout I could not have given it in the morning. This doesn't mean you can't do a hard workout in the morning. If you do, however, take a long warm-up to make sure you have the essential physical and psychological readiness.

Some runners prefer to "get it over with" or feel that a morning workout better simulates races, most of which take place in the early hours. But I have to concentrate on that special emotion that motivates me to run hard. It means toughening myself and preparing for the discomfort and fatigue that are a necessary part of pushing myself to run fast. Despite the many years I've run hard workouts, the emotional aspect is always intense. Hard training is never done casually; I never lose the fear or the nervousness. This is why I am usually edgy all day long—tense, preoccupied, apprehensive.

I take hard workouts very seriously and try not to have a busy schedule on the days I am doing them. I take a nap beforehand, if possible, to make sure I feel rested and prepared to run hard. (If you can't nap, try taking a short rest or "meditation break" at work, in which you concentrate on relaxation.) After the workout, my nervousness is replaced by a positive feeling of fatigue, a sense of relaxation after the hard work is done, and satisfaction in having conquered a challenge and done good training. This emotional cycle shows why a hard workout is just as important for mental development as for physical development.

These quality workouts are the heart of my training program and may vary according to an upcoming race, but the structure I have described in both this and the intermediate chapter is what I do year-round. How you train, of course, depends on your goals, schedule, temperament, and resilience. Although I have always trained hard all year, it is not necessarily something I recommend. Several top Norwegian coaches who have analyzed my training over the years feel it is too intense and too rigid. Looking back, it is easy to see this mistake, and I have tried to correct it over the years, to take more rest, especially in regard to the marathon. Therefore, I recommend hard work, but perhaps with one complete rest day every week or two and periodic light training weeks. Track runners often take months such as October and November easy, or inclement seasons could be lower-key periods of training. After such a rest period, you are usually hungry to start more intense training.

THE TRACK

The roots of every great runner, and all great running, are on the track. Everyone can benefit by using the track, which I do at least once a week. This goes for the beginner as well as the advanced, but the better the runner, the greater the advantage and necessity of track training.

If the road is the playground, the track is the classroom. Track running is tough. Believe me, it's harder to run six-times-a-mile intervals on the track than the same workout along a tree-lined road. But run on the track and you'll likely find the same effort on the road feels like a jog!

Track is very structured, very exact. It is the essence of discipline. It teaches you to use concentration, tempo, and rhythm, and it improves form by forcing you to be efficient. There is no scenery—no distractions—and no variation; it's just you and that quarter-mile oval. Sound challenging? If you want to know how tough it is for me, just look at me in my track races in the photo section.

Track competition isn't necessary, but participating in an all-comers track meet can be a good quality workout, a great experience, and an excellent way to improve. I no longer seriously compete on the track, but about three to five times a year during track season I use various track races for sharpening.

DOUBLE WORKOUTS

I was one of the first female runners in Norway to do double workouts, which I started in 1974. This is when I began to run in the morning. At that time everyone on the street stared at me. They weren't used to seeing someone run that early, especially a woman. Now no one even blinks.

I'm often asked at clinics if twice-a-day running is necessary for the advanced runner. Especially with the popularity of endurance sports, people are looking for the improvement they believe they can get with greater training volume.

The purpose of double workouts is to accommodate more training by dividing the volume into two sessions. However, this doesn't mean splitting a single session in two. According to most experts, doing one ten-mile run, for example, is better than doing two five-mile runs. Double sessions are relevant only to those runners doing more than about seventy miles per week and who have been running at least several years. For anything less than this amount, one run is sufficient. Although single workouts can be just as effective for most advanced runners, in my case, to stay on top I've got to do doubles.

One of my double sessions is always a shorter, easier-paced run, between thirty minutes and an hour. However, doing doubles does not necessarily mean doing two runs a day, every day, week after week—even I don't run fourteen times a week. My program varies between eleven and thirteen sessions per week. If you want to add sessions, begin by running doubles on recovery days, not on quality training days. Start with additional easy runs of about thirty minutes, twice a week, and use the "10 percent rule," adding no more than that amount as you increase. Give yourself time to adapt gradually, especially if you are an older runner.

Trying to squeeze in a second workout can mean sacrificing important recovery time, and it doesn't pay to do that if the quality of the single run suffers. Doing doubles means a morning run, and if you have to cut out necessary sleep, it isn't worth it. Quality is the main goal of your program, and that quality is contingent on proper rest and recovery.

For most people with full-time jobs, twice-a-day running will probably not be productive. When I was teaching and doing these workouts, I was chronically tired. Doubles are more easily accommodated by students and by those with part-time or flexible jobs. There is a point of diminishing return, when any added volume becomes counterproductive. That point for me is over ninety to a hundred miles, but for some advanced runners, it can be as little as fifty to sixty miles.

SUPPLEMENTARY TRAINING

Double runs apply to a very limited group; however, a runner at any level can do double workouts using another sport. More running is not the only way to increase your training and conditioning. With the advent of "cross-training," a term popularized by the triathlon that refers to training in different sports, there are other options to just running more miles. For example, a daily run can be supplemented by swimming, bike riding, cross-country skiing, using a rowing machine, or weight lifting. Cross-training also distributes stress to various parts of the body, allowing recovery and reducing the risk of injury.

Cross-country skiing best duplicates running, while swimming is a good overall workout and an excellent therapy for a runner's tired legs. You can even do the running motion or other exercises in the water, which saves the legs from pounding and also functions as resistance training. I've used a stationary bike when I'm injured, but I generally don't do cross-training if I'm healthy, as double running gives me all I can handle. You should realize, however, that while supplementary training can make you a stronger and better athlete, I feel it has a limited value as far as specifically improving your running. Remember, if you do more training, it should not compromise the quality of your running.

There is a good deal of controversy over whether weight training is useful for advanced runners. While some runners do it, my feeling is that it's generally unnecessary for distance runners. When I was running the quarter mile and the half mile on the track, I trained with free weights. This weight training is good for running a fast half mile, but not for running a fast marathon.

On the other hand, light weights are useful for general strength and to strengthen certain areas as a preventive measure against injury—for example, the lower back or the quadriceps (front thigh) muscles, which support the knee. Analyze your running: for example, do you tire or feel pain or stiffness specifically in the calves, quadriceps, or hamstrings? It could be useful to strengthen these areas. Consult a health club staff member or other expert for testing to determine any weaknesses and useful exercises.

Rather than do general weight training, I think it is more useful to be sport specific. If you want to work on the upper body, besides doing push-ups, be sport specific by using ten-pound dumbbells and swinging your arms in a running motion for one to two minutes at a time. Chapter 14 includes good general strength exercises with weights.

With the trend toward track training for distance runners, some are also doing track drills. Circuit training, a series of calisthenics and strength exercises like exaggerated hopping, skipping, and bounding, are commonly used by sprinters and some middle-distance runners. These exercises can improve form, but be careful to avoid injury, especially by overdoing it with high mileage and calisthenics. Keep the exercises light, and start very slowly, which will give your body time to adapt.

There are a growing number of devices on the market used as training aids. Ankle weights should never be used while running, as they can damage tendons and ligaments and throw off the stride. For a time in 1981 I tried weight gloves, but the habit just didn't stick. Hand weights are used by some runners in the States, but I rarely see them in Europe, and I feel they interfere with good form. The American Running & Fitness Association advises against running with weights because they increase the chance of injury, place additional stress on the body, and throw off your gait. If you want to work out with weights, the association suggests doing it after you run.

With an understanding of the function of supplementary exercises, you can create a well-rounded program and become a better overall athlete. But keep in mind: while more cycling, weight lifting, or swimming may make you a better cyclist, weight lifter, or swimmer, only running will make you a faster runner.

Racing

At this level, you race for competition. You're usually not out there just for a jog, to see if you can go the distance, or to socialize. You're

MY SAMPLE TRAINING WEEK

	Morning 5–6 A.M.		Afternoon 4–5 P.M.	
Monday	10–15km (6.2–9.3 miles)	40–60 mins	10–15km (6.2–9.3 miles)	40–60 mins
Tuesday	10–15km	40–60 mins	6–8 × 1,000m intervals, 1–2 min rest breaks (pulse 180)	
Wednesday	10–15km	40–60 mins	rest	
Thursday	10–15km	40–60 mins	Fartlek, approx. 13km (7.8 miles), several 500m sprints	
Friday	10–15km	40–60 mins	10–15km	40–60 mins
Saturday	10–15km	40–60 mins	15–20 × 300m sprints (pulse 180)	
Sunday	20–33km (12.4–20 miles) fast-pace distance run		rest	

running against the clock or your competitors. This section includes the components of advanced racing that will help make you the best runner you can be and give you the winning edge.

The higher your aspirations, the more complicated the race becomes and the more finely tuned you must be. All the elements in the preceding chapters become even more crucial for the advanced racer. Take the race warm-up, for example. My sense of readiness from a warm-up is dependent on everything I do—down to my shoes and socks. I begin my warm-up with my training shoes, doing a few pick-ups to get loose. Then I change into my racing shoes and my socks right before the start, doing another few pick-ups to feel the contrast. This ritual comes from my track days, when I used to change into my spikes. The act of putting on lighter shoes is a small but important touch, my way of telling myself, "Now you're ready to race."

Advanced racing offers a tremendous variety for the brave and hearty, and I encourage you to try different types of races in addition to those on the roads. The benefits of track have already been mentioned. Cross-country is my favorite event. It's running in its original and most challenging form, over hill and dale. No matter what or where you race, the following applies to you.

PACING

Pacing is the primary ingredient of successful racing. The type of pacing you use in a race depends on personal preference, experience, and an understanding of physiology. Some people prefer running fast in the beginning and hanging on to the end, while others have greater success with even pacing or negative splits (running the second half of the race faster than the first half).

Although there is not complete agreement, scientific studies have shown that even-paced racing is best in terms of oxygen consumption and mechanical efficiency.* Most world records are run at even pace, which is generally how I run and what has been my most successful method. For example, my 10km world road best consisted of the following mile split times: mile 1: 4:55; mile 2: 4:54; mile 3: 5:05 (uphill); mile 4: 4:58; mile 5: 4:58; mile 6: 5:08. All my marathon records were run at even pace, except my first one, in which I went out conservatively and ran negative splits. The world marathon record at the time of this writing, by Carlos Lopes (2:07:11), consisted of half-marathon times of 1:03:24 and 1:03:47. Ingrid Kristiansen ran 1:10:09 and 1:10:57 for her 1985 world-record marathon of 2:21:06. Both are amazingly even.

My experience in going out fast in races has usually been disastrous; while running even-pace I usually pick other runners off, which means they started too quickly. In my opinion, it's best to be in control throughout the entire race, which is something you lose when you've gone out too fast and must struggle to finish. Psychologically, it's better to pass than to be passed. Negative splits can also be effective in certain circumstances. Especially if you don't know what you're doing, start conservatively. In this case, or if the race is tactical, it may turn out you run negative splits. In a tactical race like the World Championships, I held back in the beginning but ran my last 10km in under thirty-three minutes. This is in the range of the times I usually run for 10km races!

PEAKING

To do your best in a race, you must peak for it. Peaking means preparing to be at your very fittest and freshest for a specific race. It's

---

*David L. Costill, *A Scientific Approach to Distance Running* (Los Altos, CA: Tafnews Press, 1979), p. 71.

the ability to combine the right training with the right timing. Bob Sevene, Joan Benoit Samuelson's coach, defines peaking technique with one word: focus. This means that every aspect of a runner's life—workouts, other races, daily habits—is focused on the important race. To peak you must cut back on training volume, sharpen your speed, get sufficient rest, and maintain consistency in your general routine—avoiding anything that may negatively affect your race effort.

Peaking traditionally brings to mind a long buildup toward a long-range goal. It also implies that for every peak there must be a valley. In the case of Lasse Viren, for example, the acknowledged master of peaking, all his training was geared exclusively toward the Olympic Games. Between the Games his performances were relatively mediocre, but in the 1972 and the 1976 Olympics he won unprecedented double gold medals in the 5,000 and 10,000 meters. The traditional system of peaking is ideal for most Europeans because we have two distinct seasons, cross-country and track. Though I peaked for major races in these seasons, I always preferred to avoid the valleys, instead maintaining a consistently high level of year-round training.

When I began running road races, which are not seasonal, I found my system appropriate for racing well all year long. My belief is similar to that of Australian national distance coach Pat Clohessy, who feels that traditional peaking is unnecessary. Clohessy, coach of top runners such as Rob de Castella, thinks it's too risky to sacrifice everything for a distant goal and that sustaining this pressure also takes the enjoyment out of running. He believes in having long-term goals but that they can be reached by running well over an extended period of time.

I made a necessary exception for Helsinki and Los Angeles, for which I peaked in the traditional sense. Each was a yearlong project, in which everything was planned around that one race. Mentally, it was very tough, and, of course, it's always very risky. With few other races for which to taper and rest, it is easy to do too much and get injured. For shorter races it isn't so bad, but to peak for a marathon this way is very intense.

This does not mean, however, that you shouldn't attempt to peak at all. For important races I try to peak by planning well ahead and not doing anything to jeopardize my effort. All the traveling I did in 1985, for example, was not conducive to peaking. It was a calculated risk, and it contributed to my close defeats in important races, such as the Crescent City Classic and the L'eggs Mini Marathon.

Rest is an important element of peaking, no matter how you train. My system means I am never in poor shape, but perhaps the decision not to taper a bit more in training means I have never reached my best shape, either. Looking back, I realize I may have peaked better if I had rested more, and if I could do it again, I'd have rested more during my years on the track. Of course, this is much easier to see in retrospect, and so much more is known about training today than there was back then. At the time I thought I was resting, but what did I know? It wasn't as if I had a professional coach; it was only Jack and me. Most Norwegian experts who have since analyzed my career now concur that I've never given myself a chance to truly peak. Perhaps this is why I've always run best after recovering from illness or injury, when I was forced to rest. Those became my best peaks. Generally, though, my system works for me. I'm used to it and satisfied with the results I've achieved with it.

Some top runners, especially track runners, take holidays during which they don't run a step for up to two months. Maybe I don't do that because I'm afraid I would like the vacation too much! Jack thinks I could use a break, especially after a marathon, but if I can, I run the very next day. I have chosen to train hard all year round because it suits my goals and maintains what I feel is my necessary routine, whether or not that routine is most conducive to a particular system of peaking. You, too, will have to make the choice of which system of training, and peaking, best suits you.

You should realize, however, that peaking is not as easy as making the decision to be in great shape on a specific day. As I mentioned before, you can follow all the rules of race preparation and still not have your day. So desired is the often difficult and elusive peak that some athletes are using an unfair advantage to try to obtain it. Blood doping, in which an athlete gets an infusion of his or her own blood that has been previously withdrawn, is an attempt to induce a peak. The athlete's oxygen-carrying capacity is increased by the greater number of red blood cells from the added blood.

Sometimes I think hitting just the right peak depends on biorhythms, something out of our control, since, obviously, a day on which absolutely everything comes together is rare. That's why I don't try to hit a true peak more than two or three times a year. How many races you decide to peak for depends on how hungry you are. But if you are too ambitious, you risk burnout. You can only find so many times in which you are physically and emotionally able to peak for a race. Choose them sparingly and carefully.

STRATEGY

An important aspect of the race for the advanced runner is the plan of attack. Almost every top runner has some concept of strategy before the race. Despite prerace comments like "I'll just see how the race develops," experienced runners are rarely so random in their approach. I make these same comments to the press as other runners do, even though we all have at least a basic race strategy. Of course, none of us wants to give it away! My general plan is always to go with the leaders and gauge strategy by how the race takes shape.

Developing a strategy is based on many factors: your strengths and weaknesses, the competition, the length of the race, the course, and the weather are among them. A good knowledge of these factors will help you formulate the best strategy. For example, my strength is my experience, my ability to run well up and down hills, and that I can still run well in warm weather. My weakness is that I am probably less hungry, especially than newer runners. If I were to anticipate this lack of hunger as a potential problem, I would establish a big enough lead to keep someone from getting the psychological motivation of being in contact or in a head-to-head competition.

In addition to assessing my own strengths and weaknesses, I base my strategy on my competition. For example, Joan Benoit Samuelson likes to go hard from the start, to get rid of her competitors as soon as possible. Her ability is her strength; that's what makes her a great marathoner, so it's important not to let her get away. Wendy Sly is difficult because she's so versatile; she has both endurance and speed. In her case, I have to hope she'll make a tactical error, like going out too fast. If Olympic 3,000-meter champion Maricica Puica is in the race, I have to try to take the sting out of her kick by tiring her out before the end. Among others, these are the runners I respect, who are all mentally tough, and to whom I must gear my strategy. In terms of setting strategy, it's more difficult for me now than it used to be, as my competitors are different from the Russian women. At least I knew what to expect from the Russians. They always ran on the track as a team, sitting on the pace and sprinting the last lap.

Strategy is different for each type of racing. For cross-country, it's the runners against each other and the terrain. The clock is never a factor. A hilly course in any race gives me an advantage because hill training is unavoidable in Oslo, so I have trained myself to charge the upgrades. Traditionally, road races have not been tactical, as in track, especially in the women's field. It has usually come down to one woman against the clock, with the emphasis on setting records. Fortunately, this is changing, as I, for one, am tired of it. I'm glad to run against my competition rather than the clock. Besides, as a purist with my roots in track, I feel records don't mean much in road races, for which the conditions always vary. The fact that a road record is technically called a world best, as opposed to a world record, obviously means I'm not alone in my opinion.

My strategy usually includes using the terrain. I try to run as fast as possible going downhill, despite the fact I still brake a bit because I don't like the pounding. On turns I take the shortest distance, even though it slows me down a bit. It takes less energy to pick up the pace again than to make up the distance by taking a wide angle around a turn. However, swinging wide might be better if you're going very fast or if the race is crowded.

Often, you'll be forced to take some strategic risks. In Helsinki I had to consider the warm weather and the hilly final part of the course when I took the risk and let several different leaders go at various points. I banked on my feeling that the race would be decided after eighteen miles and that what happened before that point was not significant. Of course, that strategy did not work in Los Angeles, where Joan Benoit Samuelson ran away after three miles and I was never able to catch her.

As the race unfolds you may find yourself changing your strategy. A midrace change of tactics is most difficult, as you must be in sufficient control to make decisions and respond to your competition. The following are some tactics you may use once the gun goes off.

Surging

Surging is a sudden and drastic increase in pace for the purpose of pulling away from your competition. This change of pace breaks the rhythm and concentration of the runner(s) near you and forces the competitor(s) to respond to your move. A surge forward often "breaks" another runner mentally as well, creating the impression you're too strong to be followed. Often, the element of surprise can be the most effective. Surge when your competition may least expect it, like going uphill, where runners traditionally slow down and try to conserve energy. A surge is more common in a tactical race like cross-country, in which it is especially advantageous to use the terrain. In the 1983 World Cross Country Championships, in Gateshead, England, I took advantage of the fact that the Russian women had gone out very fast, and pushed an uphill toward the end of the race. I maintained the pace of that surge, left them behind, and won the race.

However, you should be aware that the change of pace surging requires is more physically demanding, as it contradicts what I have said about even-paced running being the most economical. Surging is a competitive tactic and not relevant to running a good time. It can be tremendously effective, but if you intend to use it, be prepared by practicing it in training.*

The Kick

A kick can be the most potent tactic in a race. You can let another runner lead while you sit on the pace, then take it all with this one technique. By using the kicker's technique of drafting off the runner in front and letting that person do the physical and psychological work, you conserve energy. All things being equal among competitors,

---

*Sample workouts to practice surging: Vary the pace within each interval, ¾-mile repeats comprised of ¼ miles in 75, 68, 75 seconds; or ½-mile repeats with 220 yards in 35, 35, 30, 35 seconds.

the kicker will win the race. However, it's one of the most difficult tactics to master. To use a kick, you have to convert from a distance runner to a sprinter—to make a complete change in form, stride, rhythm, and speed. This is tough anytime, but especially at the end of the race, when you're most tired.

The kicker has both a physical and a psychological advantage. According to Rod Dixon, being "the hunter rather than the hunted" was what worked to his advantage in his 1983 New York City Marathon win, in which he outsprinted Geoff Smith in the final quarter mile. Dixon felt he could still win with only 385 yards to go, and what gave him this confidence was his track background. "A miler's kick does the trick," as he put it. Despite Dixon's years of experience, I'm sure he'd admit this technique is a gamble. Be careful about relying on a kick in this way. It's much smarter and safer to run a good pace throughout the race. Many a top runner has depended too greatly on the kick to coast through the preliminary rounds in the Olympics, only to miss sprinting into one of the top places, thus failing to make the final.

I wish I had more of a kick in my track days against the Russians. No matter what I did against my rivals, their kick got me every time. My dream race, the World Cup 3,000 meters in 1977, was my only major race as a successful kicker. Finally, I could attack from behind instead of struggling to hold the lead. I kicked in the last 300 meters in forty-four seconds, my fastest ever. It was one of the rare times I ever felt in control in a major track race.

The good kickers are blessed from birth with natural sprinting ability. I've even seen beginning joggers with this ability. But you don't have to be a born sprinter to use a kick. It's one thing to be a sprinter and quite another to be able to sprint at the end of a six- or ten-mile race. As with surging, you can practice your kick in training. The necessary leg speed can be developed with short interval workouts, and to develop your ability to shift gears at the end of a race use your long interval workouts.*

---

*Sample workouts to practice kick: ¾-mile repeats comprised of ¼ miles in, 75, 75, 68 seconds; or ½-mile repeats with 220 yards in 42, 42, 42, 34 seconds. (Both workouts are also excellent practice in pacing.)

POTENTIAL PROBLEMS:
OVERTRAINING

Overtraining is perhaps the greatest risk to an advanced runner and is often the most difficult problem to prevent and diagnose. First of all, overtraining isn't as clear as a specific ache or pain, bruise, or swelling. Second, it is only recently a recognized, widespread problem because of the advent of much longer and harder training. The risks of overtraining are inherent on the advanced level, as the ambitious runner has a tendency to try to push the body and mind beyond their limits. Experts say every mile run beyond forty per week puts a person further into the danger zone in terms of injury, and overtraining also becomes one of the risks. I wish I could give you a scientific formula on how to prevent overtraining, but I'm still looking for one myself! To a great extent, it can be avoided by knowing your body and by using common sense.

What exactly is overtraining? One aspect commonly overlooked by even the most advanced athletes is that it is both physical and mental. It is caused by training as well as everything else that happens in daily life. Overtraining means overstress, and stress is a part of almost everything we do. If you race too much, or combine even minimal racing with a busy job or other burdens, you'll likely encounter a number of overtraining problems. One of the first signs, and a more subtle one, is a loss of sharpness. I did it all before the 1983 New York City Marathon—trained, traveled, worked—but instead of being sharp on the starting line, I found myself flat and tired. Even though I won the race, if the competition had been tougher, I may not have had the ability to overcome a challenge.

Overtraining is wasted training. It means piling on hard workouts without total recovery and, therefore, without maximum benefit. The difficulty is that it's often not immediately clear that this training is wasted. Just because you manage to escape from illness or injury doesn't mean you're not overtrained. Looking back, I think I would have run just as fast in the 1976 Olympics by cutting out 25 percent of my training. The year prior to the Games I ran up to 100 miles a week and didn't miss a single day. With a full-time job as a teacher, an hour commute to and from work, playing basketball when I taught physical education, and two workouts, my body and mind just couldn't absorb it all. I was always tired, but it took me almost ten years to realize I was overtraining.

You have to be especially careful not to overtrain when you're highly motivated. When aiming for a serious race, a common mistake is to spend it all in training. We have a Norwegian expression for runners who do well only in training or small competitions. "Wednesday runners" they're called, as important events are almost never held in the middle of the week. Remember, it's the race in which you've got to do well. They don't give out prizes for training.

The same advice holds as true for the advanced runner as for the other levels: when in doubt, underdo it rather than overdo it. I know when I can't push anymore by the feeling I get in my legs and the way I breathe. Usually, heaviness in my legs goes away after I get moving, but when I can't shake that feeling I know I'm due for a rest. Norwegian physiologist Professor Sigmund B. Strømme, Ph.D., suggests that if you want to determine overtraining more scientifically than judging by a subjective feeling, use heart rate as a guide. Take your pulse regularly to determine your usual rate under various conditions: at rest, after a interval, or during a steady, comfortable run, a jog, or riding a stationary bike. If that usual rate becomes consistently elevated for several days, you are likely overtrained and should cut back.

How do you know when you're overtraining? The problem is that there's usually a time lag between the act of overtraining and the resulting state of being overtrained. You have to learn by experience to recognize the early warning signs. Unfortunately, this is something you probably can't understand until it happens to you. Even the most experienced of us tend not to believe that our bodies could ever fail, until they do.

In the last several years, I have begun to take blood tests to determine overtraining, which are administered by Dr. Leif Roar Falkum and Dr. Thor Øistein Endsjö, the Norwegian Track & Field Federation doctors. This is a biological control method effective for elite athletes. There are two types of tests, both of which originated in Finland. The one I use evaluates the levels of two hormones, cortisol and testos-

Here I am at six months (April 1954), with my two "guardians,"
brothers Jan (right), age nine, and Arild, age three.

As a three-year-old spectator at
the Holmenkollen,
Oslo's famous ski jump.

My mother finally had a girl,
and she was determined to
make her look like one!

My two nephews, Geir, age seven, and Terje, age four, wanted to get on the track after the Norwegian Track & Field Championships in 1976. Their aunt had just won the King's Trophy for the best performance of the meet for the fourth year.

Midway into the 800 meters in the Norwegian Junior Championships, July 19, 1971, just shy of my eighteenth birthday. *(Photo Courtesy of* Norsk Telegrambyrå*)*

After winning the 800-meter race, I received the award for the best performance of the meet, with a time of 2:11.5. *(Photo courtesy of* Norsk Telegrambyrå*)*

My first victory in a senior Norwegian championship, in 1971. I won both the 800m and the 1,500m. *(Photo courtesy of Norsk Telegrambyrå)*

The look of effort reveals what it took for a win, a personal record (4:10 for 1,500m), and the King's Trophy for the best performance of the meet in the 1974 Norwegian Championships. Close on my heels is the girl who routinely had beaten me for two years.

The Norwegian Cross Country Championships in 1976, my fifth national cross-country win in a string of fifteen such titles.

On the way to victory in my "dream race," the World Cup 3,000 meters in 1977. In the pack are Jan Merrill (USA), Ulricke Bruns (East Germany) in third, and Lyudmila Bragina (USSR) in fourth, then world-record holder in the distance. *(Photo by Knut E. Holm)*

True cross-country, over hill and dale and through the mud, is the toughest and most challenging form of the sport, and it's also my favorite. This 1978 World Cross Country Championships marked the first time Norway sent a women's team to the event. I led from the gun and won the 5-kilometer race, my first in a series of five World Cross Country victories. *(Photo courtesy of* Verdens Gang*)*

This photo, taken on the last lap of a 3,000-meter race in Bislett Stadium, says it all about my life and career: concentration, effort, support from Jack—and success. I ran a lifetime best of 8:31.75 for the distance, which was also a world best in 1979. I am particularly proud of having run the 3,000 meters under 8:40 nine times. *(Photo courtesy of* Verdens Gang, *by Tore Kristiansen)*

I was twenty-one and Jack was twenty-seven on our wedding day, June 26, 1975. We just made it to my neighborhood church after getting lost on a long run that morning. Forever romantic, we spent our "honeymoon" doing an interval workout on the track the following day. *(Photo courtesy of* Norsk Telegrambyrå*)*

One of the sweetest moments of my career, winning the 1983 World Championship marathon in Helsinki, making me the first person to win the first event of the first ever World Championships! It was a race so perfect, at a distance so tough, that it remains the only marathon in which I have ever run that I didn't think about dropping out at some point. *(Photo courtesy of Adidas Germany)*

What do you do the day after winning a gold medal? Following the 1983 World Championship marathon, the Norwegian newspaper *VG* gave me a choice for a photo essay: to meet the prime minister of Norway, or to go shopping and they'd foot the bill. I chose to shop, and here I'm wearing the outfit I bought. *(Photo courtesy of* Verdens Gang, *by Hans Olav Forsang)*

Leading the pack of the 1980 L'eggs Mini Marathon, a race of over 8,000 women. *(Photo by Paul A. Spinelli)*

Looking back, I never realized at the time the accomplishment of this 1980 L'eggs Mini Marathon, a world road record of 30:59.8. No one, including myself, has come close to matching my time on the roads, and only Ingrid Kristiansen has matched it on the track. It was probably the best race of my life. *(Photo by Paul A. Spinelli)*

Running alone over a hilly Central Park course in the 1980 L'eggs Mini Marathon 10k, my competition was the dreaded clock. I had set a standard in those days always to run faster than I ever had, to set another world record. *(Photo by Paul A. Spinelli)*

Being crowned with the traditional laurel wreath after the 1979 New York City Marathon, the day I became the first woman to run under 2:30. Crowning me is Mayor Ed Koch, who has declared me "a New Yorker by adoption." Standing near me is four-time winner of the race Bill Rodgers, and behind him is race director and New York Road Runners Club president Fred Lebow. Mae Rudin, standing to my immediate right, presented me with the winner's award, the Rudin Trophy. *(Photo by Paul A. Spinelli)*

Victory. The Falmouth Road Race, in Massachusetts, in August 1980. *(Photo by Paul A. Spinelli)*

My "support crew," from left to right: Jan, Jack, Arild, Geir. *(Photo by Gloria Averbuch)*

2:27:33 — and Waiting

There may be more important indices of women's progress in recent years but probably none so dramatic as 2 hours 27 minutes 33 seconds. That was how long it took Grete Waitz, a 26-year-old Norwegian teacher, to run the New York Marathon in Sunday's heat. It is no act of disrespect toward Bill Rodgers, the men's winner again, in 2:11:42, to dwell on Mrs. Waitz's time. Not only did it make her the first woman to finish. Not only did it break her own world's record for the 26-mile, 385-yard distance. It meant that in just 15 years, the women's record has improved by *one hour*.

Progress has been slower on the bureaucratic side. For years, many people thought it was physically unwise for women to undergo so punishing a test. It was not until "K. Switzer" let her hair down that people knew that a woman had run the Boston Marathon for the first time. Women were not allowed in the New York Marathon until 1972. Now, with marathons springing up all over the country, women runners have become steadily more welcome. Next September, they will be admitted to the famous 52-mile London-to-Brighton ultramarathon.

But not the Olympics. Never mind that Mrs. Waitz's 2:27:33 would have beaten half the male Olympic marathon winners, and all the men who ran in the 1970 New York Marathon. The Olympics still do not recognize women who run 26 miles. Indeed, the longest Olympic race for women covers one metric mile.

It is too late to do anything about it for the 1980 Olympics in Moscow. But it may still be possible to right matters in time for 1984 in Los Angeles. One standard objection to new events is that they take precious space and schedule time. But that objection cannot apply to the marathon. Adding 20 or 30 women to a race in which 70 or 80 men are already likely to run would hardly crowd the streets of Los Angeles. New York's streets handled 11,533 marathoners Sunday.

Others think too few women are involved in the marathon to justify an Olympic event. Let them note that there were 1,800 women in Sunday's race. And others still feel, out of machismo or paternalism, that women athletes just cannot keep up with men. Let them remember the name Grete Waitz and the numbers 2:27:33.

It's nice to make sports headlines, but this *New York Times* editorial (October 23, 1979) was a special honor.

terone. In overtraining, the ratio of cortisol to testosterone increases. (The other test measures the level of creatine phosphokinase. An increase in this serum enzyme indicates muscle damage.) Six months to a year after I began testing, a curve was made to determine my optimum training. Although there is no conclusive evidence that the test I am given is effective, when a reduction in training intensity has been prescribed by Dr. Falkum, together with a proper regimen for fluid intake and diet, it has resulted in an improvement in a relatively short time. It should be pointed out that additional life stress is a significant factor in the results of these tests.

BURNOUT

Burnout is the result of extreme or consistent overtraining. I categorize it in two types: mini and maxi burnout. The mini version occurs when you ignore overtraining, which is the warning: a persistent staleness, illness, or exhaustion from which recovery can be reasonably short if the warning is heeded and training is curtailed. The maxi burnout is another story. This is the case in which the word "burnout" truly lives up to its name: a complete collapse in running, both physical and mental, from which it can be a very long road to recovery.

Preventing burnout means reducing both physical and mental stress. This stress can become a vicious cycle. Overtraining can cause lack of success in running or racing, which in turn creates a depressed, washed-up feeling. Overtraining in a determined effort to improve compounds the situation, so that both the initial problem and the incorrect remedy work together to make a runner feel even more tired, negative, burned-out. To avoid this cycle, make sure you have the proper perspective about what you are doing (see Chapter 9).

Constant monitoring is extremely important. Keep guard over yourself both physically and psychologically. Continually check for the signs of overtraining, which are discussed in Chapter 5. Our memory of what we have done and can do is often contradicted by what's written in black and white, so use your training diary as a conscience.

Know your body—how it reacts, recovers, strengthens. This is yet another reason to keep your training consistent. There's a normal, expected type of fatigue and recovery time, and you need to be able to recognize what's normal and what isn't. If you continually change your workouts, you'll have trouble recognizing it. You may feel a different or unfamiliar fatigue in different parts of your body. Do not ask the body to adjust to so many varying kinds of stress.

Never try to overcome fatigue by force. Don't push through training or a race. Relax, reduce the training, skip the race. The worst mistake, and one of the most common, is driving yourself in anger, trying to push even harder. I'm guilty of this myself, even after all these years. As recently as in 1984, I defiantly pushed through a series of workouts and races, after which my blood tests showed I should have been in bed.

If you're in doubt about your training, beware. Doubt is your safety device, telling you it's time to cut back. If you're wondering whether you ought to run just one more interval, the answer is probably no. Don't do it just to prove you're tough or to make yourself tough. There are better times to test your strength. And don't do it just because it's on your schedule. I decide on training one month at a time but never hold myself too strictly to what's on paper. I constantly ask myself, "Will this help me?" If I'm tired, the answer is no. In fact, I know that workout can likely harm me.

Watch for the "blahs." Keep your training consistent but varied. Don't always run the same workout, in the same place, in the same way. Try some creative speedwork. For example, doing intervals trying to catch a partner, interchanging the lead, or using a handicap system if you're on different levels can add an element of fun and camaraderie. I've even heard of runners who do fartlek by playing tag. Even though training can be hard work, take time to "smell the roses." Sometimes on my easy days I do a little sight-seeing on the run, or I'll drive twenty minutes in order take a run in the forest. It's good just to be in nature.

Don't overrace. This is perhaps most important to the advanced runner, for whom racing is the bread and butter of the sport. The advanced runner draws on great resources of strength to race and has learned to a great extent to overcome fatigue and pain. Racing means "going to the well," in runners' lingo, and you can only go to that well so many times. Dig down too often, and you'll find that it's dry.

Avoid boredom in racing. Don't continually run the same distances. I mix my race distances and still run an occasional 1,500 or 3,000 meters for variety. If you're moving up to longer distances, don't do it too fast. Younger runners should take their time before running longer distances and the marathon. You can get stale very quickly when you've done it all too soon, when there are no new goals or challenges. After all, I could see it this way for myself: after all these years, I've done it all. It's just a replay. Quite frankly, even the Olympic Games loses some of its thrill after three visits. But I've never lost my motivation, because I've always been able to add something new to my program—from track to cross-country to road races and the marathon. And I've run only ten marathons. I know I haven't reached my prime in the event. I know I can run faster.

Don't be overambitious. Alberto Salazar learned the hard way about sensible training. He has a prescription I like: "If you want to run your ideal marathon, for example, ask yourself what you think would be the maximum, absolute, top mileage you can run. Then chop 20 percent off that!" Salazar goes on to suggest that we overtrain because we're greedy—trying to get everything out of our bodies that we can.* Training sensibly means treating yourself with respect, respecting your limits as well as your ability.

Although I have come to consider my mini burnouts as occupational hazards, luckily, I have never had a maxi burnout. However, the list of world-class runners who have is a long one, headed by former world-record holders like Patti Catalano, Allison Roe, and Alberto Salazar. As of this writing, none of these runners has made a complete recovery, although they're still working on it. They illustrate the risk for runners at all levels. Caught up in the cycle of success, it's hard to slow down, to step back and take a breath, get perspective. Now they must reroot themselves and get back to the simplicity and consistency that originally allowed them to develop their athletic talent.

*Hal Higdon, "To Everything a Season," *The Runner*, March 1985.

7

Mind Power

We all may have different levels of physical ability, but there is one aspect in which we are equal: the capacity to develop our mental ability. We all can be equally mentally focused, disciplined, and determined. While there is a limit to how much physical training any of us can do, the mind is an area of unlimited potential, and one that has a powerful influence on performance. I call it mind power.

Our mental capacity is so enormous, experts say we have not even begun to tap it. This is true in all endeavors and illustrated dramatically in sports. The mind–body connection seems clearest to me when I consider races in which I did well despite the fact my running was not up to par. It's so much more emotional, more memorable, to succeed in a race for which I was not 100 percent fit. That's why I cried after the 1984 Olympic marathon—to win a silver medal when the day before I could hardly walk because my back hurt so much was one of the most emotional experiences of my career. This is why I so well understood Joan Benoit Samuelson's tears of joy and relief after she won the 1984 Olympic Marathon trials only seventeen days after knee surgery. It is this race, above even her Olympic victory, that she calls "the race of my life." What makes these experiences so memorable, and so remarkable, is that they are largely achievements of mental will.

120

The recognition of the mental edge is the reason the field of sports psychology is growing so rapidly, an area in which the Eastern Europeans have long excelled. The majority of top athletes practice some form of mental conditioning, and a number of them even claim that their success on any given day is 80 percent to 90 percent dependent on mental readiness. Mental preparation consists of various factors, such as motivation, goal setting, visualization, relaxation, and concentration, or focus. Understanding and developing these techniques will help you run your best in the same way that training your body does.

Motivation is a key factor in mental preparation. Once you have developed the initial motivation in your running, you must work on maintaining it. Sustained motivation is essential to achieving your potential. This is why goal setting is so important. To keep your motivation high, use mental stimuli. Find what gets you psyched and surround yourself with it: posters, sayings, photos, running magazines, videos. The more you see it, the more you remember it. For example, you might put up a sign on your wall, or a note on your mirror or in your wallet reminding you of your goal time. Ingrid Kristiansen put up pictures of her competitors by the treadmill she ran on before her world marathon record. One runner I know uses his goal marathon time as his access number for an automatic bank machine. Some people are inspired by reading about or knowing other athletes. When I was a girl, it was Wilma Rudolph and later a top East German track runner named Gunhild Hoffmeister.

VISUALIZATION

Visualization, also called positive imagery or guided imagery, is mentally picturing yourself achieving your goals. Visualization helps build a positive attitude and heightened sense of self-esteem. Every training run, every day, sets a pattern for what follows—mentally as well as physically. What do you think about when you run? Do you daydream or sort out personal problems? On my easy runs, I may use the time to relax and let my mind wander, but never in hard workouts or races.

Some running should be different mentally just the way it is physically. Spend at least some of your training time, and other parts of your day, concentrating on what you are doing and visualizing your running success.

The more detailed and specific your visualization, the better. Picture the upcoming race course and your competition. I visualize myself in relation to other runners, and if I know the course is hilly, for example, I will think of pushing uphill, then downhill. Create a mental image of yourself as a powerful athlete. Imagine yourself driving up the hills, sprinting to the finish in a good time or ahead of your competition. While seeing yourself running the race, concentrate on form—feeling and looking strong. Recalling detailed sensations can be very effective in creating a vivid image: the sound of your breathing, your feet hitting the pavement, wind blowing on your skin and through your hair as you run. The more time you devote to visualization the better, but practice at least twenty minutes, three times a week, while relaxed in a meditative state and also on the run.

Visualization does more than just occupy your mind; it can actually affect your performance. This has been proven in numerous experiments. In a demonstration featured on the ABC-TV broadcast of the 1984 Winter Olympics, a ski racer was wired with electromyographic devices and told to visualize skiing the course. His muscles actually mimicked the physical response to a downhill run.

When you first begin using visualization, you may find that some negative thoughts force their way into your mind. You must learn to push that negativity away, even though it may be difficult. If I have a cold or other problem, I try to disassociate it from my race and keep it from negatively affecting my attitude. Keeping a positive frame of mind was especially difficult for me in 1982, after I had dropped out of two marathons. Although the rumor that I was "washed-up" helped fuel my determination to prove I wasn't, I must admit it still affected my confidence in my next marathon. Positive focus was very difficult, but I worked hard to concentrate on my especially strong desire to do well. If you do picture the adversity, try to make use of it in a positive way, by picturing yourself overcoming any obstacle on your way to success.

MENTAL TOUGHNESS

Mental Toughness is the ability to push when it hurts, to fight for success, to dig down when you're empty and come up with more. It is a test of your will, in which you ask for and get the most of yourself in a race. Mental toughness is developed with good mental preparation, and it requires a combination of *concentration, discipline, self-confidence*, and *aggression.*

Concentration

I concentrate so deeply when I run that I am totally unaware of what goes on around me. I don't see the surroundings or other people or hear anyone talk. In fact, if Jack or Jan isn't there to warn me about mud puddles, potholes, or other obstructions by tapping my arm to get my attention, I run right into them.

A lapse in concentration can mean the loss of valuable seconds or even minutes in a race. Nowhere is concentration more important than on the track, which is where I learned it. A track race goes so quickly and is so intense, you can't afford to lose concentration for even a second. A problem like my diarrhea in the 1984 and 1985 New York City Marathon resulted in not only discomfort and embarrassment but a loss of concentration. Although I was thinking more about my stomach than running a race, I just kept going and tried to ignore it. Once you've made up your mind to continue running, you must continue to concentrate, battling anything that distracts you from your race effort.

Discipline

Training prepares you to race. It's that simple. And the discipline of training is what readies you for the race. This is why I get up for my first training session at 5:15 A.M. every morning. Believe me, there are many cold, dark Norwegian mornings I would rather stay in bed, but I know the discipline of going out develops the same toughness I need in a race. A few mornings of indulging myself here and there, and I would lose that edge that I maintain by keeping this routine. Winter in Norway forces a runner to be disciplined. There are times the snow is so deep that I am forced to run in boots. I recall a snowstorm so severe that the only clear patch of ground I could find was a quarter-mile long. I ran back and forth on that space for eight miles.

I'm not suggesting my 5:15 A.M. regimen is necessary for you, but some kind of consistency and discipline contributes to mental toughness. Keep in mind that sticking to your routine will also help you develop tenacity and confidence. One of my coaches used to insist on doing workouts even in the ice and snow. "We cannot simply skip workouts," he said. "Life is not without problems. Athletics is the same."*

Self-confidence

Although training prepares you physically, it alone cannot give you the winning edge you need in a race. Something else has to make you push when your body says no. For that you must rely not only on your mind but on a trained mind. The mental psyche that visualization helps develop is part of that training, but it won't work if you're not confident.

Being tough requires tremendous self-confidence. This confidence is crucial in athletics. You may be able to fake confidence in other

*Amby Burfoot, "Grete," *Runner's World*, March 1981.

aspects of life, but you can't fool your own mind or body—and they're what count in running. If you aren't truly confident, you're missing the major ingredient of becoming a winner.

You must always have the attitude "I can do it." When I go into a race, I never think negatively. Once I'm on the starting line, despite any lingering doubts, I constantly work on convincing myself I can win. Quite simply, if you don't believe in what you're going to do, you won't do it. Your mind is like a computer; if you program it to succeed, it will. It has been proven many times that to a great degree we are what we think we are, and we achieve only what we think we are capable of achieving.

Aggression

To be tough, you've got to be aggressive. Aggressiveness means being able to assert your presence in the race, being in control. Don't be hesitant, timid, doubtful, or intimidated by others. Develop the ability to take command. Be an actor, not a reactor. Run according to your own plan. Let the others race according to what you do. I feel more confident and in control knowing the other runners in the field are watching and waiting to see what *I* do. Mary Decker Slaney is an example of an aggressive runner. Everyone thought it best for her not to run from the front against the Soviets in the 1983 World Championships. Few runners win track races from the front, and she had rarely raced the powerful Soviet women. But Mary runs all her races from the front, and she ran that way in Helsinki—her way—and won both her races.

It was in cross-country that I really learned to be aggressive. The starting area is very narrow in international cross-country, and you have to spring to the front to get good position and to avoid being trampled. It's a race with a lot of elbows. In addition, because cross-country is always tactical, aggression is a key factor. I'm naturally a lot more aggressive when my opponent is a human being rather than a clock.

I lose my aggressiveness when I go into a race lacking self-confidence and conviction. This has cost me the chance for a victory. In the 1984 Olympics I was so troubled by my back problem that my usual focus on winning was replaced by the fear of not being able to run at all. When Joan Benoit Samuelson took the lead, I did not respond until it was too late to catch her. Later, I realized it was probably a mistake to have let her get so far in front. As I said before, it's important to go to the starting line thinking positively. Without that necessary mindset, I didn't make a bold move. Mentally, I had lost my edge.

So many runners have approached me with questions or problems about being mentally tough. It would seem by the number of them who are women that this is more difficult for them, as most women don't grow up encouraged to be aggressive. However, I think it is also difficult for many men. Maybe they're just less open about it or more reluctant to talk to me, especially because I'm a woman. Athletic toughness and aggression are not natural for many people, but anyone can develop it if his or her confidence level is genuinely high.

Aggression is part of sports and part of life, and it's important to realize that "aggression" is not a dirty word. It's what makes a good athlete and a champion. It's also important to appreciate that aggression and self-confidence are benefits of sports that remain with you long after the race is over. Those who excel in running are often those who excel in other aspects of life as well. They are equipped with the traits that enable them to take risks, try new endeavors, and achieve greater success.

No Pain, No Gain

You can't be mentally tough if you're not a fighter, and you can't be a fighter if you can't take the pain. This pain is not the enemy, rather a discomfort you have learned to endure as part of your achievement. It's running's biggest cliché, but it says it all: No pain, no gain. It's also been said that everything else being equal among competitors, the winner is the person who can sustain the pain the longest. Surviving is one of the elements of successful racing. People constantly tell me my races look easy, that I look relaxed, but that doesn't mean I'm not hurting! The truth is that every race hurts, from the 10km to the marathon. I just don't make a point of announcing it. Like every competitive runner must, I accept pain as a necessary part of success.

Training helps you to accept the pain, to overcome the fear and discomfort. When you realize that you are in control of your pain and that you're prepared for it, it becomes "friendly" pain. Often, I feel more able to push myself in a race when I realize that although I hurt, so does everyone else. I'm not the only one struggling. That's part of the camaraderie. It's always the most tired bodies, in a state of temporary collapse after a hard race effort, who are the first to put out a hand and congratulate each other beyond the finish line.

Sometimes, however, nothing can prepare you for the pain, especially a kind you've never experienced. Then only your toughest mindset can make you endure. In my first marathon I was in such pain near the end that I was almost running and crying at the same time. Nothing could have prepared me for the 1983 London Marathon, either. It was the first time I had to cut back in training before a marathon. A lingering injury had prevented me from putting in enough of the necessary long runs, and by the final miles of the race, I felt that lack. My entire body ached; my legs were numb. "You're on record pace!" Jack shouted. "I've just got to concentrate on finishing!" I yelled back. It wasn't until the final quarter mile that I realized I could get the record. "You can stand this pain a few more minutes," I told myself. Then I literally closed my eyes and kept repeating, "Only another minute." I had to use everything in my warehouse of mental skills. My mind had to want what my body didn't, and it was my mind that pushed me to that world-record time.

8

The Marathon

MY FIRST MARATHON

I came to the starting line of my first marathon feeling lost and lonely. Instead of the predictable 400-meter oval track with just a few familiar faces, I was standing on a huge bridge with thousands of strangers. As everyone began to take their places, moving like a school of fish in a familiar stream, I realized I didn't even know where to stand on the quarter-mile-long starting line. Amidst what looked like more chaos than I'd ever seen, I approached a bearded man standing in a jeep shouting orders from a megaphone. Pulling on his pant leg to get his attention, I asked, "Mr. Lebow, where do I go?"

This, you may ask, was the "start of something big"? It was my first road race, my first marathon, and my first run over twelve miles. I had a win and a world record, and I broke all the rules, every one of them that I've emphasized so strongly here! True, I had made some mistakes in the race due to inexperience, but, obviously, I had also done something very right. The marathon may have been foreign to me back in 1978, but it was still a version of the craft I had practiced for over ten years.

Although Fred Lebow could tell me where to stand on that warm October day, nobody could have prepared me for what lay ahead over the 26.2 miles. That's what I'm going to do for you—give you the best view there is, the one from hindsight. First of all, the difference between my marathon and what you face today is the wealth of information. Although running 26.2 miles should not be taken lightly, it seems it has become extremely complicated. There are enough books, magazines, stories, and legends (mostly, of the dreaded wall or other forms of death or dying) to fill an entire library. I'm beginning to think people can be too educated. I hope to help strip away some of the confusion and the mystique and to simplify what is admittedly a challenging endeavor.

The first lesson my experience in the marathon taught me is to be well prepared. Obviously, I wasn't, and that story gets even better. Back to the streets of New York. As I clicked off the miles of the marathon, actually beginning to enjoy myself, I made the common assumption a novice sometimes makes before the twenty-mile mark. "Hey, this is easy. When do we start really running?" I wondered. The pace, so much slower than I was used to, felt like a jog. Little did I know what lay ahead. Luckily, I had made a very smart decision to go out slowly, because I made plenty of other mistakes for which a careful approach helped compensate.

One of the biggest was that I didn't drink anything. I had never drunk during a race, and although I tried now I realized this, too, required practice. The water bounced out of the little cups, up my nose, all over my face, and onto the ground—everywhere but in my mouth. The orange slices that were passed out along the way provided my only relief, but they certainly weren't enough to prevent dehydration.

By sixteen miles, I had really picked up the pace. The crowds on First Avenue were wonderful. An almost deafening cheering went on for miles. I had never experienced anything like it. I was really flying. Then at about twenty-one miles it began, that dull ache in my quadriceps. I turned to a runner next to me and asked how far it was to the finish. "Five miles," he said. "What's five miles?" I asked myself. As a European used to kilometers, I thought five miles could have been to the moon, and by this time I was too tired even to attempt to compute the distance into something understandable.

Every time I turned a corner, I looked for some trees—the sign of a park that I knew meant the finish. By now it had really begun: the pain. I hurt all over—my legs, my side, my shoulders. Never had

I hurt so much. I was almost crying. Odd feelings overtook me: anger, frustration, depression, then anger again.

When I finally crossed the finish line, it wasn't with a sense of joy and ease, the way the media portrayed it, but with sheer relief and a lot of anger. "I'll never do that again!"* were my angry first words to Jack as I threw down my discarded shoes.

If this doesn't sound like the thrill of victory, it's because it wasn't. In retrospect I can say, sure, it was great to win, especially with the added bonus of a world record. It was the beginning of a new and wonderful road racing career. But that's not what I was thinking at the time. If I were to glamorize the experience, it might make nice reading, but it wouldn't be what stands out in my memory, nor would it be very instructive to you. It's more important that you learn what I had to about the marathon—the hard part. No one needs to learn how to handle what's good, the sense of excitement and accomplishment. It's achieving those feelings that's sometimes tough.

By the time I hit my stride in the event, the marathon had become quite a status symbol. It's now a feat millions of people have accomplished, and they say it—with everything from marathon T-shirts and certificates to hats and coffee mugs. When I first started running in Norway, a marathon seemed very odd, impossible for all but a small group of men. It was in the United States that the marathon began to seem accessible. After Frank Shorter won the Olympic marathon in 1972 and the masses hit the roads, the attitude toward the distance totally changed.

In competitive American society, the marathon presented the perfect challenge. With the emphasis on the individual and the fitness boom, marathon mania was born, helped along by the media. Sure, I understand the glamour; I have only to look at what the marathon has done for me. However, I have always felt that if Americans, especially novices, better understood the sport, they would have started by running shorter distances. Sure enough, they're learning this now.**

---

*It's funny, but I also swore I'd never run another 3,000-meter race after my first one.

**The number of Americans finishing 10kms has increased dramatically since 1978, while the number of those finishing marathons has dropped off. In 1984, 229,000 did 10kms; 100,000 did marathons. Source: *USA Today*, March 20, 1985, and The National Running Data Center.

To begin with the marathon is to start at the wrong end. I recommend a couple of years of running the shorter distances before trying a long one. In fact, Jack had been running twenty years before he ran his first marathon.

This may come as a complete surprise, but the truth is I really don't like running marathons. Twenty-six and two-tenths miles is definitely not my favorite or ideal distance. The five- to ten-mile range is more like it, and it's probably the distance at which I am best. When people ask what my favorite part of the marathon is, I tell them it's the last 300 yards! The marathon takes long preparation and is a high-risk event. The effort of concentrating for two and a half hours is extremely difficult. If my mind wanders for even a second, I must force it back. Run competitively, it is especially tough. If I could run one in three hours and just enjoy the scenery, maybe I'd feel different, but in my position that just isn't possible. Despite what the press says, the marathon has never been easy for me. In fact, the World Championships in 1983 was my only marathon so far in which I didn't think at some point about dropping out of the race.

Now that I have sufficiently frightened and discouraged you, I will talk about the flip side. It's the sense of accomplishment and the spirit of the event that make the marathon worthwhile. In New York, the atmosphere is what makes the race really special for me. The crowds are great—so inspirational. Everyone shouts my name: even the cab drivers recognize me! Sometimes I feel more like a New Yorker than a Norwegian. In addition, it is precisely because the marathon is so challenging and so difficult that I undertake it, and since it has become more prestigious as a championship event, I find even more reason to stay with it. Running a marathon can be rewarding for you as well, if you are well prepared and sensible about your expectations.

One thing is certain: you will never forget your marathon—for good or for bad. It is the day on which you put it all on the line in your ultimate test as a runner. This race has given me some of my greatest and most satisfying moments. In fact, without that fateful day in 1978, I would not be where I am today: there would be no gold and silver medals; I would not have written this book.

WHY RUN A MARATHON?

Effective marathon training means following every principle outlined in this book, and doing so even more closely than for any other race. These principles—such as pacing, tapering, fitness, training, concentration, realistic goals, patience, control, and relaxation—are doubly important for the marathon.

What disturbs me more than anything about the marathon fad, though, is seeing people run it who aren't prepared. Maybe this is unfair, and I'm sure there will be people angry that I'm saying it, but I don't feel a normal, healthy person needs six hours to finish the race. This isn't running; it's surviving. If you aren't an older or a disabled person, any longer than five and a half hours is just too long. The Stockholm Marathon has a cutoff point of five hours, and I agree with it. If you need longer than that, you should train more and try again when you're ready, or stick to shorter races.

Considerable attention has been given in this book to discussing your motives as a runner. Early on I advised the beginner that I think one's motive for running should be personal—not something a person does for family, friends, or social prestige. This is even more true of a marathon. A number of people do it because "everyone else does," or on a dare or a bet. I admit I ran my first marathon because Jack talked me into it, and all it got me was very angry and two incredibly sore legs! However, I continued to run marathons based on my own desire: because the event is a challenge, I was motivated by success, and I felt the longer distances suited me better than the shorter events on the track. There's no better or more inspiring a goal for the serious runner than a marathon, as long as you're truly motivated and well prepared.

RESPECTING THE DISTANCE

It's not called a marathon for nothing!* This event has humbled many, among them some of the best runners in the world. Nothing made that clearer than a look at Geoff Smith stumbling along to victory in the 1984 Boston Marathon as he clutched the cramps in his thighs, the price he paid for a foolish early pace, or me in Boston 1982, when I was slowed to a walk and finally a stop by twenty-three miles, literally unable to continue. Alberto Salazar, Dick Beardsley, and Allison Roe, among others, toppled from the heights of marathon victories and records, broken but wiser for the experience. Now no one treats the event lightly, and gone are the days when most top runners dared to predict times and records.** This race is too unpredictable. It can defy all logic, break all the rules.

Don't forget that the marathon is not over until you run all 26.2 miles. It's easy to run twenty miles; it's the last six you have to respect. If you don't, you're simply not going to make it—at least in any meaningful sense of that phrase. The most common mistake people make during the race is to think only about the moment, instead of two hours ahead. Twenty miles is where the race really begins.

My idea of respecting the distance is reflected in the fact that other than in the Boston Marathon I have never set out to run for time, to break a world record. To run well and win, yes, but never specifically for time. If a record happens, it happens, but I never make it my aim. Of course, I am aware at certain points if I am on record pace, but paying close attention to the clock is just too stressful. The few times I have run races specifically for a record, the pressure was just too great. Running this way, I'm never relaxed, and I'm so concerned

---

*A disputed legend has it that in 490 B.C. a messenger named Phidippides ran from Marathon to Athens to carry word of the Greek victory over an army of 30,000 Persians. As the story goes, he proclaimed, "Rejoice, we conquer," then dropped dead.

**Runners such as Geoff Smith and Ahmed Saleh in the 1985 New York City Marathon, and Ingrid Kristiansen and Joan Benoit Samuelson in the 1985 Chicago Marathon all attempted world records, and all in the same fashion: going out at what turned out to be a suicidal pace. Most folded. Benoit Samuelson came closest with a PR of 2:21:20 but was initially on 2:14 pace.

about splits that I can't pay careful enough attention to my body. It's one thing to try for a time in a shorter race but quite another to try it in a marathon. Besides, I left the track for the roads to get away from the emphasis on running for time. On the track you can't get away from it—every lap time is shouted in your ear.

I initially enjoyed road racing because it lessens the focus on times. A record is a nice bonus, but no matter how many road records I set, they don't outweigh the victories. A record can be broken, but a victory is forever. This doesn't mean a record has no meaning. I still get geared up knowing there is the possibility of a record, and I feel thrilled if I get it.

Respecting the marathon distance means being aware that running for time is a gamble and that if you try it, you've got to accept the risk. So many things can go wrong. It's not like a 10km, for example; you're more in control for 6.2 miles than for 26.2. A lot of runners calculate their marathon splits and do everything to reach them, despite the conditions or how they're feeling. I had hoped for a personal best in New York in 1985 but gave up that plan as soon as I felt the heat, which reached 70 degrees only an hour into the race. A marathon is the kind of race you must take one mile at a time, being flexible enough to adapt to the unknown and the unexpected.

YOUR FIRST MARATHON

What makes a successful marathoner? They are the same qualities that make a successful 10,000-meter runner or a successful anything: discipline and dedication. Of course, there is a degree of physical ability, but almost everyone can run a marathon. In fact, a common coaching expression is that a sprinter is born, but a distance runner is made. It's important to keep in mind that every marathon is different—location, weather, course, crowds—and every marathon is a learning experience; you can never learn too much about the event. For example, over the years I've learned different things about New York: to use the hill leading onto the Queensboro Bridge at fifteen miles as a landmark to pace myself, and not to get carried away and run too fast up First Avenue, a straightaway of crowd enthusiasm.

How long you need to prepare for the event depends on your conditioning and athletic background. You should be running regularly for a minimum of one to two years before you contemplate a marathon, and you should have reached at least the level described in the section for intermediate runners—the first stage for which I outline some quality training. Quality training is still important for the runner who isn't concerned with time in the marathon, who just wants to go the distance. Every runner can benefit from even moderate speedwork. With speedwork, those who do run for time can get faster, and others can run the distance more comfortably and efficiently.

Many novices fear the marathon distance. They hear so much talk and advice, they can't help but feel somewhat intimidated. Believe me, it's not as bad as it sounds if you are well trained and run a smart race. Long runs should prepare you physically and mentally, and give you needed confidence. Although my experience sounded a bit overwhelming, I was never really afraid. First of all, I had no idea what to expect, and in that way ignorance *is* bliss! More important, however, I went out slowly and ran conservatively, which gave me the security of knowing I was in control. One of the greatest dangers for the inexperienced marathoner is to get carried away in the beginning and be undisciplined about pace.

No matter how well prepared you are, you may still experience anxiety and doubts. Even I feel that way. Weeks before a big marathon I begin to question myself. "Why do I train so hard? Why must I always be so tired? Why do I make life so difficult for myself?" I get into one of my moods—throwing my training gear all over the house, congratulating myself on being an ex-marathoner. Of course, I'm up for my 5:30 A.M. run the next day.

Marathon training is no great mystery. Don't throw your current training out the window in search of that "magic" marathon program. The basic training principles I have outlined are the same for every race. My marathon training is fundamentally the same as my 3,000-, 5,000-, and 10,000-meter training, except the mileage is higher. The importance of maintaining quality training for a marathon is illustrated by the fact that most of today's top marathoners have also been top track runners. The major difference is the addition of a long run once a week leading up to the race, approximately fifteen to eighteen miles. You should build up your long run slowly, the same way you have built to your present mileage, and make sure to get used to running on asphalt if you aren't already. The hard/easy rule still applies for marathon training, and you should allow for some days off if you're running fairly low mileage. At forty miles a week, you might try taking off the day before a long run. It's not how many miles you run but how they're distributed that counts. It may be more beneficial to run every day if your aim is fitness, but not if you're goal is a marathon.

Do some shorter races leading up to the marathon. Whether it's for time or just to go the distance, other races are valuable. They are important as intermediate goals, for achievement and confidence, and to prepare you for the big day. If you're an experienced marathoner, do some runs at race pace and good efforts in shorter races. I run a few races leading up to a marathon, and my final tune-up is a short road race a week before.

Be especially careful to avoid injuries, and watch out for overtraining. Any change in training should always be made slowly, and be careful of the increase in mileage for marathon training, which is especially risky. In addition, the bigger the event, the more we tend to push ourselves in training. This is an important time to pay special attention and listen carefully to your body. For marathon training, the basic warnings still apply: when in doubt, do less rather than more. Be even a bit more conservative as you approach the race. First and foremost, get to the starting line healthy. While I trained my hardest for the Olympics and the World Championships, I was also especially mindful of rest and not to overdo it. I made sure not to do any endorsement work (or go to meetings, which I can always do without since they're primarily just talk. I always come out of most meetings just as ignorant as before I went in!). On the other hand, I continued with my daily chores, which I enjoy and don't find taxing.

I am frequently asked what I eat before a marathon. I do not use the typical carbohydrate-loading diet including depletion (several days of a no- to low-carbohydrate diet followed by a diet high in complex carbohydrates the last several days before the race). Studies in Norway have shown that well-trained athletes don't derive any benefit from this diet. Many runners now omit the depletion and follow only the second phase of the diet, the carbohydrate loading. I don't even do that, as I don't like to change anything in my regimen. Besides, I normally eat a high-carbohydrate diet, anyway. I don't like pasta, so while I may eat two potatoes rather than my usual one to add some carbohydrates, I don't deliberately change what I eat at all. By the way, carbohydrate loading does not mean stuffing yourself. It refers to the type of food, not the quantity. I never eat a big meal the night before any race, as it usually just gives me trouble the next day. Actually, I find it better to eat a bigger lunch and lighter dinner the day before a marathon. It's best to read up on all the latest diet recommendations, because while mine may be good for me, it's very subjective.

RACE CONSIDERATIONS

As I have mentioned, each marathon should be considered individually, and you must be more flexible in the marathon than in shorter races. Watch the weather. Especially if it's hot, you must adjust your goals. You can't beat the heat by sticking doggedly to your game plan. I've made the mistake of starting too quickly in hot-weather marathons, like New York in 1984 and 1985. This is one of the prices I pay for not paying attention to split times, preferring to run as I feel or sacrificing good pacing to the tactical necessity of tiring my opponents early in the race. There are times the clock can be very important, especially to keep yourself under control in the early stages of the race.

Practice drinking fluids in training. If you plan to drink anything else in the race in addition to water, like one of the electrolyte solutions (sports drinks), try it in training as well. Remember my experience in my first marathon? Even if the water would have ended up in my stomach, I wasn't trained to run with it there. Drinking fluids during the race is extremely important. I'm convinced that if I had taken more fluids in the hot Boston Marathon, I wouldn't have had the cramping in my legs that forced me to stop. The need for electrolyte drinks is controversial, but after tests I have undergone, I am convinced of their value and have begun regularly drinking one during the marathon in the last few years. Since the 1981 New York City

Marathon, Jack hands me a bottle of XL-1 about every three miles, mixed to various strengths depending on the weather. Since hypoglycemics (those who suffer from low blood sugar) sometimes experience moodiness, it has occurred to me that since I'm not usually so emotional, the anger and depression I felt in my first marathon could have been caused at least in part by low blood sugar. Beware, however, of the drawbacks of these drinks in the race. Ingesting sugar delays the absorption of fluids, critical on hot days. (This is why I drink a weaker solution, diluted with water, in warm weather.)

The fatigue in a marathon is not like the kind you feel in races at shorter distances. It comes on much more slowly. The first place I feel it is in my quadriceps, usually after about two hours of running, for the last twenty-five or thirty minutes of the race. It's the pounding and the loss of muscle glycogen reserves that cause this fatigue, and the aim is to postpone it as long as possible. That's what long training runs prepare you for.

This last half hour of the marathon is always difficult for me. It's usually the point at which I start to talk to myself. I tell myself to relax each specific part of my body: neck, shoulders, arms. Then I may repeat some words like "steady, push" to keep up the pace and my confidence.

Hitting the wall. I have always claimed I never really hit the wall, but that must have been what happened in my first marathon. It was caused by a combination of factors: inexperience, insufficient preparation, and dehydration. The last five miles I really had to struggle. However, though no one says a marathon is easy, you don't have to hit the wall; and even if you do, it doesn't mean it's immovable. I still believe that for the well-trained runner there is no wall. Of course, it can get tough at around twenty miles, but it doesn't have to be as dramatic as hitting a wall.

I have not addressed dropping out of a race up to this point, because I don't believe in doing it unless it's absolutely necessary. As far as I'm concerned, in shorter races it's not reason enough to drop out because you're uncomfortable or because your time isn't to your liking. Part of the discipline of racing is to see it through to the finish, to stick with it, regardless, to take the good with the bad. Dropping out can also become a very bad habit. Once you've quit, it's easier to do it the next time. It can also cause a "choke" syndrome, which makes it very hard to give a 100 percent effort in future races.

My advice on dropping out of a marathon, however, is somewhat different. Because of the length of the race, there's a much greater potential for serious problems. Every marathoner must expect some potential problems, but 26.2 miles is a long way to go if something serious goes wrong. There's a difference between difficulty and danger, and you will have to learn to judge for yourself what would necessitate stopping. The race is not worth risking illness or injury. You have learned the natural feeling of pain or fatigue from pushing your body in training, which is a discomfort you must expect to endure. There's also a type you can't.

I have never dropped out of any other road race but a marathon. When I did drop out of those two marathons, I knew I had to. In one of them I was injured, and whether or not I could have endured the pain, continuing was not worth the risk of further physical damage. The other one was an easy decision: I simply couldn't move any farther. This is why it's so important to listen to your body. A hint of what was to come occurred at fifteen miles, when my legs began to tire, too soon for that to happen. By twenty-three miles my body simply shut down.

The case of Gabriella Andersen-Schiess staggering to the finish line of the Olympic marathon in Los Angeles created a tremendous controversy. Public debate centered on whether she should have been taken off the course by medical personnel. Another person in another race might have dropped out, but she didn't—after all, it was the Olympics. But I think she should have been pulled off. There's a point at which the risk just isn't worth it, even if it is the Olympics. If she had become dangerously ill or been severely affected by heatstroke, what then? Then there's the other side: if she had been the first runner, or even running her best time, what then? It's impossible for me to answer that with any surety. My initial reaction is that the leader can't be pulled out. Although I know it is dangerous, if it were me and I were on my way to a win or a personal best time, I would be angry if someone pulled me out. I suppose I'm not completely rational about this problem. That's why it may be best to let medical officials in the race decide what to do.

I'm certainly not advising you to drop out of a marathon, nor am I predicting you'll have to. As I've said, it's just wise to be prepared for everything. My guidelines for running a marathon are the same as those I've given for training: what you do is a matter of personal judgment and experience. Don't necessarily determine what to do based on another person's advice or experience, because we are all so different in what we can handle. After all, one runner's wall can be the point at which someone else picks up the pace.

The chapter for intermediates addressed the issue of not having "your day" in a race. This is terribly difficult when it happens in a marathon for which you have prepared so long, but again, it is something you have to be prepared for, while not letting that possibility undermine your confidence. You prepare properly and hope for the best, knowing you're taking a risk. Finally to reach Los Angeles and the first women's Olympic marathon only to end up with back trouble was one of the biggest frustrations of my career. It just shows how something totally unexpected can happen. Who could have guessed that the soft mattress I was sleeping on in Los Angeles would have caused a muscle spasm in my back? Aside from that problem, I was in the best shape of my life. The day before the race I experienced every predictable emotion. Finally, I cried myself to sleep, exhausted. Of course I took it hard. This was the Olympics, and I had hoped to win a gold medal. But it was all part of the marathon gamble. If you're going to run the race, you have to look at it that way. Remember, just as things can go wrong, they can also take a turn for the better. After all, I still won a silver medal.

RECOVERY

A full and careful recovery from a marathon is extremely important, and the novice must be as mindful of this as he or she is about other aspects of the race. Recovery measures should begin the moment you finish. After you finish, keep moving, get warm, and drink water. The biggest problem for me is that I have to stop immediately after the race for interviews, questions, and ceremonies, so I always try to compensate by walking the mile or so back to my hotel. Another recovery measure is diet. Most runners are concerned about loading up with carbohydrates before the race but fail to replenish afterward. I eat the same diet after the race as I do before. The following days I maintain a state of active rest. I walk or jog and get a massage within a day or two if my legs aren't too painful to be touched.

More people probably get injured from insufficient recovery measures than from the marathon itself. Keep my own motto in mind: It's a waste of time to train to be a better runner for at least two weeks after a marathon. I take a long recovery after a marathon, especially after a tough one. As I'm like so many "fanatic" runners who don't like to take days off, I don't use my diary for at least two weeks after the race. It isn't important what I do, and I don't want to be pressured by my diary reminding me I've missed training time.

Just as every marathon is different, so is every recovery. After my first marathon, I couldn't run for three days; after the next several marathons, I was out the next day. Following my disaster in Boston I couldn't run for twelve days, and for the first three my legs hurt so much I had to walk down steps backward. The day after the Olympic marathon, a brisk forty-five-minute walk felt good. After one cool-weather marathon, I have run as far as seven miles. That, however, was an exception.

The first two weeks I run how I feel but never do any quality work. I begin with a comfortable jog for twenty to twenty-five minutes and increase step by step, until I am back to normal training, usually about three weeks after the race. However, just as it is clear from my varying types of recovery that every race is different, so is every runner. Your body takes a lot of abuse over 26.2 miles. Don't be in a hurry to put it through any more. If you are edgy about total rest, maintain a program of active rest, which you should do, anyway, as it speeds the recovery process. Supplementary training in other sports or physical activities is a good alternative to running.

Two to three marathons per year is the most I recommend, no matter what level runner. My entire career to this point consists of only ten marathons. Physically, I could run two or three, but mentally, I'm not prepared for more than one a year. When I did three marathons in seven months in 1983, it was the first time I'd ever done more than two in a year, and it was one too many. To be motivated and to do well, I have to really want to run the race.

You don't have to do a marathon to be a serious runner, and the event is not for everyone. However, if you want to run one or improve your time, you might consult an experienced runner or coach for training advice and see the Recommended Reading (page 249) for suggested reading. For an idea of how I train, the following are my schedules leading up to four of my major marathons.

New York City Marathon 1982

(Two distances indicate double sessions. All training done in Norway, with steady runs at approximately 6–6¼ minutes per mile, unless otherwise indicated. Two numbers indicate double sessions.)

OCTOBER 4–24

Monday, *10/4* —7 miles; 8 miles

10/5—8 miles; 7 miles

10/6—7 miles; 8 miles fartlek (2-mile warm-up, 4 miles of 300–1,000m hard, 2-mile cool-down)

10/7—18 miles (long run)

10/8—7 miles; 9 miles plus 15 × 100 meters

10/9—7–8 miles

10/10—9 miles; 7 miles

Monday, *10/11* —6 miles; 3 miles, 6 × 1 mile on the track (at 5–5:10 with ¼-mile recovery), 2–3-mile cool-down

10/12—18 miles (long run)

10/13—8 miles; fly to New York

10/14—fly from NY to Hampton, VA; 7 miles

10/15—6 miles easy

10/16—10km road race in Hampton (32:24); 5-mile cool-down
10/17—6 miles; 6 miles

Monday, *10/18*—10 miles; fly from Hampton to NY

10/19—6 miles, 6 miles
10/20—3 miles; 10 × 300m with short rest, 2–3-mile cool-down
10/21—6–7 miles easy
10/22—6 miles easy
10/23—5 miles easy
10/24—New York City Marathon, 2:27:14

World Championships, Helsinki 1983

Monday, *7/18*—7–8 miles; 9 miles

7/19—6 miles; track intervals, 4 × 150m, 4 × 200m, 2 × 400m, 5 × 200m
7/20—7 miles; 8–9 miles
7/21—7 miles; 2 miles easy, 5 miles fast, 2 miles easy
7/22—7 miles; 8 miles
7/23—6 miles; 5 miles easy
7/24—20 miles (long run)

Monday, *7/25*—6 miles; 7 miles

7/26—6 miles; 8 miles
7/27—6 miles; 2–3 miles, 4 × 1 mile with 500m recovery, 2–3 miles
7/28—13 miles (long run)
7/29—6 miles plus 5 × 150m pick-ups
7/30—2 miles, 3 miles fast (time trial 15:23), 2 miles easy, 5 × 200m, 2 miles easy
7/31—10 miles

Monday, *8/1*—7–8 miles

8/2—10 miles fartlek
8/3—3 miles, 9 × 300m, 3 miles easy
8/4—6 miles easy
8/5—4 miles easy
8/6—World Championships Marathon, 2:28:09

London Marathon 1983

(IN FRANCE, 3/28–4/3)

Monday, *3/28*—5 miles; 8 miles

3/29—7 miles; 7 miles
3/30—6 miles; 2 miles, 7 × 1,000m (1-min. rest), 2–3 miles easy
3/31—13 miles (long run)
4/1—7 miles; 7 miles
4/2—6 miles; 8 miles
4/3—6 miles; 3 miles, 13 × 500m (30–45-sec. rest), 2 miles easy

Monday, *4/4*—6 miles; 7 miles

4/5—2 miles, 4 × 1 mile, 3 miles
4/6—10 miles
4/7—18 miles (long run)
4/8—3 miles, 10 × 300m, 3 miles easy
4/9—7 miles; 5 miles easy
4/10—4 miles easy; Norwegian Cross Country Championships (3 miles)
   1st place, 5-mile cool-down

Monday, *4/11*—14 miles (long run)

4/12—no running, tired and trouble with right knee
4/13—3 miles, 10 × 300m, 3 miles easy; knee hurts

4/14 and *4/15*—no running because of knee (cortisone shot and naprosyn: anti-inflamatory)
4/16—6 miles easy
4/17—London Marathon, 2:25:29, world best

New York City Marathon 1984

Monday, *10/8*—8 miles

10/9—8 miles; 7 miles
10/10—6 miles; 10 miles
10/11—7 miles; 4 miles easy, 4 miles fast
10/12—8 miles
10/13—11 miles
10/14—20 miles (good pace)

Monday, *10/15*—7 miles; 8 miles

10/16—10 miles
10/17—6 miles; 3 miles, 5 × 1 mile, 2–3 miles easy
10/18—10 miles; fly to NY
10/19—fly from NY to Indianapolis; 6 miles easy
10/20—3.1-mile road race (15:30) in Purdue, IN; 5–6 miles afterward
10/21—9 miles (Purdue); fly to NY; 5 miles (NY)

Monday, *10/22*—10 miles

10/23—7 miles
10/24—8 miles
10/25—3 miles, 10 × 300m (25-sec. rest), 2–3 miles easy
10/26—no running, don't remember why
10/27—5 miles
10/28—New York City Marathon, 2:29:30

9

Balancing Your Sport and Your Life

Running and sport add a different dimension to your life, no matter what your level, and this change isn't just temporary. It's one that must be accommodated as long as you run, likely for the rest of your life. Running is more than a hobby; it's a lifestyle, and at no time has this become more possible and more significant than in the eighties. But like any major life change, it takes some adjustments to keep everything in balance.

Running offers many rewards. It keeps us healthy, makes us feel good, and offers social and recreational possibilities. But there's a limit to what running can do. It can't solve your personal problems or the world's, and contrary to popular belief I don't think it boosts your love life. You can run for a better life, but not to escape the one you have or create one anew. As logical as this all sounds, unfortunately, there are increasing numbers of people who run for all these reasons— the wrong reasons. They run obsessively, believing that more of a good thing has got to be better, more positive, more powerful. They simply lose their balance. "Whatever I didn't get in the rest of my life, I'm still chasing it," admitted one self-confessed running addict.*

A certain style of American fitness is illustrated by the extremely

*Tom Jarriel, "The Fitness Obsession," *20/20*, ABC-TV, July 16, 1984.

popular Jane Fonda approach. "Burn, burn!" she tells you as you work your muscles in search of that pain. Maybe this is a good approach for those who need such intensity, but for most people I think it's too frantic, too life-disrupting. It's not the approach to being a good runner and to making your running a permanent, harmonious part of your life. You can regard your running with an appropriate intensity, but that must be balanced with a sense of calm. Hard/easy, stress/rest— it's a life prescription as well.

There's a big difference between commitment and fanaticism, and knowing that difference is the key to finding your balance. Obsession is a growing problem among runners, and, ironically, especially among the more experienced. One study of negative addiction in runners showed the phenomenon increased greatly in the group running four years or longer, as opposed to those running one year or less.*

Creating and maintaining a harmonious balance is largely contingent on organization. This applies to your inner life as well as your outer life, and it is an important aspect of being a good runner. A balance of emotions provides the kind of steadiness needed to excel. I've known runners whose performances were erratic because they were that way emotionally: on a seesaw—high or low, impulsive, or hyper. Athletes can be emotional about their sport: this is often what drives them to excel, but even people who depend on strong emotions, like artists or actors, know that some control of those emotions is necessary. This is true for athletes as well.

You should set realistic priorities. Before you even attempt to construct a training program, ask yourself how it will fit into your life. Running is my full-time job, so I do what I must to do that job well. How much time and energy can you realistically devote to your running? What does it mean to you? How important is it, for example, to run that three-hour marathon? Does it mean making sacrifices to the point where you have to consider whether it is more important than your job, your friends, and your family? How much are you willing to devote emotionally to your goals? You may be dedicated and goal-oriented, but it takes more than that to achieve those goals. It takes a realistic approach. The more involved I am in a race, the less

* B. J. Hailey and Leisa A. Bailey, "Negative Addiction in Runners: A Quantitative Approach," *Journal of Sport Behavior* #5 (September 1982).

energy I have for others, the more selfish I am forced to become. These are very stressful times, both for myself and for those around me. These periods simply must be tolerated, but I realize that, so I am very careful to accommodate them.

To maintain balance, you must be skilled at planning your time. If it's a busy week, you'll have to make adjustments in your training. (Remember that training time must also include rest time.) If training is a priority, of course there must be some sacrifices, but you can't abandon your responsibilities, either. Obviously, you'll need to use both foresight and flexibility to balance your priorities successfully.

If you work ten hours a day, you're not going to be able to do the kind of training required for an ambitious goal. You can't go out and put in a good workout just because your program calls for it. On a busy day, you should run for relaxation. A three- or four-mile jog is what you need, but, of course, that's not going to give you a three-hour marathon. Like getting to know your body, sometimes you have to realize what's unrealistic by personal experience. More than one runner has been humbled by overambitious goals or by trying to achieve even reasonable running goals that become unreasonable in the context of a hectic life.

Even after you firmly establish your priorities, they will likely change with time and experience. Running is my number-one priority, but not in the same way it was ten years ago. I have built my life around my running: I still do. Almost nothing comes before it—almost.

There wasn't always an "almost." When I was younger, running was everything. All I did was train and do my schoolwork. I never took time out; I had no social life. Running and winning don't mean quite the same thing after a while. Especially now that I've reached my goals, that burning importance isn't there. Unlike before, I'll skip a workout if necessary. Even the Olympics, the center of my life at eighteen, lose some of their glow for the thirty-two-year-old who has been there before. Of course, I still work hard and am inspired to stay at the top. I always want to excel, to work hard for a goal—but the years have a way of changing the emphasis on that goal.

I am a runner, but not twenty-four hours a day. I am also a wife, a sister, a daughter, an aunt, and a businesswoman. My running means a lot to me, but it will never come before my family, for example. When Jan's wife, Kari, was in the hospital for two months in 1984 for a serious back operation, I helped with their children and the house, despite the fact I had to sacrifice some of my Olympic training. However, I felt what I was doing at the time was so much more important.

I have always tried to live a normal life. Even with the fame and attention, I have remained the same shy, quiet person, despite the many demands on me to take on a role more befitting a "star." Being true to my personality has helped me to keep my balance and not get swept away by the attention or overwhelmed by the pressure. I am not unlike some other top runners in this regard, and I think it is one of the keys to our longevity. When Carlos Lopes, Olympic gold medalist and world marathon record holder, was asked how he has been so successful for so many years, he answered that in addition to his training, goals, and determination, he has held on to his personality. "I'm not running because I want to be a star or because I'm looking for prestige. I'm the same guy as when I started competing fifteen years ago."*

You simply cannot devote yourself 100 percent to running. It's a formula for disaster. When I first got serious about running, I was equally serious about my studies, then about my teaching. And luckily, for most of my career, life's necessities have always prevented me from focusing solely on my sport. First I had school, then I had to work to make a living, and I've always kept my own house in order. Despite the fact that I now make a good living from my running, I still find other things to occupy me. I do my own cleaning and shopping, participate in some running promotions, answer abundant amounts of mail, and, when I can, I help my brothers at work. There's always something to keep me busy.

Once personal priorities are established, you must consider how they fit in with the people in your life. A number of runners have problems in their relationships because of their sport. In fact, the divorce rate among runners is three times higher than the national average.** This is a sorry situation, but a predictable one. A troubled relationship is one of the risks of getting too involved in running, or in anything for that matter. This is especially the case when people don't share the same interest or don't show understanding and respect

---

* Amby Burfoot, "Carlos Lopes in His Prime," *Runner's World* (April 1985).
**Gloria Averbuch, *The Woman Runner*, (New York: Simon & Schuster, 1984), p. 33.

for each other. After all, a runner's life must seem crazy to an outsider. Who can understand all those miles, early in the morning or late at night? Why the constant fatigue, the early bedtime, the apathy toward socializing? Obviously, there have to be some compromises with a runner in the house.

If you expect to share stress and pressure with a partner, you'd better have a stable, supportive relationship. If I were the type of woman who had a different boyfriend every month, it would destroy my athletic career. In fact, I would have never made it as a runner without Jack. For those who want to get to the top, I can tell you that without the support of your spouse I don't think you're going to make it. I really admire the rare athlete who goes out and trains ten to twelve times a week without the support of his or her spouse. I couldn't do it. Living with a runner can be difficult for even the most secure couples. This is why they have to be especially careful to keep up constant communication.

Instead of merely tolerating the runner's lifestyle, a nonrunner should be encouraged to use the activity to add, rather than detract, from the relationship. The runner should be sure not to exclude the nonrunner, which can, and does, frequently happen. Running can be a joint interest, even if one person doesn't run. Make a race a family affair. Bring the children to watch mom or dad, and have a picnic afterward. Use a holiday to travel to a race. Many major road races even have special travel packages for both runner and family. Consider a running camp, an ideal vacation for the family that enjoys the sport and a healthy atmosphere.

On the home front, make compromises. My sister-in-law Kari does not share the interest in running of her husband and sons, so she has her own time to go out with friends while my brother does the dishes and washes clothes. And although we never thought we'd see it happen, with time Kari has found her niche in the running world, helping at races and with the administration of our club.

Of course, it's more difficult for the woman who runs and the man who doesn't. It isn't a traditional situation, to say the least. The husband has to be very secure and supportive in a society in which situations like this are rare. Jack is exceptional in this regard. He's had to put up with a fairly ego-threatening life with me. Not only has he sacrificed his own career to help mine, but he suffers some annoying comments and questions. ("Can't you keep up with Grete?" is one of our favorite in the "most stupid" category.)

Jack is trained as an accountant but now works in promotions for Adidas. He feels he will have to forgo developing his career to any great extent as long as I am competing seriously. In 1985 he took a year off to accompany me on my travels, acting as both a buffer and an agent. Jack was probed in detail by Gloria about his feelings, as it is understandably hard to believe a man in his situation might not be threatened or jealous at times. Here is how he responded. "Actually, by taking off this year [1985], Grete and I have much more time for each other than we had before. That's been a nice experience. I suppose this arrangement would be difficult if I were very intent on a career of my own, instead of taking care of Grete's. Does being in the background bother me? No. I have never felt the desire to be famous; the recognition I get through Grete is more than enough. At one time I wanted to be a good runner myself, but I realized I didn't have the talent. I've been able to see Grete do the things I was unable to do. It has given me a great deal of satisfaction, and I take pride in her achievements."

Perhaps this seems too idyllic to Americans, but the way we see it, Norwegians are generally much more easygoing compared with Americans, whose strong competitive nature can extend even to marriage. Sometimes couples seem to compete even in their running. It may be difficult to separate the competition for money, prestige, or success from the rest of life, but it has to be done. Life in the "real world" is about competition, a road race is about competition—but a marriage isn't!

While I'm on the subject of running, balance, and family, it seems appropriate to discuss children. Children need to get up from their video games and the television, so it's great to see that some parents are encouraging them to run. Yet unlike their parents', children's fitness levels are worse today than they were ten years ago. In the 1983–84 school year, only 36 percent of 4 million American children achieved the "basic goals" of the President's Physical Fitness test, down from 43 percent in two earlier testing periods. And several studies show that up to 40 percent of children between five and eight years old already exhibit at least one symptom of heart disease risk factors such as obesity, high blood pressure, and inactivity.* Yet despite the poor fitness showing, 20 million American children take part in organized sports.** Perhaps there's something wrong with the approach to these sports.

From what I've seen in the States, many children who run are going about it in the wrong way. They need proper guidance from their parents. Running isn't meant to be a career for youngsters, not even their only sport. Young children before puberty should be encouraged to engage in different kinds of sports for enjoyment and to develop overall fitness. In running they should stay with the shorter distances and low-key training. This is the way I was brought along, and I strongly believe in it. I've heard the same statement from other top runners, like Joan Benoit Samuelson.

It's shocking and distressing to me to see young children in road races being pushed by their parents. Unfortunately, the "little league syndrome" is also part of the running scene. I'm not against competition for children, because they'll face it all their lives, but that competition should be among their peers, not in road races with adults. If young children do compete, special care should be taken to make sure they develop positive feelings, rather than insecurity or fear. The emphasis should be on fun. Win or lose, they should continually be encouraged, but at the same time any seriousness about their competition de-emphasized. This is the type of atmosphere I benefited from in the running club when I was young.

As a runner, would I encourage my own child to run? Not directly. As running and racing are such a major part of my life, I would bring the child into my world so that perhaps he or she would see the enjoyment and spirit and be drawn into it independently, but I would never force or even strongly coax the child. When my young nephews saw us run, they wanted to take part. By the time Geir turned twelve, he began wanting to run longer road races. Instead of telling him why I felt it wasn't a good idea, I turned it around to the positive side and talked a lot to him about my respect for track. He soon got the message.

---

* Amby Burfoot, "Johnny Can't Run," *Runner's World* (September 1985).
** Steve Huntley, with Ronald A. Taylor, "Keeping in Shape—Everybody's Doing It," *US News & World Report* (August 13, 1984).

Although today he does an occasional road race, his interest is where I think it should be. At sixteen, he is one of Oslo's best track runners in his age group.

I'm especially against children running long distances, like the marathon, for the physical as well as emotional risk. In my opinion, the minimum age for a 10km should be fourteen or fifteen, and eighteen for a marathon. I was twelve years old before I even ran as far as 2.6 miles, which is the same distance of the Grete Waitz Run I started in Norway. By age sixteen I ran only six times a week in training, and never farther than 10km (6.2 miles).

The following guidelines are a compilation from conferences in which European coaches presented their views on children's running.

1. Specializing in middle distances (800m to the mile) should not take place before 13–14 years of age; long distances (up to 10km) not before 15–16 years of age.
2. Young runners should have well-rounded training before specializing. (For example, I competed in the high jump, sprints, and even the throwing events.)
3. Aerobic, or endurance, training is important for young runners, but it should only be done easily.
4. Young runners should be careful with anaerobic training (what I have called quality work). Hard anaerobic training should be avoided before puberty, and once begun, increased only in small doses from year to year.
5. Strength and sprint training are good for young runners.
6. Long-term planning is crucial to prevent early peaking and burnout.

PERSPECTIVE

One thing that astounds me about the running boom is the incredible seriousness with which so many runners regard their sport. When they're not doing it, they're talking about it or thinking about it. Sometimes, frankly, I feel it's just too much. I understand the obsession, because no one knows better than I do what it's like to live with running all day, every day. It's this strain that has created for me a true love/hate relationship with the sport. Obviously, the love side wins out, and it does so because I have the proper perspective. This is the key ingredient to balance.

If you have the proper perspective, it's much easier to deal with success and failure. Ten years ago, I wasn't able to put running in that perspective. But time and age change a person. The 1976 Olympics felt like the end of the world. Now, of course, I know it wasn't. The running world that seemed so big then is actually quite small. Now, for example, if I get injured and can't train for three weeks, it may seem like a disaster to me personally, but it's not a disaster for Norway or the rest of the world. As we say in Norwegian, I must "put my finger in the earth and see where I am." The same day I'm feeling low, I may see someone without a leg or tune in to the evening news for a dose of reality. That sure puts things in perspective.

I try to be a positive thinker, to look on the bright side. A person in my position has to be this way to keep perspective, because while success at the top can be sweet, failure can be equally bitter. Positive thinking means being confident and upbeat, but realistic at the same time. You have to combine optimism with realism—aspiring to the highest goals while recognizing certain limits. This may seem like a contradiction, but at times so is keeping perspective when you're a serious runner.

One of the greatest benefits of coming from a modest background and culture is that I have never expected too much. I've always been pleased with what I've accomplished and with what running has given me. Elite runners often say that the bottom line is their enjoyment of the sport, and I'm one of them. I couldn't go out and run 100 miles a week if I didn't enjoy it. I think it's important always to remind yourself of the simplicity of the sport and that it should be its own reward—despite how lofty your goals or how great your achievements.

Perspective should especially be part of every race. If the race goes well, like everyone, I'm happy. But when it doesn't, I have learned to accept it, let it go, and look to the future. Since my days on the track, people have always expected me to be devastated after a loss. They often assume my failure to get emotional is a sign of apathy. It's not apathy at all; it's control. That's how I keep my perspective. Looking through my scrapbooks, I found a quote from a newspaper article before the 1976 Olympics that's simple but says it all: "Life goes on, even if I don't succeed." When people prod me about being upset, I say, "What should I do, get into bed and cry?" Sure, I'm a little angry and disappointed, but I just vow to come back stronger next time. I've seen people fall apart over their running, and not just the elite. I'm referring to the "weekend athletes" as well—those who have invested far too much ego in their running.

No one knows better than I do how painful a failed effort can be. First of all, your defenses are down after a bad race, which is more tiring than a good race. Emotionally, as well as physically, you have put it "on the line," summoned all your strength. Being this vulnerable, you can be devastated by a failure. Sometimes you remember those losses better than the victories. Believe me, I remember each time I have been beaten, and by whom, since I began road racing in 1978.

It's never easy to lose, to fail to meet your expectations. I'm better at it now, but it's always a battle. I've been competing internationally for sixteen years, over half my life. Running has been a great teacher, an infinitely wise master. Eventually, I learned that the fierce desire to win is only part of the game. Of course, I always want to win, every time I race. But if I don't, I know I'll go on enjoying the competition and strive for future success. You must remember that your willingness to face the consequences of the race is one of the conditions of stepping up to the starting line.

When you aren't satisfied, haven't succeeded, you tend to torture yourself. "What went wrong? Was I overtrained, not aggressive enough? Was it the course, the weather, my shoes?" It's one thing to learn from your mistakes, but dissecting and second-guessing your effort is a waste of time. It can destroy your confidence, not to mention make you crazy! If you've done your best, you must be content. Then it's time to look down the road to the next race with renewed determination.

In the 1981 New York City Marathon, I was forced to drop out at fifteen miles with an injury. I knew at the start of the race that I might not be able to finish, but I had to try. I watched the remainder of the race on television in my hotel room as Allison Roe went on to break my world record. I could have asked myself all kinds of questions about what went wrong, speculated with all the ifs. But in giving the race all I had, I felt satisfied. I had done everything I could, and there was no use hitting my head against a wall.

In the 1985 L'eggs Mini Marathon, I lost by a mere three seconds. That was tough. One less tactical error, a few more yards, and maybe...If only I'd been beaten by fifteen seconds; that seems like an ocean. But I have to look at it differently. I ran as hard as I could, and I can learn to live with anything if I've done my best. Without the ability to "regroup," I could not have come back several weeks later to win two major races, with one course record and the other just two seconds off a record.

If you see your running as lifelong, it's important to keep this perspective. When the race is over (or the workout, or an injury, or any pitfall), it's over. Now you must continue to get on with life and to live with yourself. Do you dwell too much on failure? Do you see only the negative aspects of your situation? Were you constantly complaining or depressed, impossible to be around? Remember that what endures longer than victory or failure are your attitudes and behavior.

If a runner can't be gracious to fellow competitors, that person has to do some major introspection and make some serious changes. Bad sportsmanship is prevalent on every level, and it can quickly and severely damage an athlete's reputation. This is what happened to Mary Decker Slaney. When she fell during her 3,000-meter race in the 1984 Olympics, destroying her chance for a medal, she publicly took out her anger and disappointment on Zola Budd, whom she accused of causing her to fall. In my opinion, this was a case of bad sportsmanship. Despite how badly she wanted that gold medal, she should not have let her frustrations take control of her. She went too far. Such an experienced runner who has been on a world-class level for so long should know better. She should have waited and calmed down before making announcements to the press. When you are disappointed and angry, you say things you likely would not say after you have calmed down and had a chance to think. Eventually, Slaney reconciled with Budd, but it's a shame that both of them were greatly hurt by so much pain and anger.

Several of my major losses have come at times when I was ill and unable to race in my best shape. When I lost for the first time to Ingrid Kristiansen in Norway, I was overtrained. And when I lost my first L'eggs Mini Marathon, in 1983, I had a sinus infection. I think it is unfair to the athlete who wins if I were to announce my troubles after the race. It's a lowly attempt at detracting from that person's victory. Just as I try not to dwell on a loss for long in private, I would not have gone on worldwide television after the Los Angeles Olympics and talked about my back problems. Besides, once we are on that starting line, we are all equal. No excuses.

Of course, you need a special attitude to beat someone in a race, but you've got to have some humility, too. I'm afraid that sometimes the only way to be humbled is to get beaten. For the first two years that I was a serious track runner, I lived in the shadow of another Norwegian girl, always being beaten by her. It was probably good for me. This is why I believe stars who rise too fast are often in trouble. They haven't paid their dues along the way. They're not prepared for what happens when they lose and don't get the adulation they're used to.

Running is not like a team sport. You *have* to be egocentric. But you also have to separate the race from the rest of life; you shouldn't become an egocentric personality. For example, you can still be friends with your competitors. I'm not friendly with Wendy Sly on the starting line, of course, but off the road I most certainly am. How can I be angry at people for beating me because they run faster than I do?

Keeping things in perspective doesn't come easily, I know. Just ask the young girl who used to cry when she didn't win. But I know now that proper perspective and a healthy attitude are absolutely necessary to be both a good competitor and a good person. Not only has this realization helped me to endure the drastic ups and downs of a running career, it has given me a deeper fulfillment from the sport and a better understanding of myself.

MANAGING STRESS

Managing stress is important for achieving balance and succeeding not only in running but in everything else as well. Being in control of stress better equips you to handle pressure and prevent burnout.

This has been one of my aims since my first days on the track, when I realized I'd have to learn not to internalize the pressure if I were going to be able to live with it. Since that time, managing stress has been a major factor in my running success and longevity. From what I have seen in the world of sports, and in the competitive, fast-paced world in general, it is a necessity for everyone. Stress has conquered many a runner, and just as you can't get away with too much stress in life, you certainly can't get away with it in running.

I have been under tremendous pressure since 1970, when I first became a Norwegian national champion. The fact that there are so few world-class athletes in my country compounded the problem. Once I began to represent Norway internationally, it seemed as if everyone's eyes and hopes were upon me. A certain amount of pressure is always part of the serious runner's life. Today I feel stressed when my running suffers from doing too much business or promotion or when something unexpected comes up, like getting to a race and discovering I'm expected to do a clinic or photo session. It's not just a reduction in training that helps solve stress-related problems; it's careful planning and prioritizing.

Although I can't eradicate the pressure, over the years I have learned to reduce some of it. Before a race, for example, I take the focus off myself by emphasizing the ability of the other runners. At press conferences I say I'm in good shape, that I'm optimistic, but I always shake my finger and add, "But you never know!" It's no longer just me against the clock; the competition is often tough, and it never hurts to be cautious, not to promise what I can't be sure to fulfill. If I were publicly to predict a world record, for example, it would put unbearable pressure on me.

This example applies to you as well. Don't put the weight of the world on your shoulders. Reduce the expectations you have of yourself and those of others around you. Be careful about broadcasting your intentions. It's great to be confident, but let your race achievements speak louder than your words. In my case, I try to lessen the unreasonable expectations of the journalists. I always put things in perspective by reminding them that while, of course, I have a chance to win, so many things can happen in a race. If they understand the difficulty of what I do and who I'm up against as competition, they are less likely to take it for granted that I will automatically succeed.

If you don't take your success for granted, neither will your friends, family, or coach. By the way, the pressure to succeed in such an individual sport as running can be greatly helped by being on a team or with a group. A team offers support and can take some of the emphasis off a single running performance.

Part of the pressure you feel about the race comes from fear. Sometimes, like animals, I think we run fast out of fear. Some kind of fear response is probably natural, but it can be destructive if it becomes the wrong kind of fear, like that of not pleasing other people. Not until I was older did I realize what so frightened me about a race. Partly it was anticipating the pain I had to go through, but it was also partly the fear of not pleasing other people. In my case, if I have a bad race, everyone knows it. It's splashed all over the newspapers and on television. This is why, as I mentioned in the very first chapter, I had to decide to stop running to please other people. So must you. It's enough of a burden to want to run well for yourself, let alone for anyone else. Try not to be concerned with how others view or judge your running. Besides, if you ask yourself who is putting the pressure on, you'll realize that it's likely only you.

These measures may help take the pressure off, but they certainly contradict what I've seen as the American way. In a society in which being number one is everything, understatement is not exactly a top priority. I find many of the top American runners very confident, almost too confident. Some of them freely predict wins and world records. I have met many world-class American runners who proclaim, "I'm in great shape. I think I can win." Maybe this is a way to scare their competitors. Frankly, it goes totally against my grain. On the other hand, although I could never talk this way, I sometimes admire these athletes. Maybe if I were more like this, I'd have greater self-confidence. However, I'm not willing to sustain the pressure this attitude invites.

Have a winning attitude, by all means. Believe you can do well, but keep it to yourself. I have never made such a bold public statement, but I will do it now to make my point. I honestly believe I will win every race I enter. I have to believe that. I just don't go around saying it. First of all, it's not a typically Norwegian thing to do. Second, I think the need to proclaim invincibility is often a sign of insecurity. Some runners do it just to convince themselves.

Don't think that the pressure doesn't get to me. When I read in the paper that I'm expected to win or break a world record, it makes me crazy with nervousness. Sometimes I purposely don't read the paper. Even though I realize the pressure is coming from outside, not from within me, it doesn't alleviate my anxiety. This is when I get a lot of help from Jack. We sit down and talk it out. I tell him how nervous I am, that I feel people expect too much from me, and I fear not being able to meet those expectations. Jack helps me accept that this is just the way it is. He tells me to try to ignore the pressure, to concentrate on the race. "After all, when it comes down to it, it's not a disaster if you don't win or break a record," he says with a smile. Even though none of this is new, these talks are very important to me. Without them, I know I would brood, and internalizing just makes it worse.

A runner's ambitious personality often means that person is more susceptible to general life stress. Some stress is good. I know I wouldn't run as well without a degree of tension. However, the effects of destructive stress also carry over to running. This is why I'm especially fortunate to have a Norwegian attitude. But I, too, have to be careful about general stress, which may be the reason, for example, that I'm such a light sleeper. Here are some methods I find useful to control stress.

Take regular meditation or nap breaks, the same type I take before hard workouts. Most days I spend up to an hour in a state of semisleep: a light, not deep sleep. If a nap is impractical, take one or two twenty-minute meditation breaks. Sit in a dark room in a relaxed position with your eyes closed, and concentrate on letting tension seep out of your muscles. When you get good at it, you can do this kind of meditation anywhere.

I have stressed that I lead a simple, ordered life. Not only does that make me feel happier and more secure, but it greatly reduces stress. Sudden or constant changes in life patterns, like diet, training, job, or personal relationships, are extremely stressful. When I spent much of 1985 traveling, often changing places every five days, I suffered colds and other minor illnesses, and my conditioning went up and down like a yo-yo. When major changes do occur, accommodate them by slowing down and taking it easy. Use your running as relaxation rather than as a workout. Hard running and life stress just don't go together.

We all need simply to lighten up at times. That's why I went ice skating before the 1980 New York City Marathon and why I often pass the time before a race with my family, if possible, playing volleyball, cracking silly jokes, or marveling over the crazy game shows on American television.

A sense of humor and spontaneity are good "life lighteners" and do a lot to relieve pressure and stress and to provide some perspective. People are usually surprised to discover how spontaneous I can be. After the 1984 New York City Marathon, a middle-aged spectator approached me to offer congratulations. I was feeling so good that the race was over, and so happy I had won, that I put my marathon finisher's medal around her neck and gave her a kiss. It is a moment I'm sure we will both treasure.

10

Coaching

Whether to be coached is a decision many advanced runners face at one point or another. This can mean anything from formal training to casual advice; it does not necessarily require you to join a team or hire a professional coach. There are plenty of local teams, clubs, and classes continually popping up in the United States that offer instruction and advice by everyone from experienced runners to university coaches. The more serious you get, the more helpful it can be to work under someone's watchful eye. Especially in a solitary effort such as running, the encouragement and support of a coach can be invaluable. Coaches offer not only training advice but inspiration, and for many athletes, a coach has added value as both mentor and friend.

Although the level of coaching is much more advanced and there are many more professional coaches today than when I began running, I have been lucky to have had good, supportive coaching throughout my running career. I am basically independent after so many years of training, but coaching input is still beneficial. Since 1983, I have worked with Johan Kaggestad, the Norwegian national long-distance coach and also Ingrid Kristiansen's personal coach, in addition to Jack, who serves primarily as my advisor. Johan creates a program, which Jack and I adapt according to various conditions and circumstances.

Another important aspect of coaching entails follow-up. On my level, it is important for someone like Jack to take care of the details, like organizing training, races, and medical care. You may want to find someone to recommend various races or to help you with such things as applications, travel, or lodging. The following are some further points about coaching based on my own experience.

In my opinion, the single most important criterion beyond a coach's qualifications is a good athlete/coach relationship. This relationship is based on good communication, a factor that often tends to be overlooked. You're not a novice or a child who needs to be guided by strict direction or who should blindly follow orders. Coaching should be based on mature, two-way communication. A lack of this communication is often the cause of improper training that can result in injury or burnout and is probably at the root of most failed athlete/coach relationships.

Take it upon yourself to make this essential communication your responsibility. You can't expect the coach to know how and what you're feeling. He or she may be experienced, but no one knows your body and mind better than you do. If you constantly communicate to the coach how you feel and what you're thinking, that person can best help you to learn and improve. Be honest. Don't be too proud to say you're tired, thinking you're tougher if you don't complain. If you don't communicate with the coach, he or she may reasonably assume you are absorbing the work and that you can do even more. This is obviously when problems begin.

If possible, you should take an active part in constructing your program with the coach. Even if you're fairly new to running and being coached, you're still the best expert on you. Establish a healthy exchange of ideas. It's very tempting to develop blind faith in an expert, to surrender yourself to the coach's wisdom. This is one of the reasons I'm always careful not to take advice from someone I don't know and who doesn't know me. I'm too obedient. Right or wrong, my sense of discipline makes me inclined to do whatever I am told. And like many runners, I've been tempted by new coaches or training schemes in an effort to find a greater winning edge.

Whether you are given a training program or take one from a book, you should thoroughly understand that program: its content, aim, and philosophy. If necessary, question a coach or an experienced runner about your training. If you do just what's on paper without understanding why, not only do you risk doing the wrong workout, but you are missing an important educational aspect of your running. In order to learn the various approaches to training and what best suits you, the rationale behind the workouts should always be clear. There are different ways to do workouts, depending on your aim. For example, if you see "10 × 150 meters" on paper, like most runners', your instinct is probably to go out and run ten times 150-meter intervals as fast as you can. But what if the point of this workout is not speed but to practice rhythm and technique: running up on the balls of the feet with slight forward lean, perfecting the arm swing? What about "4 × 1 mile"? Is the point to run as hard as you can or to practice your pace for an upcoming 10km race? Without a thorough understanding of it, the workout may lose its intended value. This is why a coach can offer proper guidance—helping prevent the inherent danger of just "going by the book" or following another person's program without individualizing your approach.

Be careful in any situation in which you are coached in a large group, where the workout is always the same for everyone. Make sure the training fits your individual needs. Be careful as well of group workouts that lack sufficient control or discipline, where the runners continually stray from the plan in an effort to outdo each other. Some competition is natural and good for motivation, but you don't want to run each other into the ground. This can happen no matter how mature or intelligent you are. No one wants to come in last, no matter how good the effort or the time, so be strong enough and wise enough to do what you know and feel is right. While the others may be tired or injured from training, you will have saved yourself for the race.

It is very important that the coach get to know you personally—how you react physically and emotionally, your personality as well as your abilities. This knowledge becomes an important part of that person's ability to guide you. Frankly, some of my coaches never really knew me. As a coach, Jack has known me the best, largely because he understands my disposition and is able to relate it to my running. Most important, he knows even better than I do when I've had enough, something some other coaches have not understood. As I'm generally not one to cut short a workout or complain that I'm tired, I can't count on myself as a guide.

To establish the type of communication I have described, it takes a while to get to know someone well enough. For this reason I think you have to work with a coach for at least a year. Meanwhile, as you're getting to know one another, you obviously must have a certain amount of trust in that person. Some things you'll have to do on faith, based on the coach's reputation and a positive instinct about the person.

Usually, with time and experience, you can monitor your own program if you wish and use the coach more as an advisor and for moral support. Also, if full-time coaching is not practical or available, you may want to seek partial or temporary advice. After years of training, Joan Benoit Samuelson knows what to do, but a coach still gives her guidelines and support. Jack functions in the same way for me. I do, from time to time, seek a closer relationship with a coach. This is how I started with Johan Kaggestad. When I decided to concentrate more on the marathon, a significant change in my training became necessary. I consulted with Johan, and because it worked out well I have continued to confer with him, especially if I am in doubt about some aspect of my training.

There are many reasons a coach can be important. Outside of your family, no one can be more understanding or supportive than a good coach. A coach and/or team also gives you the opportunity to pursue a more serious athletic career and try something you may have missed while growing up. But the giving must go both ways to make the relationship work; with mutual understanding and respect, it can.

A coach can be a significant factor in your motivation and success; however, don't have unreasonable expectations of that person. You are the one ultimately responsible for your own success. As tennis champion Chris Evert Lloyd has said, "A coach can teach you how to play, but you have to teach yourself how to win."

11

The Training Diary

HOW AND WHY
TO KEEP A DIARY

For runners on every level I recommend keeping a diary, and I *highly* recommend doing so for the advanced. The higher your level, the more involved and complicated your training. A diary serves not only as a record of what you have done but as a guide to what to do in the future. Because you invest so much in your sport, the diary is also important in its function as a coach, psychiatrist, and conscience. It gives you the opportunity to contemplate your training and to be counseled by it.

A diary provides you with knowledge and perspective. When I look back in my diary and recall the patterns and changes in my life, I can see how they have affected my training. However, it takes at least six months to a year to get this perspective. For this purpose, the diary is an important part of your long-term memory, recording the information for use when it will best make sense to you. The diary is often a runner's most accurate judge, as our memory of what we do is selective, but what's in black and white never lies.

The diary helps you analyze cycles of training. By examining my diary, I have noticed a pattern in the last several years that has greatly helped in planning my races. While I'm always in good shape in November, December, and February, I have a slight down period in March and April. This is probably due to the stress of travel, but it may also be related to other factors that can better be understood by continuing to monitor this trend. This type of observation is why keeping a record should not be restricted to only certain time periods. There is always an ongoing need to keep a diary.

A diary is important to keep track of the variety of workouts, conditions, and feelings. Of course, if you run the same course every day, the same distance and pace, you probably don't need a diary. World-class distance runner Mark Nenow doesn't need one. Here is his training, according to a popular running magazine: afternoon, 10 miles; evening, 7 miles; Sunday, 15 miles—the same thing week after week. Sound simple? But don't believe everything you read about top runners' diaries. I've talked to runners who never even heard of the training diaries attributed to them until they were published in a magazine.

A diary is a great inspiration for me. While preparing for the 1984 Olympic marathon, I frequently looked back to my training the year before for the World Championships, one of my best races. I duplicated the preparation that had given me success, and got added psyche by making parallel progress. The diary can also simply help get you out the door when you're not motivated. After all, it's awfully hard to have to write, "Didn't train today—didn't feel like it."

In many ways a diary can give you the confidence that may be missing. If you could always run another race, or even a time trial, you probably wouldn't need a diary to give you that confidence. But, of course, this isn't practical. If you are in doubt about what you can do, look through your diary. Focus on your good workouts. Realize that if you're able to do all those workouts, you must be able to do well in your race. Deep down I may feel I can run well; Jack can try to convince me, but nothing gives me confidence like my diary. Of course, this can have the opposite effect if you're not careful. When I'm feeling negative, I seem to see only the bad workouts. Even if there's only one out of ten, I'll zero in on that one.

A diary is valuable to keep you from overtraining. That's why I call it a conscience. It's the reminder that says, "Stop, you've done enough." Even with all my experience, I often don't understand why I'm tired or why I didn't race as well as I had planned or thought I should. Then I look back over the last few weeks in my diary and all the miles I've done, and it's clear. For years I claimed I hadn't run very much when I was young. Then I looked back at my diary for the year I was seventeen. It was surprising to see how much I had actually done and how much I had forgotten. Because training has a cumulative effect over the years, keeping a diary right from the beginning of your running career can be extremely useful.

Don't fall into the trap of making your diary a curse rather than a blessing. A common mistake is to compete with it, as if it were something to conquer. The runner wants to boast, to impress it—to fill the pages with as many remarkable achievements as possible. In 1976 I got into a groove; I couldn't leave an empty spot in my diary. It just looked bad. One winter day I was doing repeat 1,000-meter intervals in Oslo on the snow and ice. I kept slipping, and my Achilles tendon began to hurt, but all I could think about was what I wanted to write in my diary: "Today I did eight times 1,000 meters." What happened afterward was of no concern, as long as that page looked good, so I kept on going. Four days later I was still sidelined with a sore Achilles.

Your diary should be your friend and your helper, not your adversary. If the only reason to go out and run is to record it in your diary, you'd better toss it out. The diary shouldn't dictate your program. It's a reflection of your training, not a motive for it. I've discovered this problem with other runners as well, even those who should know better.

One of my good friends I met years ago while running track is Olympic silver medalist Markus Ryffel, of Switzerland. He once admitted that despite a sore calf he forced himself to finish a track session so he could write it in his diary. He knew the best thing was just to quit, but the diary loomed over him, a crazy obsession. He got the entry he wanted, all right, and an injury that kept him out of running for a long time afterward. (Now that I have shared one of his failings, I would like to add that it was Markus who unknowingly saved me from making a big mistake of my own. Years ago, he befriended this lone young woman in Australia for two weeks of competition, who, lacking the independence to make it on her own, had telephoned Jack begging to come home. "Call the race organizer and tell him my father died!" I pleaded. To this day, I am thankful to Markus for extending his friendship, thus curing the loneliness and enabling me to enjoy one of my best two-week periods of racing and travel.)

Since 1970 I have kept a diary and have depended on it for all of the above reasons. My diary is a record of my entire career, and I continue to learn from it. In fact, it has been the source for a great deal of material in this book. In the samples of my own diary I include here, you will notice I did not record details on the conditions and how I felt. I remember feeling at the time that I didn't want to take the diary too seriously. This is a mistake I regret having made, and I recommend that you include those details for yourself.

In 1985 Kai Møller, women's national coach of Norway, completed a comprehensive study of my early diaries. It is intended that this study will be used to aid the young girls he coaches. I have discussed in detail my training since beginning road racing, in 1978, and these diaries record what I did up to that time. As I have continually stressed the cumulative aspect of training, I think they are especially useful in understanding my entire career. One significant point this analysis illustrates is that while I have had great periods of consistent success, like most runners, I have also had periods of stagnation. It is during these times that some people quit, so this is when one really needs patience. Early in the book, I promised to teach you what I know about running through my mistakes as well as my victories. So for good and for bad, in black and white, here they are!

Day	Date	Type of training November 1981	Miles	Time	Comments
Mo	9/11 AM	Normal run steady	7 mile		(6:15)
	PM	2-3 miles warm-up. 6×1000m. 2-3 miles cooldown	8-9 mile		Fragnerparken (3.10 3.15) V: indes yet. (1/2 min break)
Tu	10/11 AM	Normal steady run	8 mile		Near home — met Ekeberg
	PM	3 miles easy + strengthening workout	3 mile		
We	11/11 AM	Normal run	7 mile		Near home — pavement
	PM	2-3 miles warm-up. 8×500m. 3 miles	8 mile		Fragnerparken 1/2min break. no snow.
Th	12/11 AM	Normal run	8 mile		Near home
	PM	Normal run	7 mile		Vidar training
Fr	13/11 AM	Normal run	7 mile		Met Ekeberg
	PM	3 miles. 15×100m accelerations on 3miles	7 mile		Supermarket area — pavement
Sa	14/11 AM	Very easy run	7 mile		Felt tired, heavy legs.
	PM	No running			
Su	15/11 AM	Normal run	7 mile		Near home
	PM	Normal run	3 mile		Near Jan's home
		Total miles this week	91 miles		

Week no.: _____

adidas ®

We're running serious

Day	Date	Type of training April 1982	Miles Time	Comments
Mo	19/4	Boston marathon	23miles	Dropped out because cramp in the quadriceps
Tu	20/4	No running, could hardly walk	0	
We	21/4	''	0	
Th	22/4	18 miles bike couldn't even jog	0	
Fr	23/4		0	
Sa	24/4	6 miles walk	0	
Su	25/4	12 miles walk	0	

Total miles this week __23 miles__

Week no.: _____

adidas
We're running serious

Day	Date	Type of training March 1983	Miles Time	Comments
Mo	28/3	Easy run	5miles	after boatride to Kiel
		Normal steady run	8miles	In Sessen Germany
Tu	29/3	Steady run	7miles	Seesen
		Steady run	7miles	Adidas France (Landersheim)
We	30/3	Easy run	6miles	Landersheim on the track
		2miles warmup 7×1000m continuous running 7.23 3.8mils	8mils	(3.02 -3.01 -3.03 -3.03) 3.40 on the easy
Th	31/3	Easy long run	12miles	along the river in Saverne
Fr	1/4	Normal steady run	7miles	Landersheim
		— "	7miles	Saverne
Sa	2/4	Easy run	6miles	Landersheim
		Steady run	8miles	Saverne (rain)
Su	3/4	Easy run	6miles	
		2.3miles 13×500m 2-3miles	8mils	On the track 30set rest (133.35)

Total miles this week 95 miles

adidas ®
We're running serious

Week no.: _____

Day	Date	Type of training	Miles	Time	Comments
Mo	28/1	Normal steady run	6 miles		Bermuda
		Run at a good pace	6 miles		— " —
Tu	29/1	Normal run	8 miles		Travelling from Bermuda to Miami.
We	30/1	2-3 miles warm up, 3 x 5 x 300 m, 3 miles	8 miles		Series slow · med. fast
		Easy run	4 miles		Felt it in the quads".
Th	31/1	Easy run	7 miles		Miami
Fr	1/2	Normal run	6 miles		Miami
Sa	2/2	3 miles warm up, 10k Orang Bowl,	9 miles		Warm (32.44) placed 2nd
		Didn't do cool down, because of cramp in the legs.			after Lynn Williams)
Su	3/2	Very easy run	9 miles		Miami
					Travelling to Tampa

Total miles this week 65 miles

adidas

We're running serious

A SUMMARY AND ANALYSIS OF MY CAREER TRAINING, 1971–78

1971/72
February/March: types of most frequent workouts.

Short intervals:	a. 30 × 200m, 10–15-sec. rest, or
	b. 45 × 100m, 10–15-sec. rest, or
	c. 15 × 300m, 15-sec. rest.
Long intervals:	a. 2 × 1,000m + 2 × 800m + 2 × 600m, 3-min. rest, or
	b. 8 × 500m, 3-min. rest, or
	c. (often) 8 × 400m, 3-min. rest.

All of the above done on outdoor track.

Long runs: most of the sessions between 11–14km (6.8–9 miles). Parts done over hilly terrain.
Supplementary training: cross-country skiing—16–30km (10–18 miles).

April
Same type of training, but in addition:
Hill work: 3 sets of 4 × 500m (fast). 5-min. rest between sets.

Summary: *Long runs:* high intensity, between 6–12km. *Hilly courses:* often very tired. *Speedwork/intervals:* many repetitions, high intensity, short recovery. Short recovery also when running long intervals.

Summer Training

Short intervals:	a. 25 × 100m, 20-sec. rest, or
	b. 50 × 100m, 20-sec. rest.
Long intervals:	3 × 1,000m (time, 3:10), 5-min. rest + 2 × 600m (time, 1:43–1:46), 5-min. rest.

Tempo runs: a. 1 × 400m (61 secs.) + 1 × 300m (45 secs.) +
 1 × 200m (29 secs.) + 1 × 150m (21 secs.)
 or
 b. 7 × 200m, high speed, 3–4-min. rest, or
 c. 2 × 1,100m, "speed changing" (i.e., 100m fast,
 100m moderate), 10-min. rest.

Breakdown of Training Sessions

	November		February		April		July		August		September
	1971	1973	1972	1974	1972	1974	1972	1974	1972	1974	1972*1974
long runs over 10km	30%	60%	28%	63%	23%	24%	9%	25%	16%	37%	43%
short runs under 10km	14%	15%	15%	18%	3%	24%	19%	40%	0	29%	35%
fartlek	18%	5%	8%	3%	24%	9%	9%	5%	6%	0	0
long intervals	3%	5%	18%	6%	10%	9%	5%	5%	0	0	0
short intervals	21%	7.5%	18%	10%	13%	19%	14%	11%	13%	11%	11%
tempo runs	0	0	0	0	0	0	12%	4%	35%	11%	0
time trials	0	0	0	0	0	0	0	0	0	0	0
hill work	0	0	0	0	10%	3%	0	0	0	0	0
competitions	0	0	3%	0	7%	6%	24%	10%	19%	12%	11%
x-country skiing	0	0	0	0	0	6%	0	0	0	0	0
*strength training***	14%	7.5%	5%	0	10%	0	0	0	5%	0	0
sprints	0	0	5%	0	0	0	8%	0	6%	0	0

*Did not keep a diary after the Olympics until Nov. 1.
**Light weights and calisthenics.

1971/72
Number of Training Sessions

	NOV	DEC	JAN	FEB	MAR	APR	MAY	JUNE	JULY	AUG
long runs over 10km	8	8	12	9	8	7	7	5	2	5
short runs under 10km	4	3	2	5	1	1	1	—	4	—
fartlek	5	3	5	3	3	7	6	4	2	2
long intervals	1	3	8	6	8	3	3	2	1	—
short intervals	6	5	6	4	4	4	4	5	2	4
tempo runs	—	—	—	—	—	—	4	5	3	11
time trials	—	—	—	—	1	—	—	—	—	1
hill work	—	—	—	—	—	3	1	—	—	—
competitions	—	—	—	1	—	2	2	3	5	6
x-country skiing	—	1	2	—	3	—	—	—	—	—
strength training	4	3	3	2	4	3	1	—	—	1
sprints	—	2	2	2	—	—	—	—	1	1
total # of sessions	28	28	40	32	32	30	29	24	20	31

Summary: Intensive training the entire year, also during competition season in summer. In addition, many races.

1973/74
Number of Training Sessions
(beginning October 14, 1973)

	OCT	NOV	DEC	JAN	FEB	MAR	APR	MAY	JUNE	JULY	AUG	SEPT
long runs over 10km	11	24	13	9	24	19	9	12	11	12	16	15
short runs under 10km	3	6	12	19	7	12	9	9	17	16	13	12
fartlek	—	2	—	—	1	—	3	2	4	2	—	—
long intervals	—	2	1	—	2	6	3	4	—	1	—	—
short intervals	2	3	3	1	4	4	7	3	3	4	5	4
tempo runs	—	—	—	—	—	1	—	3	5	2	4	—
time trials	—	—	—	—	—	—	—	—	—	—	—	—
hill work	—	—	—	—	—	—	1	1	—	—	—	—
competitions	—	—	—	—	—	—	2	2	2	4	4	4
x-country skiing	—	3	1	—	—	1	2	—	—	—	—	—
strength training	5	3	3	—	—	2	—	—	—	—	—	—
sprints	—	—	—	—	—	—	—	—	—	—	—	—
total # of sessions	21	43	33	29	38	45	36	36	42	41	42	35

Despite the increased percentage of long runs noted in the chart, 800m times did not change, but a big improvement occurred in the 1,500m and 3,000m.

Comparison of Training

total # of sessions	Nov	Feb	Apr	July	Aug
1971/72	28	32	30	21	31
1973/74	40	38	36	41	42

Summary: Increase in training, but same number of competitions.

Autumn/Winter 1973–74
Sample training week, November 1973

Mon	*Nov*	*26*	Long run, 14km (9 miles)
"		*27*	Fartlek ("speed play"), 14km
"		*28*	Long run, 14km
"		*29*	A.M.—short run, 9km (5.6 miles)
			P.M.—8 × 1,000m (time, 3:35–3:44), 1-min. rest
"		*30*	Long run, 14km
	Dec	*1*	Intervals, 25 × 300m (15-sec. rest)
"		*2*	A.M.—short run, 9km
			P.M.—long run, 14km

Week's total: 110km (68 miles)

Sample training week, February 1974

Mon	*Feb*	*4*	Long run, 14km (9 miles)
"		*5*	Long run, 14km
"		*6*	Long run with alternating speed, 14km
"		*7*	Long run, 14km
"		*8*	Long intervals, 4 × 1,000m (1-min. rest) + short run 6km (3.7 miles)
"		*9*	A.M.—long run, 10km (6.2 miles)
			P.M.—long run, 10km
"		*10*	Short intervals, 25 × 300m (15-sec. rest)

Week's total: 105km (65 miles)

Summer 1974
Sample training week, July 1974

Mon	*July*	*8*	A.M.—short run, 6km (3.7 miles)
			P.M.—intervals, 20 × 200m + 12 × 200m (10–15-sec. rest and 5-min. rest between sessions)
"		*9*	A.M.—short run, 6–7km (4 miles)
			P.M.—long run, 12km (7.5 miles)
"		*10*	A.M.—short run, 7km
			P.M.—tempo run, 1,000 + 800m + 600m + 400m (dirt road), 5-min. rest
"		*11*	A.M.—short run, 6–7km
			P.M.—long run, 12km
"		*12*	A.M.—short run, 7km
			P.M.—fartlek, 12km
"		*13*	Short run, 7km and slow 5km (3.1 miles)
"		*14*	Long run, 12km

Week's total: 111km (69 miles)

Sample training 1973/74
Last 2½ weeks before European Championships, Rome

Fri	*Aug*	*23*	A.M.—short run, 7km (4.3 miles)
			P.M.—long run, 13km (8 miles)
Sat	"	*24*	A.M.—short run, 7km
			P.M.—long run, 13km
Sun	"	*25*	A.M.—short run, 7km
			P.M.—long run, 13km
Mon	"	*26*	P.M.—Track, 1 × 1,000m (time, 2:47.5) + 1 × 600m (1:36.1) + 1 × 300m (43.6), 7½-min. rest
Tues	"	*27*	A.M.—short run, 7km
			P.M.—long run, 13km
Wed	"	*28*	No training, leg pain
Thurs	"	*29*	20-min. jog
Fri	"	*30*	Long run, 13km
Sat	"	*31*	Track, 1 × 1,000m (time, 2:42.6) + 1 × 600m (1:34.9) + 1 × 300 (43.1), 7½-min. rest
Sun	*Sept*	*1*	Short run, 8km (5 miles)

Mon	"	2	Fartlek, 11km (6.8 miles)
Tues	"	3	Short run 8km
Wed	"	4	Intervals, 12 × 150m + 10 × 100m (10–15-sec. rest and 5-min. rest between sessions)
Thurs	"	5	25-min. jog + 3 pick-ups
Fri	"	6	A.M.—4–5km jog (2.5–3 miles) P.M.—heats (European Championships) 1,500m (time, 4:11.5)
Sat	"	7	25-min. jog + pick-ups
Sun	"	8	1,500m final, 4:05.2 (3rd place, bronze medal)
Mon	"	9	Short run, 9km (5.6 miles)

Competitions, 1971–78, Track
(*Note:* up to 1978, racing only from May to September)

1971	26	races	Mostly 800m, and also shorter races
1972	20	"	800m–1,500m
1973	29	"	Mostly 800m, eight 1,500m, and one 3,000m (a few races under 800m)
1974	12	"	800m–1,500m
1975	14	"	eight 800m, four 1,500m, and one 3,000m
1976	12	"	eight 1,500m and one 3,000m
1977	18	"	nine 1,500m, five 800m, two 3,000m, one 1,609m, and one 1,000m
1978	20	"	ten 1,500m, three 800m, and five 3,000m

Races not indicated on the track were either cross-country or a few short road races, typically two miles.

Race Analysis 1971—78

800m	YEAR'S BEST	AVERAGE OF YEAR'S 3 BEST RACES
1971	2:05.7	2:06.3
1972	2:06.9	2:07.5
1973	2:06.0	2:06.4
1974	2:03.6	2:04.2
1975	2:03.1	2:04.8
1976	2:03.8	2:04.5
1977	2:04.4	2:05.0
1978	2:03.6	2:04.3
1,500m		
1971	4:17.0	4:21.7
1972	4:16.0	4:19.3
1973	4:12.7	4:18.6
1974	4:05.2	4:08.6
1975	4:07.5	4:09.5
1976	4:04.8	4:06.0
1977	4:05.1	4:05.9
1978	4:00.6	4:03.7
3,000m		
1973	9:34.2	—
1975	8:46.6	—
1976	8:45.4	—
1977	8:36.8	—
1978	8:32.1	—

12

On Women

PROGRESS AND POLITICS

As a female athlete, I have faced obstacles from the time I started to run. It began with having to find a sports club that accepted girls, and it continued with trouble on the home front. My parents had a certain idea of what they wanted their "little girl" to be, and it did not include a budding track star. My duties were the traditional kind: washing dishes and taking care of the kitchen, and until I was ten or eleven my mother was quite protective of me in the traditional sense, always warning me not to get dirty when I went outside. Looking back, I am sure that much of my parents' early resistance to my running, and my subsequent anger and rebellion, had to do with the fact that we had very different ideas about who Grete Andersen was and what she should become.

Choosing to be a runner also meant following in a tough tradition. I recall reading that women in Greece were forbidden from even entering the festival site of the Olympic Games under threat of execution. When those who oversaw the Olympics decided to do away with the women's 800 meters after the first time it was run, in 1928, it took thirty-two years to reinstate that event alone, and sixteen more years to add any distance longer than a mile.

Norway has the same problems as other Western societies in terms of equality between the sexes. When I was coming up through the ranks of the sport, things were by no means equal between men and women. The press never came to all-women's track meets, and big international meets such as the world-famous Oslo Games had very few events for women, at most two or three. To get the same recognition both from the press and the public, a woman athlete had to be relatively much better than a man. When I was on the national level, no one paid any attention to me, although men on the same level got public recognition. It was only when I had reached the international level that I began to get any significant mention in the press. Even when I got to the top it was still a struggle. Kristen Damsgaard, my coach at the time, complained about my situation in one of the major daily newspapers: "No land in the world has a junior with a European record who does not get any support for Olympic preparation."

Even well into the early 1970s, my feeling was that women's track and field was something that existed merely as part of the scenery. The media and the public were really interested only in the men. According to what I have heard from other athletes, it was just as bad (if not worse) in the United States as in Europe, until the late 1970s, when feminism helped create greater interest in women's sports. The situation, although still not ideal, has improved.

I am often asked, usually by Americans, whether the feminist movement has helped my career. It is true that feminism had become a significant social force at the same time I made major improvements as a runner. But feminism didn't really help my career. What helped my career was a bronze medal in the 1974 European Championships and a world record in the 3,000 meters in 1975. This is what got me recognition as an athlete, and it was as an athlete that I established myself, not as a woman in athletics. I have always regarded myself first as a "professional" athlete and a Norwegian, and then as a woman. However, although I have never regarded myself as a feminist, I believe in the feminist movement and that my achievements may have contributed to help feminist development.

Although I believe athletic performance is what brought me personal recognition, feminism has had an undeniably positive effect on women's sports. The testimony I hear from women runners everywhere is always decidedly feminist. They continually tell me how important running is to them in a very personal sense and that it has opened up new doors in their lives. To do something for themselves, to become more physically and mentally fit, has given them a tremendous sense of confidence and general well-being.

I realize the effect of feminism on sports and the importance of a special spirit among women, but it is hard for me to address this issue in detail as it is not a part of my background or my culture. Running has always been a sport to me, and later a livelihood. Only recently has it taken on meaning as a social movement. But even though I am still a bit perplexed by all the significance attached to it, especially for women, I am also glad it can give so many people so much.

Despite all the advances, is there really equality between men and women in running? Although not completely, in some important ways I believe there is. The prize money for the winners is usually equal, and relative to their numbers in participation so is the money for other top finishers. The recognition for women that was once missing is now available. In fact, when I'm asked if I get equal attention in the New York City Marathon, I answer that for my taste I get too much! But this wasn't always the case. As late as 1978 and 1979, when I ran my first two marathons, the focus was still more on the men. With time and my achievements, the situation improved by 1980 and 1981. Now that the marathon is an international event for women as well as men, we have gained equal status in the event. It is no longer as it used to be, when women were regarded as just a sideshow to the men.

The best forum for women runners in my opinion are all-women's races. We women have to share most races with men, and they usually get more: more attention, more exposure, even more room. But in an all-women's race, we can have our own stage, including the media attention that is good for women's running and for all women's sports. This media attention, especially television, is a tremendous source of inspiration to other women, showing them what they, too, can do. Another benefit of an all-women's race is that it allows a woman to be able to see her competition, which is often difficult in a mixed race. Being part of an all-women's race—to be able to race with, and against, her peers—is an experience every woman runner should have. Just as this participation is important for other women, it is important for me to be able to cross the finish line as the one and only winner of a race.

An example of the growing pains in women's running is the current controversy over pacing in mixed races. Should a woman get credit for her performance if she runs with a man, being "paced"? There were those who complained about the world marathon records of Joan Benoit Samuelson and (to a lesser degree) Ingrid Kristiansen, accusing these women of being paced. This is not as controversial in Europe, where Ingrid set her record, as it is in the United States, where Joan set hers. Frankly, I can't see the reason for all the fuss. After all, men have always hooked up to help each other in races. In fact, pacesetters, or "rabbits," are an important part of track races in which records are sought. But when a woman in a road race runs with a man, whether she invites him to pace her or not, everyone cries "foul!" I can't even count the number of times that men have hooked onto me in a race, using me as a pacesetter. Nobody tries to disqualify them for being paced! So why is this such an issue for women? As far as I'm concerned, as long as a woman is moving her own legs, she is doing the work, regardless of who is running near her. It seems to me that when we are fully accepted as athletes, and not just as *women* athletes, issues like this will disappear and cease to detract from our achievements.

Women's running has changed radically since I began, and it is still changing. As the attention as well as the prize money grows, the quality of the competition also improves. Five years ago it was easy to pick the winner in a women's race, but not today. Although I was disappointed to lose the 1985 L'eggs Mini Marathon by only three seconds, I was also relieved. Finally, I could run against my competition instead of the clock. This race was a sign to me that women have climbed yet another step, reached a higher level.

Often, my name is mentioned in connection with advances in women's distance running, specifically the acceptance of the marathon as an Olympic event. This is something for which I cannot take credit, as there were so many other women who contributed to this cause by their achievements or political lobbying. Besides, I never set out to "blaze trails," nor have I ever thought of myself as a pioneer. I just ran the marathon once a year, and, frankly, I felt too much significance was attached to it. Now I realize, however, that there was a particular set of circumstances which brought my achievements into focus. The fact that I ran my marathons in New York, the media capital of the world, increased the attention given to women's running. And in retrospect, although for me what was important was simply to improve, I realize that to break 2:30, and take so much time off the marathon record, changed the nature of the sport.

I do feel, however, that now I can do something even more directly for women's running, and not just symbolically via my achievements. When I first ran the L'eggs Mini Marathon, in 1979, I was fascinated by what I saw: a race with only women—thousands of them, some the age of my mother and even my grandmother. I had never seen anything like it, certainly not in Norway, where at that time women were still sneaking out in the dark to run. I came back to Norway with a dream: to see an event like this in my own country. I am very proud of the Grete Waitz Run, which was first run in 1984 and drew 3,500 women. In 1985 this 2.6-mile fun run grew to 5,000. In the United States, that would be the equivalent of a race with 275,000 women!

Another project I began in 1984 is the Grete Waitz Foundation, designed to help talented young female runners by providing them with scholarships, overseas trips for competition, and training camps, which I also attend as an advisor. Through my own experience, I know that the teen years are a crucial age, when girls must be nurtured and encouraged, as this is the time they tend to disappear from the sport. Much of the improvement in women's running has come because of a change in social attitudes. Now that it is accepted and encouraged that women can stay in the sport indefinitely, performances are improving significantly, and young girls can see a future for themselves in running. When I started getting good at age twenty-two, it was customary in Western society for a woman athlete to retire by this age—stay home and raise a family. But much of what I have been able to accomplish has to do with the fact that I stayed with it. There weren't many women doing that when I was in my mid-twenties. A newspaper picture from those years illustrates my point. There I am, all of twenty-five years old, standing with the national team. GRETE AND HER KIDS reads the caption.

The growth of women's running is dependent both on social and political advances, but working for change must be done in a meaningful way. I received a lot of publicity for signing a petition directed at the International Olympic Committee in 1984 in an attempt to force it to add the 10,000 meters for women to the 1984 Games. At least twenty elite women runners signed as well, but the media chose to focus on me and Mary Decker Slaney. Of course, I support the inclusion of this event, but to be broadcast live from Europe on the *Today* show as one of those "suing the Olympic Committee" (I wasn't personally suing anyone!) was not the way I would have chosen to go about expressing that support. Besides, in retrospect I don't think it would have been in our best interest to have this event added at the last minute. The quality of the race would not have been nearly as good as if women distance runners had known at least two years in advance and been able to prepare for it properly. Like many other women distance runners, as I was preparing for the marathon, I would not have run the 10,000 meters. Also, this event for women is still relatively new. As of 1985, it has only recently become an international event. If the event were not run up to a certain standard in the Olympics, I believe it may have somewhat damaged the reputation of women's running.

What's in the future? As the competition gets better, I think there will be more all-women's races. I am sure race organizers will be anxious to conduct these races if they can get good competition, and especially television coverage, like the 1985 L'eggs race had on ABC Sports. In addition, I believe the women's program in the Olympics will eventually be the same as the men's: the 3,000 meters will be eliminated, and the 5,000 and the 10,000 meters will be added. However, the Olympic Committee is so slow to change, I can only hope it will happen in this century!

Ingrid Kristiansen, who holds the women's marathon record at the time of this writing (2:21:06), was fast enough to have qualified for the U.S. *men's* Olympic trials in 1980. Does this mean that women will one day catch up to men in long-distance races? Even though we'll surely beat a lot of them, probably not. Despite the fact I am finishing higher in mixed races, this does not mean I will eventually come in first overall. As long as women are women, I don't think they will surpass men. As long as we are physically less strong than men, it is an unrealistic question. If evolution changes things in 2,000 years, maybe this issue will be worth considering.

Whether a woman will beat men is a question that is frequently asked as women get better, faster. We wonder what our limits are. But men's times will also get faster, even though at a much slower rate. Besides, I don't think women beating men is even an important issue.

Of greater significance, in my opinion, is our own relative achievements. Our competition is against each other, not against men. Beating men is not what's relevant; it's competition among our peers. Nevertheless, if the day ever comes when a woman is the first person across the finish line, my cheering voice will certainly be the loudest!

I do believe that as opportunities for women increase the world will be surprised to see how fast we can run. Imagine what can happen when the sport has grown to the point that there are as many women runners in a race as there are men: true equality. As of the end of 1984, women still comprised less than 20 percent of the marathoning population in the United States. The New York City Marathon (America's largest, with 19,000 runners) has a women's field of about 3,000. But imagine a field in New York of 9,500 women—and Olympic events, opportunities, and attitudes that are equal as well. With opportunity, the potential exists for unlimited improvement. In fact, our achievements may exceed all expectations, even my own.

The opportunities for women in distance running have undoubtedly improved, but we still have a long way to go. One strange inequity still exists in the World Cross Country Championships, acknowledged by many as the most competitive distance race in the world, and in Europe one of the most prestigious events outside the Olympic Games. The men in this event run 12 kilometers (7.1 miles); the junior men (19 and under) run 8 kilometers (5 miles); and the women run 5 kilometers (3.1 miles)—hardly an equal program. It seems to me that if women can run the same 26.2-mile marathon as the men, we can certainly run the same seven miles in cross-country.

When I ran in my second Olympics, in 1976, the longest distance for women was only 1,500 meters. Here I was, training close to 100 miles a week and lifting weights in addition, and yet I was automatically deemed too weak to run farther than a mile. Even high school boys in the United States were regularly running twice as far in track competition. Today the choice for women in the Olympics is either 3,000m (1.8 miles) or 26.2 miles, with nowhere land in between. It took a near revolution to get the marathon in 1984, with the 3,000 meters added almost as an afterthought. I hope that's not what it will take for the other events.

THE WOMAN ATHLETE AND HER BODY

A great deal has been written and discussed about the effect sports participation has on a woman's body. In fact, I cannot recall a single interview in the past few years in which I have not been asked how my running has affected my life as a woman and what my views are on the subject—so here they are. Some basic guidelines are provided in this chapter, in addition to my opinions, but since I am obviously not a medical expert, any further information should be requested from a qualified professional. There are also several women's running books that may be of interest in the Recommended Reading (see page 249).

The purpose of this chapter is primarily to discuss my experiences and feelings as a woman athlete. What I have written here is very personal, and this is the first time I have discussed most of it publicly. It was not easy for me to write it, nor did I do so without a great deal of introspection. But I felt that if by being completely open in this book my experiences and opinions can be enlightening or beneficial to others, it is worthwhile to discuss them.

Menstruation

I have been amenorrheic (without my menstrual cycle) for ten years. It stopped in 1976, when I was twenty-three, which was also the first year I began hard distance training. My cycle had always been regular until 1974, at which time it became slightly irregular for two years, until it stopped altogether. Although not all elite women athletes are amenorrheic, it is well known that a number of them are or have been and that irregular cycles are common among them. This does not mean, however, that you will automatically become amenorrheic if you run, even if you run as much or as hard as I do. There are women on every level of training who have regular cycles and women who don't get their periods who've never run a step.

In 1981 I was part of a study in Norway in which twenty amenorrheic athletes from various sports were tested in an attempt to determine the cause of our condition. Part of the study included being given two types of hormones to induce our cycles. It worked for all but two of us, and I was one of those two. Since that time, I have conferred with a gynecologist who has found nothing wrong, and he feels, as most experts do about women runners, that when I slow down my life and gain eight to ten pounds my cycles will return. This is usually the case with women runners whose cycles are affected by training.

My amenorrhea would seem to coincide with the findings of the study in which I participated and the findings of most other such studies. Researchers in the study speculated that the condition could be caused by hard training, stress (physical or mental), or low body fat, all of which describe me and my lifestyle. (For example, I have 9 percent body fat, compared with 10 percent to 13 percent for most elite women runners and 25 percent for the average sedentary woman.)

My menstrual period used to affect me as it does many other women. For four or five days before it I would get back pain, become bloated, and gain weight. Hard workouts on these days were impossible, and if I did do intervals, they were not very fast. Racing was out of the question.

One of my last periods coincided with a 1,500m race for the Nordic Cup in Finland in 1976. I was bleeding quite heavily and had stomach cramps, which forced me to drop out of the race. In fact, I bled for many days afterward, as if I had gotten all the cycles I had missed that year at once—perhaps all the cycles I would get for years to come.

At that time, a woman's menstrual cycle was not a common topic for discussion. Although it is a problem women in sports have struggled with for years, it still isn't publicly acknowledged as the reason for a bad race. Surely, it is not customarily the subject of a major newspaper story. But when I dropped out of that race, it made news: an entire page in the paper, including the reason why. I suppose it was somewhat obvious when I doubled over with cramps, and it was no secret since the team doctors also knew. So I felt it was best to be honest and explain to the press what was wrong. But I didn't expect them to print it! When I saw the headline, I was both shocked and embarrassed, to say the least.

According to one theory, my menstrual cycle may have ceased because it is not a useful function for what I do. Dr. Joan Ullyot, physician, runner, and writer, has developed what she calls the "anthropological theory of the origin of monthly cycles." She claims that since amenorrhea is common in fit, healthy young runners, whereas clockwork monthly cycles are common in the sedentary, plump population, she believes regular monthly cycles may be the result of life in an inactive society in which sedentary women have higher percentages of body fat. In addition, Ullyot feels that a woman doesn't have to bleed every month in order to be healthy.

None of this means that a woman can't run hard, and run well, at any time of the month. Women have won Olympic medals at every phase in their cycle. However, it is a concern of some women that their performance may be affected by painful cramps, bloating, or other menstrual discomfort. Certainly, I'd want to avoid this discomfort since it had forced me to drop out of a race and caused me such embarrassment when it was made public. Although I have never consciously wished not to have my period—past or present—if I knew I could lose a medal in a major competition because of it, and aspirin or another remedy wasn't enough, I would take medication like birth control pills to postpone it. This was not uncommon in the sixties, and I know of one top Norwegian athlete in those days who did try it. Unfortunately, she hadn't tested it first before competition. She got her period, anyway, and got twice as sick. Of course, I think anything like this should be done only as a last resort, and I would hope that with the newer forms of menstrual pain relievers it would not be necessary.

These days amenorrhea is openly discussed by Norwegian women runners. Women on the national team are encouraged to take it up with the coach, and they generally do. Since most of them are young and experiencing changes in their cycles for the first time, a careful approach is taken to avoid alarm or insecurity. It is stressed that this amenorrhea is a frequent but likely only temporary result of training. In most cases, the cycles of the young girls return after they finish a summer of heavy competition.

In and of itself, amenorrhea has not been proven dangerous, so I do not take any hormones for it. I would consider doing so, however, if I wanted to bring on my period in order to get pregnant. Meanwhile, my only precaution is to take calcium supplements, as current research shows a relationship between osteoporosis (a decrease in bone density) and low levels of estrogen due to amenorrhea. Studies have shown that calcium loss could affect one female runner in ten who have stopped menstruating and that significant bone loss occurs rapidly during the first years of amenorrhea.* According to leading sports gynecologist Dr. Mona Shangold, a woman, therefore, should consult with her physician immediately if she stops menstruating. Meanwhile, as long as I am otherwise healthy, I feel there is no point in worrying. The extent to which I have consulted with medical experts (I still get checked every so often) is all I can do.

Children

In the last few years, it's rare if I'm not asked if I plan to have a child. And if I'm not being asked directly, it's the first thing being asked about me. It's easy to understand why, I suppose, in an era of career women past thirty, like myself, who have put off having a family. Of course, few of them depend on their bodies for a career to the extent I do, which is why pregnancy is an even more complicated issue for me. My answer to the question of whether I'll have children is usually something vague like, "I'll see when life gets back to normal." The truth is, I honestly don't know if I want a child and, because of my amenorrhea, whether I can even have one.

I suppose I'm like many women in a similar situation. We say we'll consider it eventually, pushing the subject aside, not wanting to make a decision. Right now I don't feel competent to raise children. My lifestyle—with all the travel—doesn't fit the life of a mother. Besides, I don't feel a motherly instinct, at least not at the moment. Certainly it's not for lack of love. I've been part of my three nephews' and one

*Running & FitNews, Vol. 2, No. 4 (December 1984); Vol. 3, No. 9 (September 1985).

niece's lives since they were babies (the oldest is now sixteen), and I love them as if they were my own.

I really like my life the way it is now. Sometimes I feel pressure from other Norwegian women: "When will you live a normal life?" I'll enjoy my lifestyle as long as I can, because this type of life will never return once it's over. Other women runners who have had babies, such as Ingrid Kristiansen, say to me, "You'll change your mind after you have a baby." But I don't want to try it as an experiment, to have a baby without serious, deliberate consideration. For one thing, if I'm going to be a mother, I feel I should take care of my own baby. Why give birth to a child and have someone else take care of it? I know having a family will put limits on my life—not being as flexible and independent—and right now I don't want those limits. That may sound cold or selfish, but I would be less than honest if I didn't say it. It isn't my time to be a mother. To feel or do otherwise because society says it's my time wouldn't be fair to me or to a child.

Despite what liberated American women have been led to believe, I don't think we can "have it all." There has to be a compromise. If it's a matter of having a job, being a runner, and being a mother, I think for most women maybe two of them are possible, at most, but certainly not all three. In my case, I can do only one. If it were enough to do one workout a day, not struggle to stay on top, I could probably combine my running with another pursuit. But to be on an international level, to train twice a day, makes it very hard to combine running with anything else.

Some women athletes fear the physical change of being pregnant. This is absolutely not the case with me. I don't fear inactivity or find becoming big frightening or distasteful. For one thing, these days we know that fit women can maintain a modest exercise program during pregnancy, and I would certainly be one of them. Pregnancy represents for me a different fear. At this point in my life, I feel if I were to take a break from competitive running, even for this relatively short time, it would become a permanent break. I don't think I could come back. My motivation would be gone. I have been fortunate to have achieved so much in sixteen years, but the hunger to stay on top does not last forever. Pregnancy would probably signal my time to retire, and it's actually retirement that is the dilemma for me.

This does not mean I have ruled out having children. After all, I just turned thirty-two; I'm not "over the hill" yet! As far as I'm concerned, it is completely possible to have children later in my life, and I don't envision a problem having them even in my late thirties. I am confident that this is one of the benefits of being in good physical shape. I also feel free to make this decision because I am not in conflict with Jack about whether to have children. As in everything, his sensitivity to my feelings makes me feel more secure. Besides, if and when we do have a family, we have to work out some conflicts. Although it is not uncommon for a man in Norway to stay home to take care of children, Jack doesn't feel he wants to do this. The way I see it, everyone has to give something, so we would have to create a mutually agreeable arrangement before we started a family. One job we could share or our own business would be ideal.

Pregnancy

It is not extraordinary for Norwegian women to remain physically active throughout pregnancy; in fact, it's part of our heritage. My mother worked up until the day I was born. These days, it is also not uncommon to see pregnant women exercising in Norway. Exercising during pregnancy makes perfect sense to me. After all, for years doctors have advised women to do some exercise during pregnancy, and most mothers-to-be end up being more health-conscious and active during this time than when they aren't pregnant. In fact, exercise during pregnancy may help prevent common problems, like fatigue and low backache. An analysis of women who complained of these problems revealed that they had a history of inactivity, poor abdominal muscles, and long-term delivery complaints. Exercise can help alleviate these problems as well as help control weight gain, return the belly to normal after childbirth, improve posture, decrease constipation and varicose veins, lessen sleep difficulties, and increase energy.*

Obviously, I can't talk personally about an experience I've never had. Therefore, I will use examples of other top Norwegian women

Running & FitNews, Vol. 3, No. 11 (November 1985).

runners who have children and whom I know well. One of them is Ingrid Kristiansen, who has been the focus of intense interest because of her incredible athletic accomplishments since giving birth. One word describes her pregnancy: remarkable.

Ingrid had never trained as much as she did for the 1983 World Championships. By the winter of 1982, she was up to 200 kilometers a week (125 miles). By Christmas she began to feel a little ill, which she naturally attributed to training, or having caught a bug in the medical lab where she worked as a technician. Nevertheless, she competed in some small races and went on to win the Houston Marathon in 1983 in 2:33. After this race she really slowed down, feeling extremely tired in her legs and body, and having difficulty training. This time she attributed it to all the travel and postmarathon fatigue.

Eventually feeling better, she continued to train heavily and raced a 10km and 15km, spending time in both Norway and the United States. However, when she struggled to a disappointing thirty-fifth-place finish in the World Cross Country Championships in Scotland, Ingrid finally realized something was happening with her body. Believe it or not, it was a "happening" she didn't discover until she was in her fifth month!

Ingrid's menstrual cycle hadn't been a clue, as her periods were sporadic at best. And her IUD, it turned out, obviously didn't work. "Looking back, I think I sensed something was wrong," says Ingrid. "But when you train so many years, you're used to the ups and downs." Although Ingrid was nervous because she had trained so hard while pregnant, after only three hours in labor and a very easy delivery, she gave birth to a healthy boy, who was named Gaute. The same principles that got her through her hard workouts and races came to Ingrid's aid in the delivery room. "Relax, relax," she repeated to herself throughout her natural childbirth. "I believe the birth was easier because I was in good condition," she adds.

Ingrid had no problems exercising throughout her pregnancy, which she did up until the last day. She did so with her doctor's permission, of course, who told her to take it easy and let her body tell her how much to do—and in the case of running, how fast. After the birth, she built back very slowly to previous levels and worked out a program that compensated for the fact that she was heavy with a lot of milk. (She nursed her son for ten and a half months.) She scheduled her workouts so she could feed Gaute at 5:00 A.M. and be running by 6:00 A.M..

In August Ingrid gave birth, and in January 1984 she ran the Houston Marathon again, this time in a personal best of 2:27. I think the main reason she came back so soon is that, in essence, hers was such a short pregnancy. After all, she ceased serious training for only four months.

Ingrid believes it was not the physical act of giving birth that necessarily helped her running but the emotional change in her life. "I have always been training, and I think physically I was always strong enough to run fast. My improvement was more for psychological reasons. Having my son took the pressure off; it helped give me other things to think about in life. I feel more relaxed, more happy."

Ingrid's first advice on training while pregnant is to be very conservative and certainly not to begin any new sport or type of training. Although it appears she did a lot, relative to her level she ran very little. Ingrid found that combining sports alleviated the strain that running alone placed on her legs and body, so she also did stationary biking and swimming.

Although this is NOT a recommendation, here is what Ingrid did. To keep it in perspective, remember to compare it to her earlier 125-mile training weeks!

> *During pregnancy:* Morning—stationary bike and 40-minute swim. Afternoon—a 30-minute run four times a week.
> *After giving birth:* 10 days after birth—15–20-minute jog a day for one week, then two times a day for 20 minutes, which increased to 30 minutes after 1½ weeks.

Randi Langøgjelten Bjorn, the Norwegian record holder in the 800 meters (2:01.7), was also twenty-seven when she gave birth. She agrees with Ingrid about the mental break it gives. Says Randi, "Pregnancy gave me a mental rest from training, which I'd been concentrating on all my life." Randi illustrates how each case is different. Unlike Ingrid, her pregnancy was planned, and giving birth was difficult. But like Ingrid, she looked forward to exercising. "I never doubted it was the right thing to do. When the doctor said not to do anything I hadn't done before, that was all I needed to hear. NOT to train would have gone against his advice."

Although she exercised throughout most of her pregnancy, when running became uncomfortable at seven and a half months, she walked and biked. She also did stomach, back, and leg exercises throughout the entire time (which she resumed the very next day after the birth). After over fifteen hours in labor, her son was delivered by cesarean section. "The doctor tried to tell me my muscles were too tight from training," she says, "but I don't believe it. My mother had the same problem giving birth." Because she did have such a difficult delivery, Randi took it very easy afterward, working back to full training two and a half months later. Like Ingrid, throughout the two years after giving birth, Randi was also training well. In 1985 she won a significant victory in the Norwegian National Championships in the 800 meters.

There is a great deal of speculation on whether giving birth somehow enables a woman to run faster. For years Eastern European women have been making comebacks after having babies, many of them running better than ever. But for those in Western society this experience is new. Although there is no proof that the physical act of giving birth improves performance, Ingrid went on to do what no other athlete has ever done: hold three world records simultaneously in the 5,000m, the 10,000m, and the marathon—all within two years after the birth of her son.

Some say the hormonal changes associated with pregnancy cause a woman to get stronger. Others speculate it is psychological, primarily a result of the mental and physical rest from serious training. Could it actually be the physical aspect of giving birth that makes a woman run faster? After all, all periods of rest from serious training don't result in such improvements, and there are so many examples of women for whom improvement after childbirth has happened—including Ingrid and Randi—that I have to believe there's some truth to it.

Many people still wonder if it is safe to exercise during pregnancy. Researchers at the Melpomene Institute for Women's Health Research, in St. Paul, Minnesota, have been studying exercise and pregnancy since 1981. Their research shows that 90 percent of the women in their study delivered in their ninth month—live-born, healthy infants—and that fewer children of runners had low birthweights compared with children of sedentary women.*

*Running & FitNews, Vol. 3, No. 5 (May 1985).

Each person is still an experiment of one in this new habit of training throughout pregnancy, and Ingrid and Randi are no exception. However, there are some important basic guidelines that should be followed by any woman who chooses to exercise during pregnancy.

EXERCISE GUIDELINES
DURING PREGNANCY

- Continue running only with your physician's approval. Certain conditions may preclude running during pregnancy, such as a history of miscarriages, placenta previa (the condition in which the placenta is attached too low in the uterus), heart disease, multiple pregnancies, a weak cervix, high blood pressure, obesity, anemia, diabetes, or thyroid disease.
- Run three times a week for twenty to thirty minutes per session, never exceeding forty minutes. You may also choose a program of other rhythmic exercise, including walking or moderate swimming, especially in the latter stages of pregnancy.
- Measure your heart rate during exercise, keeping it at 120 to 140 beats per minute. Your pulse should return to normal ten minutes after you stop exercising.
- Avoid overheating. Drink plenty of fluids, and wear light clothing. Do not run if you have a fever or in hot, humid weather.
- Do a good warm-up, especially the ankles, knees, hips, and lower back. Include slow, gradual stretching. Cool down by walking several minutes to get the blood circulating properly in your legs.
- Wear shoes with sturdy midsoles and extra cushioning.
- Don't try to lose weight by exercising during pregnancy. Concentrate on a balanced diet.
- If you feel pain, stop. Consult your physician for any of the following symptoms: excessive fatigue, breathlessness, dizziness, headache, muscle weakness, nausea, chest pain or tightness, back pain, or pubic pain.

• Once you have delivered, wait three weeks after a vaginal delivery or six weeks after a cesarean before resuming exercise.*

Body Image

I have never dieted with the aim of becoming thin "for thin's sake" or because it's fashionable. The way I look is a result of what I do. In fact, the only time I think about my body, except in training, is in terms of my amenorrhea. In addition, I have never struggled with the conflict of athleticism versus femininity. These are not, nor have they ever been, opposite attributes to me. I like the person I am and the way I look. Today the athletic image is probably less of a conflict, as it's so "in." It's an athletic woman's competitiveness that's still a problem for some people. All I can say is that being judged "unfeminine" because I am competitive has never stopped me, and I hope in this day and age other women feel the same.

Whether being thinner will help a person to run faster depends on each individual's body. Carrying excess weight, of course, slows a person down. But what is thin for one person may be too thin for another. It's a mistake to judge what's right by standard height/weight charts or what other runners look like. I've been beaten by runners who looked twice my size. Each runner has to find his or her level of proper weight for optimum performance. For example, I don't think I could run faster if I were any thinner. I would merely lose strength and power.

Although I do know of some top women runners who are obsessed with their weight, performance is hardly the reason most women want

*Guidelines adapted from articles in *The Runner* (Linda Villarosa, "Running & Pregnancy: Having It All," August 1985) and *Runner's World* (Janet Heinonen, "Running for Two," September 1985). Information based on guidelines from the American College of Obstetricians and Gynecologists, 600 Maryland Ave. SW, Washington, DC 20023. Exercise videotapes for pregnancy and postnatal exercise are also available through major outlets. Ask the college for further information.

to become thin. Certainly, we shouldn't be expected to cease thinking about our bodies; we are always involved with the way they function. But my impression, especially of American women, is that they think about them too much; they are far too obsessed with body image. This can be a dangerous obsession, especially as these women are role models for young girls.

Of course, I don't want to be heavy, but I certainly don't list among my goals the desire to be thin. I'll admit I've had my "growing" stage. When I was fourteen, I had a tendency to undereat, and my club coach at the time almost had to force-feed me. Like many teenage girls', my body was changing, but not to my liking. This was the era of Twiggy, when everyone's goal was to be as rail-thin as she was. Fortunately, my eating problem was temporary and not very severe, but there were other girls on the team for whom it was much more serious. Back then, none of us realized what their problem was; there wasn't a word for it. Today it's called anorexia.

Three years ago I attended a conference in Norway that included young, elite female runners. We encouraged them to express their feelings about body image, especially in these years when they experience such dramatic physical changes and tend to gain weight. The obsession with thinness is a serious problem that I have also encountered among runners in races and clinics in the States. I think the solution to this dangerous trend has to begin with honest, open discussion. Whenever I am asked about my body, which is often, I make myself very clear. "You must eat very little to be so thin!" people say. "No," I answer. "I never restrict what I eat to lose weight. If I want it, I eat it." Mine is a typical distance runner's body, and it's the equivalent size and build of a male distance runner's. No one asks these men runners if they diet to stay so thin!

Hair and Skin Care

Any woman who is active and who lives an athletic lifestyle experiences more than normal wear and tear on her hair and skin, and thus has special hair and skin care needs, both for health and appearance. At the same time you consider style, it's important to consider what is comfortable and practical for what you do.

My dream hair is thick and short, like Wendy Sly's. But if I tried to cut my long, thin hair like hers, I'd look like I didn't have any hair at all! My hair is so fine that when I used to try to curl it the curls would soon fall out, and when I tried to have a permanent it wouldn't take. So I do what is practical and reasonable. I have a style that is comfortable, that keeps my hair out of my face when I run, and that can easily be cared for. (Another reason I keep my hair long is that I spent years crying my way to the hairdresser's where my mother forced me to have it cut short.) If you're in a dilemma about the most suitable hairstyle for your activity, don't hesitate to consult with a good hairdresser about what you do and what you need. Many of today's styles are both attractive and practical to suit the fitness lifestyle.

Your skin is really a victim of the elements when you're active in an outdoor sport. Therefore, it should be protected from the sun with a visor and/or sunblock cream and kept moist against chapping in the cold. If the weather is really cold, try applying a layer of petroleum jelly on exposed skin to guard against frostbite and retain warmth. My skin is very dry from the cold Norwegian weather, so I use plain cream. I also use plain soap and cream for year-round care.

Makeup is not good for your skin when running, and I think it's also unnecessary. In general, Norwegian women don't wear much makeup, and another reason I don't use more makeup is that, frankly, I can't apply it. Sometimes when I'm made up for television or photographs, Jack tells me it looks nice, but when I try it for myself— disaster! After a run, if I'm going out, I put on mascara and a bit of powder without perfume so my nose doesn't get so shiny it blinks. (That's how Jack kindly puts it!) My nose has always been a sensitive subject. When I was young, the first thing I swore I'd do when I got older was have a nose job. But as a grown woman, I've settled for the nose I was born with—with powder, that is.

13

Diet and Nutrition

It seems there are as many recommended diets for athletes as there are athletes. In fact, diets abound for everyone—you can almost get lost in a sea of nutritional "dos and don'ts." I've noticed especially from running clinics that the vast amount of information and controversy has caused not only a great deal of confusion but a lot of radical experimenting. Finding the best diet is, of course, important, but trying them all in order to do so seems an awfully big price to pay. Just as with training, my dietary motto is simple: Be sensible and consistent.

You should, of course, be just as careful to follow a good diet as you are to do the right training. They are partners in good health. Nutritional awareness has become big in America, and that's important in an atmosphere where one is faced with so much junk food. However, I think there comes a point when you have to settle on a sensible, regular pattern of eating and then leave the preoccupation and calorie counting behind. I don't mind being food-conscious, but I draw the line at being food-fanatic. I'm fairly relaxed about my diet, but, then, I know I can afford to be. With a normal Norwegian diet, I know I eat well. I realize that perhaps Americans have to be more aware of what they eat, but I feel they think about it too much. The goal with diet, as with running, should be to live as normally as possible.

Of course, I don't want to be overweight, but this isn't the main reason I eat a proper diet. Quite simply, I *feel good* when I eat right. And because I eat right—enough bread and other complex carbohydrates—I don't have cravings for cake and cookies. People are tempted by different foods and have to control those temptations in their own ways. My lifestyle dictates many of my eating decisions: when, how much, how often. For example, I don't crave sweets, but that doesn't mean I never eat them. Especially in the summer, I sometimes have ice-cream bars, but I don't worry about it; I enjoy it! I just don't have them in excess or before a workout.

It is understandable that runners are concerned with successful weight reduction and weight maintenance. It should be clear by now that desirable weight absolutely depends on *both* diet and exercise. As I mentioned in Chapter 4, dieting alone has an extremely high failure rate for permanent weight loss, while physical activity greatly helps by leading to increased metabolism (higher calorie burning). However, it is still the combination of diet and exercise that is most effective. Just as diet alone usually doesn't work, even a great amount of exercise won't, either. In a study conducted by Kenneth Cooper at his Aerobics Center, in Dallas, a group that exercised and dieted for ten weeks lost twenty-five pounds; a dieting-only group lost eighteen; a group that did neither gained two pounds, but the exercisers who did not diet didn't lose even one pound.

My diet is based on my culture, my education, and also my instinct: I eat what I like and what feels right. The Oslo Breakfast Program, which I mentioned in Chapter 3, meant a great deal to the country and our habits. It laid the foundation of a sound diet comprised of fresh foods. Over the years as an athlete, I have learned the importance not only of what I eat but also of when and how I eat: three regular meals at regular hours and small, healthy snacks.

The recommendation for an athlete's diet (as well as a nonathlete's) in the last several years has been to increase the intake of complex carbohydrates and cut back on protein and fat. Complex carbohydrates, which should comprise 65 to 70 percent of the athlete's diet, include such foods as whole-grain breads and cereals, pasta, potatoes, legumes, and fruits and vegetables (preferably fresh). Protein, which should amount to 12 to 15 percent, includes foods like meat, fish, poultry, dairy products (milk and cheese), eggs, and soy products (tofu and soybeans). Fat, 10 to 20 percent, includes such things as butter, margarine, oil, salad dressings, and mayonnaise.

There's no magic diet for runners as far as I'm concerned. Even the marathon is no exception, although I agree with the general principles of a high-carbohydrate diet. But for every faithful pasta-loading runner, there's an athlete like Carlos Lopes, who had steak before his marathon world record. In fact—thinking it may have been my last time in the States—I'll always remember the meal I had in New York before my 1979 world marathon record: shrimp cocktail, salad, wine, steak, baked potato, and ice cream. Of course, knowing more about nutrition today, this is not the meal I would eat. I don't really change what I normally eat before a marathon. If anything, I increase my carbohydrate intake by having an extra potato at lunch the day before. My prerace evening meal is light and simple: perhaps fish with a baked potato or an omelet with bread and salad. Although I'm not recommending steak and wine—or even an omelet—it just proves that one meal is not likely to make or break a good marathon. Therefore, the same philosophy I have recommended for training and racing applies: find your own ideal diet by understanding the basic principles of athletic nutrition, then by experimenting to find what works best for you.

I try to maintain a diet that is most conducive to health and running. My high carbohydrate intake is good for me as an endurance athlete, and I've also acquired some of my habits from American runners. It was from their influence that I stopped eating red meat, cut down on eggs, and saw that a meal could consist of a salad, which I now eat regularly.

I do not eat foods that are difficult to digest before a workout or high-fiber foods like raw fruits and vegetables. This means forcing myself to close the refrigerator door on the summer berries I so love and avoiding large meals late at night, which tend to bother me on the next morning's run. Besides, putting food in the digestive system at night is like doing it before a workout: blood that goes to the stomach to aid digestion is not best utilized in repairing the muscles.

NORWEGIAN NUTRITION

The following information on Norwegian nutrition is provided by Ingrid Ellingsen Lie, a nutritionist with an interest in fitness and running, and a former Norwegian national-class 800-meter runner.

In Norway, meals containing milk, milk products, bread (as sandwiches), and cereals make up to 40 percent of the consumer's dietary intake. Our carbohydrate consumption, which is on the average 50 percent of our diet, is usually in the form of fiber-rich crackers, breads, and cereals.

As I don't like rice or pasta, my only addition to those breads and cereals is potatoes. For my money, nothing tops Norwegian wholegrain bread, which is baked fresh daily and sells for about forty cents a loaf. White bread is eaten only on special occasions in Norway; I buy it rarely, only if we have guests. It is never eaten on a daily basis, and I never eat it at all if I have a choice. However, if white bread is all that's available, I'll eat it. This is what I mean by not being fanatic.

Milk is another basic part of the Norwegian diet, as is fish, which is also a major Norwegian industry. Red meat is eaten infrequently because of its prohibitive cost. A typical meat meal consists of a much smaller meat-to-potato-and-vegetable ratio than a meal in the United States. Red meat is often combined with other products, as in the case of meatballs, which are usually mixed with potato starch. Turkey is uncommon, and chicken, considered relatively inexpensive in the States, is costly in Norway, and therefore a special weekend meal. A small, grilled chicken (which is usually how it is purchased) costs about five and a half dollars.

Although Norwegians rarely eat out (a social meal generally entails an invitation to one's home), this habit is starting to become more common, as is fast food, something that was unheard of not long ago. As Norwegian habits have begun to slip, the country has waged advertising campaigns like the one in 1983–84 that urged people to eat more whole-grain bread and like another requesting that industry cut down on the salt added to our fish and bread.

The following is a typical daily diet in Norway. It is instructive not only for the foods it includes but also for the times at which they are eaten.

Breakfast (*frokost*) (about 7:00 A.M.): whole-grain bread with butter or margarine and jam, or cheese, or hot or cold cereal. A glass of juice and milk. Coffee or tea, usually without milk or sugar.

Lunch (*lunsj*) (11:00–12:30 P.M.): *matpakke* (package lunch) —open-faced sandwiches, commonly made with salami, sausage, fish, cheese, or liverwurst—is a Norwegian institution. In a recent survey, it was determined that 78 percent of the population, from wealthy shipowners to clerks, brings a matpakke to work, wrapped in white butcher paper called *matpapir*. They also bring a thermos with something to drink, or purchase a drink in special employee cafeterias. This carry-it-along habit means that I, for one, never leave the house without a sandwich or fruit. When I travel outside Norway, it is difficult to bring a matpakke, but I always carry something with me, especially when I don't know when the next meal will be. In fact, traveling provisions is another Norwegian habit; they're called *nistepakke*. Not only is this bring-along system convenient and economical, but you also always have something healthy on hand and know exactly what you're eating.

Dinner (*middag*) (4:30–5:30 P.M.): this is the one hot meal of the day, typically composed of fish—or occasionally meat—potatoes, and vegetables.

Supper/Snack (*aftens*): an optional evening meal of something light, like an open-faced sandwich, cheese and crackers, fruit or yogurt, and tea.

MY DAILY DIET

Now that you have a view of a typical Norwegian diet, here's a sample of my own. The differences are based on personal taste (*e.g.*, I don't like milk), my lifestyle as a runner, my appetite, and lack of time and expertise in the kitchen. In other words, I'm a lousy cook!

Breakfast (6:45–7:00 A.M., after my morning run): two glasses of XL-1* immediately after running. A full bowl of thick-cut oatmeal, cooked in water, with one teaspoon of honey. A cup of tea with lemon or black coffee. (Sometimes flatbread—Norwegian crackers—with cheese.) Daily vitamin supplements, 1 elemental calcium 500 mg, 1 iron 100 mg, 1 vitamin C 1,000 mg, and 1 vitamin B complex.

Snack (midmorning): if I have a snack, it's a piece of fruit, such as an apple, pear, or nectarine.

Lunch (11:45 A.M.—12:00 P.M.): one bowl of "Homemade Two-Step Tomato Vegetable Soup" (see recipe on page 212) or a large salad. Baked potato (including skin) with cottage cheese and vegetable salt (a combination of celery salt, paprika, etc.), or bread or crackers with cottage or hard cheese. Tea or decaffeinated coffee.

---

*XL-1 resembles other sports drinks in the United States, such as ERG and Gatorade. Studies in Norway have shown that consumption of fluids during sports activities is frequently too low. Most people active in soccer, handball, cross-country skiing, and long-distance running drink less than their loss of fluid. Dehydration, or fluid loss, of 1 percent of body weight will begin to affect performance. A 5 percent loss, as is common in these sports, results in a definite impairment in physical working capacity.

I began drinking XL-1 regularly after the blood tests I take for overtraining revealed dehydration-related problems. The tests were taken following the 1983 Peachtree 10km, a hot-weather race after which I obviously did not drink enough to replace lost fluids. I drink XL-1 rather than plain water because it contains a small percentage of sugar. Drinks with too high a sugar content may actually decrease the amount of time it takes for water to leave the stomach, which is detrimental in hot weather. However, for a marathon, especially in cooler weather, the sugar (which is a carbohydrate) provides some extra fuel and can help in preventing "hitting the wall," the feeling you get when you literally run out of energy.

Snack (2:00–3:00 P.M.) (occasionally, but not before a hard afternoon workout): fruit, bread with cheese, flavored yogurt from the freezer. Perhaps one or two small pieces of caramel candy.

Dinner (6:00–7:00 P.M.): a large plate of salad (raw vegetables including red cabbage, cucumber, tomatoes, and mushrooms, and cooked vegetables such as broccoli, cauliflower, carrots, and string beans), low-calorie Thousand Island Dressing, salad seasoning herb salt, baked potato with cottage cheese or thick-sliced bread with fish paté or tuna fish, crab legs, shrimp, or caviar spread. Or, occasionally, an omelet or chicken with salad.

Snack (evening): tea with oatmeal crackers and cheese.

NORWEGIAN RECIPES

A few words in support of fish: fish is low in fat and cholesterol, easy to digest if prepared without fat, and also important for EPA (eicosapentaenoic acid) oils, shown to lower blood cholesterol. Salmon and sardines, eaten with the bones, are high in calcium, and rinsing canned fish can reduce the sodium content by half or more. Fish is a major part of my diet, and as I am forced to eat out frequently when I'm on the road I always order fish.

Fish is as Norwegian as apple pie is American. We have many varieties, which we prepare in every possible way. Fish is also very versatile. For example, I find the leftover boiled or steamed fish in these recipes to be excellent in salad.

(All amounts and cooking times may be approximate due to metric conversion.)

FISH IN FOIL

600 grams (1 lb., 5 oz.) fish
1½ tbsp. butter or oil

1   medium leek, washed thoroughly, chopped, or ½ cup onion, chopped
2   ripe tomatoes, cut into pieces
1   tbsp. fresh parsley or dill (or 1½ tsp. dried)
    salt and pepper to taste

Use whole fish or cut pieces. If using whole fish, make one foil packet. If using cut fish pieces, prepare individual packets. Oil or butter large piece of aluminum foil. Place fish and remainder of ingredients on foil. (Dill is best with trout.) Fold the foil over fish, and cook with folded side up. *To steam*, place fish packet in double boiler or directly on boiling potatoes for 20–25 minutes, a bit longer for whole or frozen fish. (For a piece 1½ inches thick, allow 30 minutes; 2–3 inches thick, 40 minutes.) *To bake*, place packet in a pan in 375° oven for approximately same times as in steamed recipe.

In the summer, I often cook fish in foil on the *barbecue*, adding any other vegetables in season. (Cook approximately 20 minutes, depending on the size of the fish. Turn fish so it cooks 10 minutes per side.) Boiled potatoes and carrots always go well with boiled fish. Rice with curry sauce is also good.

EASY-COOK FISH

600 grams (1 lb., 5 oz.) fresh or frozen fish fillet, pieces, or fishballs
1   chopped onion or leek
1   chopped red or green pepper (optional)
½   tsp. garlic powder or minced garlic clove (optional)
½   tsp. salt
¼   tsp. pepper
    parsley, as desired
1   can (approx. 1 lb.) whole tomatoes, or four tomatoes cut in pieces
½   cup water

Cut the fish in portion pieces or roll up fish fillets and place side by side in a pot. Add onion, pepper, spices, and tomatoes; add water. Simmer (do not boil) fish with lid on pot for 10 minutes.

This fish goes well served with boiled potatoes or rice, green peas, boiled cabbage, or a green salad. Serve also flatbread (crackers) or whole-grain bread.

EASY-COOK FISH IN CASSEROLE

Layer fish in an oiled casserole dish with ingredients in previous recipe and cheese (optional), and bake for 30 minutes in 350° oven. Or replace onions and tomatoes with 8-ounce package defrosted frozen spinach or mixed vegetables. Bake potatoes as fish bakes.

FISH SOUP

4	cups fish stock or bouillon
7	oz. milk
1½–2	tbsp. corn starch
1	large carrot
½	cup chopped leek or other vegetable, or 3 tbsp. chopped chives
½–⅔	lbs. fish, cut in pieces

Boil water and stock. Stir in cold milk, which has been mixed with corn starch. Add vegetables and fish. Turn down the heat, and let soup simmer until vegetables are soft and fish is cooked, about 10–15 minutes. Season to taste. Serve with bread or rolls.

This everyday soup can be made into a luxurious meal by adding shrimp or mussels.

SIMPLE BOILED FISH

2–3	liters (or quarts) water
1.5	kilos (3 lbs., 5 oz.) cod (or similar fish), cut in pieces
½	cup salt (or less to taste)

Bring salted water to a boil and add fish, lowering heat. Simmer until fish skin comes loose, approximately 10 minutes. Drain and serve with boiled potatoes and salad. Reserve water for sauces or other cooking.

WHITE SAUCE

2 tbsp. butter
2 tbsp. flour
2 cups fish water/stock, vegetable or meat stock, or bouillon
   Salt and pepper to taste
   Optional: 1 tbsp. or more paprika, curry, or dill

Melt butter in small saucepan and add flour, stirring constantly. Cook over low heat for one minute. Slowly add 2 cups liquid, stirring constantly. Add optional seasoning. Bring sauce to a boil, reduce heat, and cook for 10 minutes. Experiment with seasonings for different flavored sauces. This sauce goes well with any type of boiled or plain fish, or over cooked vegetables such as carrots, peas, and beans.

SATURDAY NIGHT PORRIDGE

Mix cooked rice with milk until oatmeal consistency. Serve hot, adding desired amounts of butter and sugar. For another typical Saturday night meal, try whole-grain pancakes (minus the syrup or jam) and tomato soup.

NORWEGIAN DESSERT CRACKERS
(also good for breakfast)

Crumble whole-grain crackers (flatbread) into a bowl. Add milk or *kefir* (yogurt drink) and jam.

GRETE WAITZ'S
NO-TIME-TO-COOK COOKBOOK

Although I wouldn't put myself in the same league with Julia Child, I have invented a few quick meals of my own.

MATPAKKE SANDWICH

Norwegian cheese is generally of two types, goat's cheese, most commonly geitost (a naturally sweet, hard, light-brown cheese with a caramellike flavor, often fortified with iron) or jarlsberg or other hard yellow or white cheese. To make this open-faced sandwich, use heavy whole-grain bread. Slice bread thick, and use a cheese cutter, a Norwegian invention that guarantees the slices will be thin. You can also make the sandwich with meat or fish. Many people use butter or margarine, but I never eat either as I don't like them.

Simply use less filling for thinner, presliced bread. Don't overdo the protein and/or fat. The majority of the sandwich should be bread. I always say that my sandwiches are bread with something, not something with bread. In fact, one of my pet peeves when eating out is that sandwiches are made the opposite way I like them—too much filling, not enough bread. I often have to pick out half the filling from the sandwich.

If you're tired of the typical fillings, try making them more creative. Add curry or grated carrots to tuna fish; blend tofu or cottage cheese with peanut butter; and/or add nuts and raisins. And you don't have to pack a sandwich. Try cereal with powdered milk (just add water), or dinner leftovers.

HOMEMADE TWO-STEP
TOMATO VEGETABLE SOUP, serves 2

1   12-oz. can V-8 or tomato juice
¼   lb. shrimp, fish pieces, or fishballs, tofu, or other protein
1   cup frozen or fresh vegetables, such as cauliflower, broccoli, leeks, squash, or ½ cup sautéed onion

Combine all ingredients and cook over medium heat until vegetables are desired softness.

BAKED POTATO MEAL-IN-ONE

Scrub baking potato thoroughly with vegetable brush to remove any dirt. Bake in microwave oven 350° for seven minutes or in regular oven at 350° for 45 minutes to 1 hour (cook a few extra for later, to reheat or even eat cold). Put ½–¾ cup cottage cheese (or plain yogurt) in hot potato and sprinkle with vegetable salt. Serve with salad.

MY SHOPPING BASKET

As the right eating requires the right ingredients, I'm as conscientious about my food shopping as I am about my eating. If you're careful about your diet, be just as careful about your shopping. Be a good consumer. Take a little extra time and effort to read labels, compare products, check for freshness.

I shop daily and enjoy the benefits of a small, family-owned neighborhood supermarket, where I know the owners and trust the quality. This market also has a kitchen, where meals are prepared that I often buy for Jack, who sometimes tires of my same old fare. (My sparse menu doesn't bother me, though. I'm a real creature of habit.)

Below are the items in my shopping basket on a daily to weekly basis:

All-Bran or Bran Buds cereal, low-fat kefir and yogurt, cottage cheese, diet Coke, mineral water, V-8 juice, tomato juice, orange juice, cheese (jarlsberg, carraway, geitost, pepper cheese, or camembert for special occasions), fish pâté (made with halibut and bass), mixed frozen vegetables, tuna (in water only), low-calorie Thousand Island salad dressing, bread, fiber crackers, shrimp, caviar spread (not the exotic type, a reasonably priced version in a tube), cold seafood, prepared chicken, salad vegetables, fruit, sweet biscuits, jam (in Norway it's more like fruit preserves, made with less sugar), decaffeinated coffee, English Breakfast tea.

TEN COMMONSENSE RULES OF NUTRITION

from the Norwegian Nutrition Council

Take time to enjoy your meals.
Balanced meals of basic foods are vital.
Don't overeat. Eat only at fixed mealtimes.
Eat more bread, preferably whole-grain.
Eat fish often, both for dinner and in sandwiches.
Eat more fruit, vegetables, and potatoes.
Use fats sparingly; eat lean.
Be careful with sugar, junk food, and snacks.
If you're thirsty, drink water.

TIPS FOR ATHLETES

Prerun eating—the rule of thumb is not to eat anything for a minimum of two to three hours before a run. Avoid large meals or foods that are difficult to digest (*e.g.*, meat and other heavy protein, spicy or fatty foods, and roughage). In general, I'll have a salad no later than four hours before a run, bread about two hours before, and a light noon meal before a hard afternoon run. Avoid anything sweet immediately before a run, which may cause hypoglycemia (low blood sugar), resulting in extreme fatigue. Experiment with different eating/

running combinations until you discover what works best for you.

Prerace—it is even more important to be careful about your diet if you are racing or doing a hard workout. For example, avoid excessive caffeine or alcohol consumption (I wouldn't have alcohol at all before a race), especially important on a warm day, as they cause dehydration. Often, nervousness and the intensity of your effort combine to aggravate your stomach. What's best for me is toast and tea, or something equivalently light, four to six hours prior to a race. Remember that what you eat before any event less than two hours in duration does not aid you in your effort.

GENERAL TIPS

Many runners fail to drink enough fluids before, during, and after exercise. Thirst is not an indicator of your need to drink. In hot weather, drink one cup of water for every fifty pounds of body weight or eight ounces for every fifteen minutes of activity. Remember to replenish fluids, but do not fall into the common trap that nutritionists such as Ingrid Ellingson Lie warn against: too many sugary drinks, whether it's soda or fruit juice. Water is the preferable drink. If you like flavor, try adding a bit of lemon or a spoonful of frozen juice.

- Limit beer and wine consumption. Up to seventy additives have been found in some beers and wines.*
- Avoid vitamin overdose. This is another habit athletes can be prone to develop. Nutritionist Lie and others caution against megadoses of vitamins.
- Eat smart when eating out.
- As I spend so much time away from home, much to my dismay I am forced to make eating out a habit. It is possible, however, to order the right type of meal. Order foods broiled, baked, or grilled, without heavy sauce—and go with something familiar (that's why

---

*Gloria Averbuch, *L'eggs Running and Fitness Guide for Women* (Winston-Salem, NC: L'eggs Products Inc., 1985).

I usually order fish). Request sauce or dressing on the side, and don't hesitate to ask how a dish is prepared. If you want to reduce the fat/calorie content, take excess filling out of sandwiches, slide some of the cheese off pizza, and take the skin off chicken. Because I am unsure of the size of the meals, which are often insufficient for a hungry distance runner, I keep snacks like crackers and fruit in my hotel room.

HEALTH AND COOKING TIPS

- Eat as much of your food raw as possible.
- Use low-fat dairy products like ricotta, cottage, or farmer's cheese, instead of cream cheese or full-fat hard cheese. Or cut the heavier variety with the lighter, using a mixture of the two in sandwiches and cooking.
- Cut mayonnaise, sour cream, or other such dressings or sauces with yogurt, broth, milk, or lemon juice (in tuna fish or potato salad, for example). Change the proportions gradually if you need to acquire a taste for the lighter version. Eventually, you may be able to do without the heavy stuff entirely. If the dish seems too dry, add more of the liquids.
- Cut salad dressing with lemon or vinegar. Try eating salad with only lemon or vinegar, emphasizing herbs and other seasonings for taste.
- Use soy products in place of conventional protein sources. Soy flakes or soy grits can be used instead of meat or cheese in such dishes as casseroles, spaghetti sauce, lasagna, Mexican food, and stew. (Presoak the soy flakes or grits, or add extra water and/or tomato sauce to the dish if unsoaked.) Tofu goes nicely with noodle or rice dishes or whipped in the blender with lemon juice, yogurt or water, and herbs as salad dressing.
- Avoid oil by using water to cook vegetables in recipes that call for them sautéed or fried. Use a steamer for other cooked vegetables, and bake rather than fry such vegetables as eggplant.
- Use water in which potatoes or vegetables have been cooked or steamed—for sauces, in bread, to cook rice, or in any other recipe

that calls for liquid. If there is no immediate use for this water, refrigerate or freeze it (in premeasured proportions if desired).

- If you use white flour, add some bran to it.
- Rinse or drain tuna fish or canned vegetables or fruits, even if packed in water, to reduce the salt or sugar in the water. Don't hesitate to rinse any food (even prepared) that contains excess salt or fat.
- Dilute juice or soda with as much water as possible.
- Cut out up to half the sugar called for in baking recipes, or replace sugar with frozen fruit juice or mashed ripe fruit, like bananas or pears. Make desserts with a fruit base rather than with such things as chocolate, cream cheese, or whipped cream.
- For healthy snacks, keep raw vegetables on hand or freeze berries, orange slices, or juice in ice-cube trays. Freeze flavored yogurt to satisfy ice-cream cravings.

14

Restoration Therapy

RECOVERY FOR BETTER PERFORMANCE

This is the era of prevention—preventive dentistry, nutrition, and medicine, which are all therapies. In fact, for many people running and fitness are a form of preventive therapy: against the illness and disease associated with a sedentary life. Rather than deal with injury treatment in the traditional mode, I have chosen to discuss restoration therapy, an ongoing system of self-care, the purpose of which is to reduce injuries, increase conditioning, and improve performance.

I have been using some of the systems of restoration therapy for years as a natural part of my training program. Other aspects, such as massage and ultrasound, I began only after many years of hard training, when it became clear I needed to be more careful to keep my body in good condition, as time seems to be taking its toll. For example, the time needed for recovery from races and hard workouts has lengthened with the number of years I've been running. If I were a car, I'd merely have the necessary parts replaced. But, of course, it isn't that easy; there's no trading myself in for a new model. I've got to keep the old one healthy, as I plan, like most of you, to be running for the rest of my life. For example, in 1981 I began treatment with two New York sports podiatrists, Dr. Lou Galli and Dr. Josef Geldwert. We don't even have this type of podiatrist in Norway.

I am very fortunate that I have rarely been injured in my career.

Even when I have been, I resorted to medication only once, and I have never had surgery. This is very rare among runners on my level, especially those who have been at it for as many years as I have. This good health profile is probably due to a variety of factors: a combination of inborn traits, biomechanics, luck, instinct, and exercise and diet habits.

However, running as long and as hard as I have been, some injury is probably inevitable. It's an occupational hazard and a risk for anyone who runs. Advice on care and prevention of injury, in conjunction with the sensible training and lifestyle habits on which I have elaborated, will keep you healthy both *in* the long run and *for* the long run.

The few times I have been injured, like most athletes, I've had to learn the hard way about cures. If I had taken better care of myself, listened to my body, and taken a preventive attitude, perhaps I could have avoided injury in the first place. Most of my injuries have come from running in the difficult winter conditions in Norway: on snow, on ice, or in mud, where the footing is poor. In fact, my first injury, shin splints at age fifteen, came from running on snow and ice. I have learned, therefore, that part of prevention means either avoiding these surfaces or taking certain special precautions if they are unavoidable.

Even after an injury would occur, in my impatience I often failed to take sufficient care and rest and so would reinjure myself. I know that time heals, but, often, I was faced with the dilemma that the time just wasn't there. The Olympics or a World Championships won't wait, and on a few occasions I have had to take my chances running while injured. It was under these circumstances that I was forced to realize there are times my body doesn't care what the event is; I simply cannot perform.

Although I knew I must run pain-free to be healed, I was always testing myself. Injury prevention is a process of learning to listen to your body communicate with you. Pain is telling you something. Don't shut out its message by ignoring it or trying to cover it up with painkilling medication.

Sometimes, however, I have not been good at listening to my body, because I didn't want to hear what it was telling me. Rest and recuperation, as for many runners, is difficult for me. I just didn't want to take time off or change my routine. After all these years I should know better, and although I've greatly improved, this failure is still one of my weaknesses. In many cases, doctors or other professionals have served me well in this regard and will likely do the same for you. If they tell me I must take time off or find alternative training to get healthy, then I'll do it. Sometimes I need to hear it from an authority. I tend to listen better, feeling more confident that the time off from serious training is absolutely necessary.

When looking for advice on or treatment of an injury, it's best to find an expert in the field. Sports-related professionals better understand me as an athlete and as a person. As far as I'm concerned, a good doctor does not enter the room smoking a cigarette, weighing 300 pounds, and then simply tell me (or any serious runner) to take three weeks off.

Marc Chasnov, a registered physical therapist with a degree in movement science and one of the experts whom I have met in the United States, was referred to me by one of his patients, world-class miler Eamonn Coghlan. Chasnov also treats other athletes, from weight lifters to dancers to swimmers, including Olympic gold medal swimmer Rick Carey. Chasnov, known as "magic fingers," is also writing a book called *Getting the Body Better* and is a proponent of restoration therapy. I believe this therapy is the wave of the future, especially with the trend toward longer and harder training in running, as well as in all endurance sports.

RESTORATION THERAPY:
A DEFINITION

Restoration therapy is also known as recovery or recuperation. It refers to the muscles and key physiological processes essential to the athlete. Restoration, however, is not meant in the passive sense; nor does it indicate the general meaning of rest. Moreover, it is a specific function, utilizing a variety of methods, many of which are discussed below.

All forms of exercise can be viewed as a breaking-down process. Restoration is a means of limiting or slowing down that process. It encourages healing of the muscles, making them less susceptible to injury, and enhances performance. The purpose of restoration therapy is to develop a better-working body and maintain health, especially for increasing workout loads.

Restoration therapy employs methods of physical therapy applied for different purposes to athletes. Traditional methods of restoration include alternative sports (*e.g.*, cycling, swimming, ballet, yoga, aerobics), stretching and strengthening exercises, and, for injury prevention or treatment, massage, hydrotherapy (swimming pools, whirlpools, baths), ultrasound (sound waves used for healing), and electrical muscle stimulation.

I have already touched on part of the preventive aspect of this therapy, the concept of overall fitness, one of the necessary foundations I stressed for beginning runners and children. According to Marc Chasnov, rather than running fifty minutes, you can likely be as effective with thirty minutes of running and the remaining twenty with exercises. My general strength comes from my training background, like running up hills and over rough Norwegian terrain. The exercises in this section duplicate that strength and are an important addition to maintaining balanced conditioning, which is especially important as you get older, when the muscles just aren't as springy as they once were.

The philosophy of restoration therapy is to cure injury by the most natural means possible. The more conservative self-help methods of healing should be tried before resorting to the more traditional methods, such as medication or surgery. According to Chasnov, although restoration therapy has been prevalent in Europe for ten years, it's likely it may not catch on in the United States for another ten. "It clashes with the prevailing attitude of the medical system," he contends. "Why use massage as a treatment when you can take a pill and see more rapid results?"

As previously mentioned, restoration therapy is active, not passive. Therefore, the prescription for injury is not rest or inactivity, but movement and alternate exercise, much like the active rest I have discussed earlier. This may mean light exercises different from running as well as nonsports methods such as massage or hydrotherapy, all of which have been shown by research to promote faster recovery. My active rest for treatment of and recovery from injury has combined stationary biking, massage, whirlpool, and, although I'm not a good swimmer, even just kicking around in the pool.

MASSAGE

Massage is one of the most widely used methods of restoration, and it functions as both a preventive and a curative means. The main purpose of massage, besides relaxation, is to enhance blood circulation and get rid of tissue wastes, like lactic acid, thereby speeding recovery.

I believe everyone who runs should be massaged. In fact, everyone who lives should be massaged! Runners work hard, and especially at the top level massage helps to counter constant stress and strain by providing a form of relaxation. It's also an important psychological aid, as runners "get something back" for all the work they put in. The hands-on approach of massage is especially significant. As New Yorker Bruria Ginton, RMT (registered massage therapist), puts it, "We are a touch-deprived society. Massage is a physical stroking of the psyche."

How do you find a good massage therapist? I know a good therapist by the way the massage feels. Some have the technique but not the touch. A good therapist can feel how your body responds and pays special attention to the tone and state of the muscles. You also get used to one another, and he or she becomes familiar with your body. In addition, according to Ginton, a good therapist will have a professional work environment and will ask questions about your medical history, specific muscle problems, and diet and exercise habits.

I didn't always take advantage of the benefits of massage, but in the last four years, with more and more miles of marathon training, aging, and having more time, I now get a massage three times a week (Monday, Wednesday, and Friday), mostly the legs, but once a week the back as well. Bruria was the first person to give me a full body massage in 1981. Since that time, I get treatment from her before and after my New York races. Marc Chasnov recommends a massage at least once a week to keep your muscles at a high level of health, most efficient, and performing better. He stresses the following areas for runners: the calves, thighs, shins, the sides of legs, the buttocks, and the lower back.

As a curative technique, massage is effective against micro traumas and injuries by working out dead blood cells and, in later stages, scar tissue. "But expect it to hurt," warns Chasnov. "A light massage is not fair to the muscles. A runner's muscles exert tremendous force over a constant time period, and those muscles should be worked as hard as they work." Sure enough, after a massage from Chasnov, I feel as though I've run 100 miles! But three days later I feel good and loose.

Get By with a Little Help from Your Friends

Although not as effective as having professional treatment, a friend can give you a massage or you can do self-massage, both of which are still beneficial to a certain degree. (See pages 234–35.) But give fair warning to a friend: it's hard work. Bruria taught Jack some massage methods, but I hesitate to ask him to use them as it's so tiring. He's good for about four or five minutes, then he loses the touch. Once in a while we trade off doing each other's legs, which is a good idea as trading a massage usually elicits more enthusiasm.

Experts have shown that self-massage during warm-up mobilizes the energy of the muscles for impending work. Often, you'll see runners rubbing their legs before a race and shaking out their arms and legs to loosen the muscles. "A loose muscle performs better," says Chasnov. "Everything should feel like Jell-O."

PSYCHO-REGULATORY TRAINING

The basic function of sports psychology is to direct you to your goals from a mental perspective. Much of this "mind training" can be done by athletes themselves with the techniques discussed in Chapter 7. One of the latest trends is the development of the field of sports psychology, which has been used successfully by athletes in every sport. Sports psychologists often use such aids as specially selected music, colors, and states of hypnosis. Among runners, Ingrid Kristiansen attributes much of her confidence to a sports psychologist she sees in Norway. In my case, Jack actually serves as my sports psychologist. Before a race we go over all the details, and although this chitchat seems informal, it is Jack's way of giving me confidence. Anyone who provides positive reinforcement, relaxation, and confidence and helps alleviate pressure can somewhat serve the function of a sports psychologist.

NUTRITION

Nutrition also plays an important part in restoration. However, its use in this context is more complex and specific than simply making sure to eat a balanced diet. The trend is toward scientific dietary analysis, using a nutritionist in order to determine dietary balance. As the body is balanced biochemically, the right chemical balance from the proper nutrition gives it the ability to recover from physical efforts. For example, it is now well known that in long races the body loses electrolytes. It was due to my blood testing that an electrolyte deficiency was discovered, and so I began to use an electrolyte-replacement drink.

EXERCISES

The following exercises are recommended by Marc Chasnov. Stretching can be divided into two types. One is static, which means the joints move only to a minor degree while the muscles stretch. This is the type commonly done by runners. The other is dynamic, or active, in which the muscles stretch as the joints move. This type of stretch moves the muscles and joints throughout the entire range of motion. For a comprehensive stretching program, begin with a set of static stretches before going on to the dynamic stretches. Make sure you are sufficiently warmed up before beginning any stretching or strengthening exercises.

Static Stretches

Hold all stretch positions for ten to twenty seconds, without bouncing. Feel a good stretch, but never push to the point of pain. Repeat each stretch about five times.

- For the *calves* and *Achilles*. "Wall Stretch." Placing hands against a wall, bend right leg at the knee and position between body and the wall. Lean into the wall while keeping the left foot flat on the floor. Stretch with the back leg straight; then, to stretch the Achilles, do the stretch with the left knee bent (see illustration on next page). You will feel the stretch shift to your lower calf when you bend the knee. Reverse legs and repeat.

WALL STRETCH

• For the *quadriceps* and *hamstrings*. "Hurdle Stretch." To do the hurdle stretch, assume the position shown in the illustration below. To stretch the quadricep, lean back as far as possible. If you can, go back until you are laying flat on the floor. For the hamstring, remain in the same position while leaning forward over the extended leg. Reverse legs and repeat.

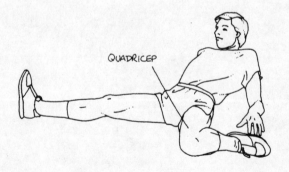

HURDLE STRETCH

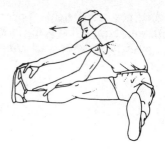

STRADDLE STRETCH
FOR THE ROTATIONAL MUSCLES

HAMSTRING

STRADDLE STRETCH

• For the *hamstring* and *back*. "Straddle Stretch." Sit in a straddle position and reach forward toward the knees or the toes, as far as you can. To stretch the rotational muscles in the back, touch the opposite hand to the opposite toe. The straddle stretch for the hamstrings can also be done with a partner.

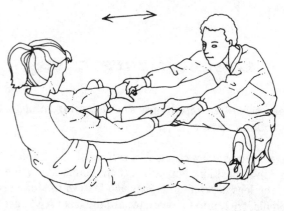

STRADDLE STRETCH WITH A PARTNER

- For the *upper body* (this is also a good posture stretch). "Upper Back Stretch." Stand in a doorway with your arms out at your sides and walk forward until your chest is pushed out with your arms extended behind you.

UPPER BACK STRETCH

Dynamic Stretches

Do between six to ten repetitions, slowly moving through the full range of motion and coming back to the start.

- For the *gluteus*, *quadriceps*, and *hamstrings*. "Split Squat." Take a fencer's lunge position. You will feel the emphasis in the various parts of the legs depending on how you lean in the lunge position. For example, try leaning forward toward the front leg to get a better stretch of the hamstring, or try lunging lower to stretch the groin. Straighten the knees and bend them to repeat lunge. Reverse legs and repeat. (This stretch is particularly effective as it works the muscles in a way that simulates the pattern of the stride. As you get more accustomed to the stretch, speed it up in order to increase the muscles' reactivity; again, this simulates your running.)

SPLIT SQUAT

• For the *Achilles*. Do the "Split Squat" with one leg elevated on a bench or chair. Keeping the foot flat on the bench, lean forward, putting the stomach on the front thigh. Lean so that the knee is positioned over the toe. Reverse legs and repeat. (See illustration on next page.)

SPLIT SQUAT
WITH A BENCH

- For the *hamstrings*. "Butt-Ups." Stand keeping your feet together and heels flat on the ground. Bending your knees, grab your ankles or calves, bringing your head as close to the knees as possible. Straighten the knees as much as possible while keeping your head on the legs. Repeat by bending the knees and straightening again.

BUTT-UPS

- For the *rotational muscles*. "Trunk Twist." Stand with your arms out and your feet apart. Twist your upper body from side to side. As the running stride entails a cross rotation pattern of the trunk and the hips, this exercise in a warm-up helps permit a looser and more fluid stride.

TRUNK TWIST

- For the *lower back*. "Lower Back Stretch." Sit with your legs apart and slide your hands down your legs until you are bent in half. Or while standing do the same, taking care to keep the buttocks over the legs, not sticking out. You can also do this exercise with your hands behind your head. (See illustration on next page.)

LOWER BACK STRETCH
(SITTING)

LOWER BACK STRETCH
(STANDING)

Strengthening Exercises

You can use the same dynamic stretching to do strengthening (except for Butt-Ups). When you can successfully do four sets of ten of the dynamic stretches, with about ten seconds' rest between sets, and you feel comfortable and the technique and rhythm are good, start to add resistance, or weight. For the Split Squat, Trunk Twist, and Lower Back Stretch, wear a weighted backpack or hold a bar or book behind your neck. You can also create resistance by holding a role of pennies in each hand, or other hand weights, or plastic milk bottles filled with sand to various weights. A partner can be used for both stretching and resistance.

LOWER BACK STRETCH
WITH A WEIGHT

SPLIT SQUAT
WITH A WEIGHT

Other common strengthening exercises are sit-ups, which should always be done with bent knees, and push-ups. If ordinary push-ups are too tough, do the modified version, putting your weight on your hands and knees (rather than feet). To stretch out and loosen the muscles after working them, do the Upper Body Stretch after both sit-ups and push-ups, and also do the Trunk Twist after sit-ups.

SELF-MASSAGE

The following self-massage techniques come from Bruria Ginton.

- One self-massage technique is "friction," designed specifically to loosen stiff or sore areas. Make a slow circular movement in which you press, squeeze, and knead with either your thumb or with your other four fingers, using your thumb as an anchor. Gently apply pressure at first, using larger circles over muscle tissue, such as in the legs, and small circles over the bony areas of the joints. Gradually increase the pressure as you rub, but never beyond the point of pain.
- Another technique is "modified effleurage," like the Swedish movement effleurage, designed specifically to increase circulation. Spread the fingers of your hands and perform a pulling motion in a rakelike manner. Again, pressure should be applied, but always lighter than the pain threshold.
- "Pressure point" massage (associated with shiatsu and reflexology) is useful for areas like the hands and feet, and is believed to relieve pain and aid relaxation in the rest of the body. Use your thumb, leaning into each point *as you exhale*. This is very important, as it is your breathing that actually triggers the relaxation mechanism throughout the body.

MASSAGE TIPS

1. You need not apply a lot of pressure in your massage strokes for effective results. When in doubt, underpress rather than overpress.
2. When doing modified effleurage, always stroke toward the heart. This facilitates blood flow. Avoid massaging in the opposite direction, which is against the flow of blood.
3. Do not massage your legs if you have varicose veins.
4. Refrain from massage if you feel you are coming down with a cold or flu or are running a fever.
5. Although you can use various general oils or creams, a specially

formulated massage oil might be best as it provides the right consistency. A good massage oil will have a pleasant fragrance, be easy to wipe off, and leave the skin feeling smooth.

GENERAL TIPS

The following is based on my experience, with the advice of Marc Chasnov.

- After a race or hard training, take a cool bath or shower, at a temperature below that of the body (98.6 degrees). Research in Eastern Europe has shown that the sooner a hot shower is taken after training, the longer it takes to recover.
- Cover your legs before and after a race or workout, even in warm weather. European track runners are very good about keeping their sweats on. Don't think it's too hot to need them. Even in 90-degree weather the temperature is still eight degrees less than that of your body. If it's hot, however, I don't warm up in sweats because I don't want excessive sweating to cause dehydration.
- Don't run in cold weather with shorts, even in races. It hampers the efficiency of the muscles. If you warm up in tights or long pants and feel comfortable, not overheated, keep them on. If you see goose bumps on your bare legs, they are too cold.
- Good posture is part of a good structural framework, and it ensures everything will work better, from breathing to digestion.
- To aid relaxation, have a massage of the back, neck, and face.

We have tried to equip you with as many resources as possible to get you from "start to finish" in your running and back again. Some additional tips follow in the Appendices. However, as helpful as this information can be, it is still only words. We know there is one thing we cannot give you, and that is the success that lies in the doing. So, here's to many healthy and happy days on the road, and may you be in it for the very long run.

Appendices

CAREER HIGHLIGHTS

Marathon Performances

1978	Winner, New York City Marathon First marathon	2:32:30 (World Best)
1979	Winner, New York City Marathon First woman under 2:30	2:27:33 (World Best)
1980	Winner, New York City Marathon	2:25:42 (World Best)
1982	Winner, New York City Marathon	2:27:14
1983	Winner, London Marathon	2:25:29 (World Best)

1983	Gold Medal, IAAF World Championships	2:28:09
1983	Winner, New York City Marathon	2:27:00
1984	Silver Medal, Olympic Games	2:26:18
1984	Winner, New York City Marathon	2:29:30
1985	Winner, New York City Marathon Ninth sub-2:30 marathon: has broken 2:30 more times than any other woman	2:28:34

Cross-Country Titles

Five-time IAAF World Cross Country Champion (one of only two women ever to capture this many titles)

1978	Gold Medal, Glasgow, Scotland
1979	Gold Medal, Limerick, Ireland
1980	Gold Medal, Paris, France
1981	Gold Medal, Madrid, Spain
1982	Bronze Medal, Rome, Italy
1983	Gold Medal, Gateshead, England
1984	Bronze Medal, Meadowlands, NJ, USA

Ten-time winner of the world's largest cross-country race, Lidingöloppet, held annually in Stockholm, 1976–85

Track Highlights

1970   Norwegian Junior Champion, 400m and 800m
        (age 16)

1972   1,500m Olympian

1974   Bronze Medal, European Championships, 1,500m

1975   World Record, 3,000m, 8:46.6

1976   Semifinalist, Olympics, 1,500m

1976   World Record, 3,000m, 8:45.4

1977   Winner, World Cup, 3,000m

1978   Bronze Medal, European Championships, 3,000m

Personal Records

800m	2:03.10	Oslo 1975
1,000	2:39.73	London 1977
1,500m	4:00.55	Prague 1978
1 mile	4:26.90	Gateshead 1978
3,000m	8:31.75	Oslo 1979
5,000m	15:08.80	Oslo 1982

Road Racing Highlights

Six-time winner L'eggs Mini Marathon (30:59.8, 1980, Current World
    Best)

1980 Winner *Runner's World* Midnight Run, 5 miles, 25:21 (Current World Best)

1984 Winner Gasparilla 15k, 47:52 (Current World Best)

Awards and Rankings

1975   Ranked number 1 in the world by *Track & Field News* in the 1,500m and 3,000m (Mary Decker Slaney is the only other woman to ever achieve this double ranking)

1977/78   Ranked number 1 in the world in the 3,000m by *Track & Field News*

1978/79   Two-time recipient of the Paavo Nurmi Award, given annually to top male and female runners by *Runner's World*

1978–80, 1982/83   Five-times ranked number 1 in the world in the marathon by *Track & Field News*

1980   One of *People* magazine's "Notable Personalities of the Year"

1982   St. Olav's Medal recipient, given by the king of Norway for outstanding citizenship (Grete is the only athlete ever to receive this honor)

1983   Volvo Prize recipient, given annually to the best sportsperson in the Nordic countries

1984   Monique Berlieux Prize recipient, given by the French Academy of Sports (Grete is the first non-French person to receive this honor)

1985   Elected to the executive board of the Norwegian Olympic Committee

Shoes:
The Tools of Your Trade

The following consumer running-shoe tips are based on information from Bill Mintiens, sport shoe product manager, Adidas, USA; Horst Widmann, advanced product research, Adidas, Germany; and from what I have learned throughout years of running and competing.

- Never run in any shoe but a running shoe. When purchasing shoes, go to a running-shoe specialty store for the most knowledgeable sales force. The staff usually knows the gear and the sport. Bring in your old running shoes if you have any questions or want advice.
- When trying on shoes, don't stand or jog on a rug, but rather on a hard surface, which duplicates the surface on which you will actually use the shoes. Try on the shoes with the type of socks you wear when running.
- Try to run in the shoes. Some stores have test models in which to run; others, especially in malls, will allow you to run outside. Others even have treadmills or runways in the store.
- Ask questions, including if you can return the shoes if they aren't right. If a problem does arise, first check your own running (*e.g.*, too great an increase in mileage or a sudden change in running surface). If you do return shoes, remember, *explain, don't complain*. You'll get better results.

What to Look for in a Shoe

- *Accurate Fit*. A shoe must immediately feel good and firm. There should be no need to "break in" a running shoe. If the shoes don't feel comfortable in the store, it's unlikely they'll feel any better later. What best suits you will depend on body size, foot type, and anticipated mileage.

- *Cushion/support.* Look for a good arch support and heel counter for lateral stability. Cushioning/support is important to every runner, but to what degree depends on your mileage, running surfaces, running style, and body build. Don't be concerned with the weight of the shoe. It is generally not the case that the lighter the shoe the better.
- *Long-term durability.* A running shoe's midsole should be resistant to compression. Polyurethane midsoles have been shown to have a slower compression rate than EVA (ethyl vinyl acetate—a midsole material) or premolded EVA shoes, a feature of racing shoes.
- *Training shoes.* A good training shoe will provide maximum shock absorption and stability. Look for all of the other above features as well.
- *Racing shoes.* The major difference between training and racing shoes is weight. If you use a lighter racing shoe, you will have to sacrifice some of the cushioning and stability of the training shoe. In racing shoes, look for flexibility and a glovelike fit. They are designed in such a way that your feet feel the ground more. Racing shoes can provide a good physical and psychological edge for those concerned with running fast, but don't feel you have to have them. By no means sacrifice the important support features of training shoes if you need them to prevent injury.

Shoe Care

- Alternate shoes. Have two to three different pairs of various styles, which may be suitable for different surfaces, speeds, and distances. What you use may be based on a subjective feeling as well. You might want a lighter shoe on a day you feel good and want to run fast, and a heavier shoe for longer distances or slower running.
- Shoes take anywhere from twenty-four to thirty-six hours to dry completely from perspiration or rain. Shoes with EVA midsoles take approximately twenty-four hours to "rebound" completely and return to their prerun shape. Always take out removable insoles, and

if the shoes are very wet, stuff them with newspaper to dry or even wooden or plastic shoe inserts to retain their shape.
- Washing shoes is not recommended, but if you must, wash them by hand with mild soap and water.
- Never dry shoes in the sun or near a heater.
- For those who prefer to run without socks (or who get sweaty feet), use a sprinkling of corn starch or powder.

Shoe Wear

- Shoes last anywhere from 500 to 1,000 miles of running.
- At about 250 miles, begin to keep a careful eye on shoe wear.
- When the soles are compressed 20 to 30 percent, it's time for a new pair.
- To check shoe wear, place shoes on a flat surface at eye level. They should maintain an even plane, not fall or rise on any side.
- Check compression by trying on shoes without the removable insoles. If the shoe conforms to your foot, it's a likely sign that compression is setting in. Or try old shoes on with new ones. The old will feel significantly flatter. Any sudden pains, often in the knees, are also an indication of possible compression problems.

Other Shoe Features

- If you run at night, buying shoes with some reflective material is strongly recommended.
- Don't be confused by various shoe-lacing systems. They all give about the same support and comfort, so choose what feels best. Keep in mind that laces will move after about four weeks due to some stretching in the shoes.

- Orthotics—these are shoe inserts designed to correct structural weakness, imbalance, or leg-length discrepancy. They are custom-fitted by a podiatrist. There is a feeling among some experts that in the past few years there has been an overuse of these devices. Manufacturers are now trying to build correctional features into the shoes for foot and leg problems.
- Sorbothane is a material used in special shoe inserts and has been shown to absorb up to 94 percent of impact shock. However, some studies have shown that with moderate to quick-paced running the compressed material does not rebound to its original state between foot strikes. For slower running and walking, however, this may not be the case. Because the material is heavy, it is recommended that these inserts be used only for impact-related injuries or problems.

Shoe Trends

- The current trend in shoe design is away from soft shoes and toward a more firm, supportive shoe in training, racing, and walking. In one test, soft-soled shoes compressed 50 percent after only 500 miles of running.
- The trend in manufacturing is to produce quality technical shoes at reasonable prices. Rather than spending $100 on top-priced shoes, you can get good running shoes in the $35–$65 price range (as of late 1985).
- The trend in women's shoes is to produce models especially made for them, rather than just men's shoes adapted for women. Although a woman can wear either men's or women's models, anyone with the classic woman's foot shape should seek out shoes designed for her.
- Another notable trend is the computerization of shoes. Technical improvements due to extensive research have combined with the computer age to create shoes with micropacers. Several manufacturers now make these shoes, which log miles, time, pace, and calories burned.
- As so much research has been devoted to the bottoms of shoes, look

for changes in the tops. A long-range trend will likely be toward changes in the upper materials of shoes, replacing nylon and leather with more breathable materials that also resist heat buildup.

My Running Shoes

- I train in several Adidas models and race in the Adidas Grete Waitz Competition and Marathon Competition. Obviously, for longer distances I wear a shoe with more cushioning, and a lighter, firmer shoe for fast running or races in the 10km range.
- My training shoes last anywhere from two to three months, averaging over ninety miles of running per week. Racing shoes last longer, as I don't use them as much. I do my hard training with racing shoes, and I like to keep a pair of racing shoes I use only for races.
- I retire my shoes when I feel they are giving me less cushioning and support, and when they look like two old pizzas!
- Because I frequently run in the mud and rain in Oslo, I sometimes wash my shoes by hand with a fingernail brush (usually at the point when I can't see what color they are). I stuff them with newspaper to dry.
- I wear short socks in summer, and long ones in winter to keep my ankles and calves warm, and to keep the wind from coming up through my pantlegs.

LIFE ON THE ROAD

Running has taken me all over the world. In nearly forty countries and countless cities, I have run everywhere from beaches and back roads to major city streets, and I've learned a lot about life on the road. Whether you run to maintain fitness or to take part in a race, running in a new environment can enrich your trip. Because I have spent as long as four to five months of the year away from home, I have outlined some tips for taking your sport on the road.

Preparing to Go

- Find a travel agent sympathetic to your way of life. Explain your lifestyle and your needs, requesting hotels situated near parks or other running areas. A number of major hotels now have some kind of fitness-related information, like running maps or health club directories, and some even have in-house exercise facilities.
- There are a number of special travel packages to major races, with provisions for the entire family. For other race information, write the race organizer, or contact the local road runners club or "Y." If outside the United States, contact the country's sports federation through the embassy or the telephone book. Major running magazines also list races abroad.
- If you are traveling to a marathon or are racing seriously, allow enough time and energy for both sight-seeing and the race effort, or de-emphasize one of them.
- Pack light. Bring running gear that's easily washable and quick-drying. Polypropylene is a good material for winter wear, and nylon running suits are functional in all weather. Pack plastic bags to carry shoes and wet or dirty gear. Take insoles out of running shoes to speed drying time. If you must pack wet clothes after a run, remove them first thing on arrival. I purchase a small box of laundry detergent or bring some in a plastic bag, and I do all my running laundry by hand in hotel sinks or bathtubs. Small items are most easily done this way. Besides, I've tried a hotel laundry for bigger items, and my gear didn't come back completely clean.

On Your Way

- Travel imposes certain physical demands to which you must adapt your running. The change in routine, airline flights, time, diet, and business responsibilities or being on your feet all day sight-seeing can all be very stressful. Travel conspires against your running, and it's often the last thing you feel like doing when you arrive after a tiring trip, especially to an unknown location. Therefore, try to do it before departure. Even if it means getting up at 4:30 A.M., I run before I travel.
- Beware of plane rides; they are more stressful than you might think. For this reason, I never do any hard or long runs before a long fight. In fact, Eastern European athletes are prohibited from training hard before a long flight.
- On a long airplane flight, walk, stretch, eat light, and drink plenty of water. If I get restless, I like to move around, and I always look for a few empty seats to stretch out if possible. I eat light—usually fish or vegetables—and drink plenty of water to prevent dehydration, common when flying and especially important for runners to avoid.
- Carry your gear on board. Ever since my luggage with my racing gear was lost before a major race, I always bring it on board in my hand luggage.

Once You're There

- Allow time to recover from jet lag. The general rule is that it takes about a day of adaptation for each hour of change in time zone. Therefore, to be on the safe side, I arrive from Norway about a week before a major race on the U.S. East Coast and allow three days from the East to the West Coast. In addition, I don't plan any hard workouts for at least two to three days after an overseas flight.
- If you can run in the morning, you'll be better off. It's best to get it done before other activities present unexpected scheduling or

fatigue. In addition, in major cities there is less traffic and fewer pedestrians to contend with in the morning. For a unique view of a city, run before daybreak.

- Be alert. Run defensively and cautiously. Don't challenge traffic signals or drivers. One small lapse of concentration can be dangerous on unknown streets or roads, like forgetting that the "right" direction for traffic is not the same in every country. In addition, make a point of asking about local customs. Many countries, for cultural or religious reasons, don't appreciate scantily clad runners. Even if the weather is warm, always bring long running pants just in case.

- Take a map, and if you're running alone, let someone know where you're going and about how long you will be gone. Carry identification, including the name and phone number of the hotel. If you're concerned about losing your way, choose a simple course, and run out and back for time. Always take money and, if you're running longer than a half hour and especially if it's hot, make sure you can get water along the way, even if you have to stop and buy it.

- Think ahead, and always be prepared. On occasions when I have been in a hotel not located near a running area, I have taken a cab to a large park. My brother Jan and I have had beautiful runs in the Bois de Boulogne, in Paris, and in a park in Dallas. The run along the Dallas lake was so peaceful. It didn't strike us just how peaceful until we were ready to leave and couldn't get a cab. We had to roam around in our shorts for a half hour before we found a telephone to call one.

Training Tips

- Don't neglect the proper warm-up and cool-down, including stretching. Leave time for your entire routine, even if it means cutting your run short. If you do supplementary exercises or find running uncomfortable in some locations, you can adapt your training to your hotel room. Try running in place (to radio music if it's available), jumping rope, or climbing the hotel stairs for a good workout, and instead of a fence or tree for stretching, try hotel bedposts or stairways.

- Be flexible about your workouts. Don't force yourself to adhere to a strict schedule in a panic about losing conditioning. It isn't worth the risk of injury or spoiling your trip. Tone down the intensity of your regular schedule to adapt for the change in routine. Any change in terrain or an erratic program, coupled with stress or fatigue, is an invitation to illness or injury. If new challenges present themselves, like mountains or beaches, don't think general fitness is enough to conquer them. Even the quality running you've been doing on a track or other hard, flat surfaces doesn't mean you are automatically adapted to racing up a mountain or running miles along sand.

- Use your running creatively. Be careful, but by all means be adventurous. There are runners everywhere; just ask for directions to a major park to find them. Use your running for sight-seeing, a unique way to experience a new location.

Recommended Reading

Averbuch, Gloria. *The Woman Runner*. New York: Simon & Schuster, 1984.
Bloom, Marc. *Cross Country Running*. Ottawa: Bhakti Press, 1978.
———. *The Marathon: What It Takes to Go the Distance*. New York: Holt, Rinehart and Winston, 1981.
Brock, Greg. *How Road Racers Train*. Los Altos, CA: Tafnews Press, 1980.
Brown, Skip, and John Graham. *Target 26*. New York: Collier Books, 1979.
Clayton, Derek. *Running to the Top*. Mountain View, CA: World Publications, 1980.
Coe, Sebastian, and Peter Coe. *Running for Fitness*. London: Pavilion Books, Ltd., 1983.
Daniels, Jack, Robert Fitts, and George Sheehan. *Conditioning for Distance Running*. New York: John Wiley & Sons, 1978.
Dellinger, Bill, and George Beres. *Winning Running*. Chicago: Contemporary Books, Inc., 1978.
———, Blaine Newham, and Warren Morgan. *The Running Experience*. Chicago: Contemporary Books, Inc., 1978.
Etchells, Andy, and Neil Wilson. *The Marathon Book*. London: Virgin Books, 1982.
Gambetta, Vern, ed. *How Women Runners Train*. Los Altos, CA: Tafnews Press, 1980.
Glover, Bob, and Pete Schuder. *The Competitive Runner's Handbook*. New York: Penguin Books, 1983.

————, and Jack Shepard. *The Runner's Handbook*. New York: Penguin Books, 1978.

Gruber, Elsa. *The Kids' Running Book*. New York: Grosset & Dunlap, 1979.

Heinonen, Tom, and Janet Heinonen. *All About Road Racing*. Los Altos, CA: Tafnews Press, 1979.

Henderson, Joe. *Run Farther, Run Faster*. Mountain View, CA: World Publications, 1979.

Humphreys, John, and Ron Holman. *Focus on the Marathon*. West Yorkshire, UK: EP Publishing, Ltd., 1983.

Jarver, Jess. *Long Distances*. Los Altos, CA: Tafnews Press, 1980.

————. *Middle Distances*. Los Altos, CA: Tafnews Press, 1979.

Lawrence, Allan, and Mark Scheid. *The Self-Coached Runner*. Boston: Little, Brown, 1984.

Liquori, Marty, and John Parker. *Marty Liquori's Guide for the Elite Runner*. Chicago: Playboy Press, 1980.

Lydiard, Arthur, and Garth Gilmour. *Running the Lydiard Way*. Mountain View, CA: World Publications, 1978.

McLaughlin, Joseph. *High School Cross Country*. Los Altos, CA: Tafnews Press, 1983.

Newsholme, Eric, and Tony Leech. *The Runner: Energy and Endurance*. Roosevelt, NJ: Fitness Books, 1983.

Olney, Ross. *The Young Runner*. New York: William Morrow & Co., 1978.

Pfeifer, Jack, ed. *How They Train: Long Distances*. Los Altos, CA: Tafnews Press, 1982.

Runner's World eds. *The Complete Runner*. Mountain View, CA: World Publications, 1978.

————. *The Complete Woman Runner*. Mountain View, CA: World Publications, 1979.

————. *Guide to Distance Running*. Mountain View, CA: World Publications, 1977.

Schreiber, Michael. *The Perfect Marathon*. Santa Fe, NM: John Muir Publications, 1980.

Shangold, Mona, M.D., and Gabe Mirkin, M.D. *The Complete Sports Medicine Book for Women*. New York: Simon & Schuster, 1985.

Smith, Bryan. *Joyce Smith's Running Book*. London: Fredrick Muller, Ltd., 1983.

Sparks, Ken, and Garry Bjorklund. *Long-Distance Runner's Guide to Training and Racing*. Englewood Cliffs, NJ: Prentice-Hall, Inc., 1984.

Squires, Bill, and Raymond Krise. *Improving Your Running*. Brattleboro, VT: The Stephen Greene Press, 1982.

Steffny, Manfred. *Marathoning*. Mountain View, CA: World Publications, 1979.

Temple, Cliff. *Challenge of the Marathon*. London: Stanley Paul, 1981.

———. *Cross Country and Road Running*. London: Stanley Paul, 1980.

———. *The Marathon Made Easier*. New York: Atheneum, 1982.

Ullyot, Joan, M.D. *The New Women's Running*. Brattleboro, VT: The Stephen Greene Press, 1976, 1984.

Valentine, Kimball. *Teenage Distance Running*. Los Altos, CA: Tafnews Press, 1973.

William Collins Sons, Ltd. *The AAA Runner's Guide*. London: William Collins Sons, Ltd., 1983.

Index

A

Achilles Track Club, New York, 47–48
Adidas, 29, 30, 32, 40
Advanced runners: balanced lifestyle for, 146–161; and burnout, 117–119; and coaching, 162–165; competitive racing for, 95–119; defined, 95; goals of, 96; mental powers and, 120–127; and overracing, 118–119; racing and, 105, 107, 111–112. *See also* Advanced runners' training
Advanced runners' training, 97–101; double workouts and, 102–103; and overtraining, 115–117; and supplementary exercise, 104–105; and time trials, 99–100; and training diary, 166–173; use of track for, 102; Waitz's sample training week for, 106; and workouts, 98–99
Age: competitive racing and, 96; running and, 47
Aggressiveness, running and, 125–126
Akti-Med, 40
Alcoholic beverages, 44, 215
Amenorrhea, women runners and, 189–192
American Running & Fitness Association, 105
Andersen, Arild, 8, 13, 15, 40, 80–81, 87
Andersen, Geir, 152–153
Andersen, Grete, 1–5; Athlete of the Year in 1974, 17; becomes Norwegian Junior Champion, 13; childhood, 11–14, 182–183; and death of boyfriend, 14–16; defeated at European championships in 1971, 14; first trip outside Scandinavia, 13–14; joins Vidar Sports Club, 12–13; lives with Jack Waitz, 17; love of competition, 11, 12; marries Jack Waitz, 17; meets Jack Waitz, 15; at Olympics in Munich in 1972, 16–17; parents' attitude toward running, 13, 14, 182–183; at teacher's college, 17. *See also* Waitz, Grete *for years after marriage*
Andersen, Jan, 8, 11, 40, 60, 80–81, 123, 148, 247
Andersen, Kari, 148–149, 150
Andersen-Schiess, Gabriella, 139
Ankle weights, 105
Anorexia, 200
Association of Road Racing Athletes (ARRA), 34
Athletes, drug use by, 34–38. *See also* Runners
Audain, Anne, 34
Averbuch, Gloria, 1–5, 6–10

B

Baked potato meal-in-one, 213
Balkan Games, 37

Baths or showers, 235
Beardsley, Dick, 133
Beginner runners, 47–65; advantages of running, 48; consistency and, 49–51; determination of proper pace, 55; goal-setting, 51–53; guidelines for, 53–56; and hurdles and breakthroughs, 61; and injuries, 61; and jogging, 54; lifestyle of, 59–65; and mood swings, 60–61; nutrition for, 63–64; and "runner's high," 59; and running form, 56; and running partners, 60; running schedule for, 62–63; ten-week program for, 56–59; and walking, 55; and weight loss, 64–65
Bjørn, Randi Langøgjelten, 196–197
Blisters, 87
Blood tests: for drugs, 118; for determining overtraining, 116–117
Boit, Mike, 16
Boston Marathon, 133
Brisco-Hooks, Valerie, 35
Budd, Zola, 156
Burnout, 117–119
Butt-ups, 230

C

Carbohydrate loading, 136–137, 140–141
Carey, Rick, 220
Cascade Run Off, 33, 34
Castella, Rob de, 55, 65, 109
Catalano, Patti, 34, 119
Chafing, 87
Chasnov, Marc, 220, 221, 222–223, 224, 235
Chicago Marathon, 1985, 133n
Children, running by, 151–152
Cigarettes, 44
Circuit training, 105
Clarke, Ron, 71
Clohessy, Pat, 109
Clothing for races, 235
Coaching, 162–165
Coghlan, Eamonn, 220
Concentration, 123
"Continuity principle," 71
Cool-down, 55, 63, 83
Cooper, Kenneth, 203
Costill, Dr. David, 73
Crackers, Norwegian dessert, 211
Cramps, 87
"Cross-training," 104–105

Cycling, 74, 104. *See also* Stationary biking
Cystic Fibrosis Foundation, 28

D

Damsgaard, Kristen, 8, 183
Defeats, 23–24, 153–157
Dehydration, 87, 88, 129, 215n. *See also* Fluid intake; Water intake
Dellinger, Bill, 68
Diary. *See* Training: diary
Diet, 117; pre-exercise, 63; pre-marathon, 136–137; and toilet needs during races, 88; Waitz's, 207–208. *See also* Nutrition
Dieting. *See* Weight reduction
Discipline, 124
Dixon, Rod, 114
Donaldson, Sam, 25, 27
Double workouts, 102–103; substitutes for, 104–105
Dreaming, before race, 81–82
Dropping out of race, 138–140
Drugs, 34–38; in Norway, 44; testing for, 34–35
Dynamic stretches, 228–231

E

Eastern Europeans: and drugs, 36–37; and sports psychology, 121. *See also* Russian women runners
Easy-cook fish, 209; in casserole, 210
Eating out, 215–216
Electrolyte-replacement drinks, 137–138, 224. *See also* XL-1
Endsjö, Dr. Thor Øistein, 116
European Championships: 1971, 14; 1974, 17; 1978, 18–19
Exercises: dynamic stretches, 228–231; pregnancy and, 194–199; in restoration therapy, 224–233; static stretches, 225–228; strengthening, 232–233; supplementary, 104–105; traveling and, 247–248; weight reduction and, 203

F

Falkum, Dr. Leif Roar, 116, 117
Falling, 84, 85, 156
Fame, impact on Waitz, 25–28
Fartlek, 72, 98–99, 118

Fast foods, 42–43, 63
Fatigue, 60–61; and burnout, 118; and marathon racing, 138; rest and, 70–71; signs of, 54, 73–74. *See also* Restoration therapy
Female athletes. *See* Women runners
Feminism, women athletes and, 183–184
Fish recipes: easy-cook, 209; easy-cook in casserole, 210; in foil, 208–209; simple boiled, 210; soup, 210
Fitness, 3; of American children, 151–152; definitions of, 41; instant, 49–50; in Norway and U.S. compared, 41–46; running and, 48; in U.S., 146–147
Fluid intake, 117, 129, 215; during marathons, 137–138. *See also* Water intake
Focus, peaking and, 108
Fonda, Jane, 147
Food. *See* Diet; Nutrition

G

Galli, Dr. Lou, 218
Geitost, 43
Geldwert, Dr. Josef, 218
Ginton, Bruria, 222, 223
Goals: for beginner runners, 51–53; scheduling races and, 89–90; training program and, 72–73
Grete Waitz Foundation, 9, 28
Grete Waitz Run for women, 8, 28, 153, 186
Grete Waitz's no-time-to-cook cookbook, 211–213
Guinness Book of World Records, The, 18

H

Hair care, 200–201
Hard/easy system, 69–71, 90
Health education, in Norway, 43
Healthwalking, 55
Heart rate, determination of overtraining and, 116. *See also* Resting pulse
High-carbohydrate diet, 203–204
Hoffmeister, Gunhild, 121
Holidays, 110
Homemade two-step tomato vegetable soup, 212

Houston Marathon, 1983, 195
Hurdle stretch, 226

I

Injuries, 61, 69, 219; and active rest, 74; beginner runners and, 54. *See also* Pain
Intermediate runners' training program, 66–94; basic rules, 69–74; and determination of amount of training, 73–74; hard/easy system, 69–71; individual needs and, 66–68; marathons and, 135, 140; and quality training, 71–73
International Amateur Athletic Federation (IAAF), 32, 35
International Olympic Committee, petition to, 186–187
Interval training, 72, 98, 118
Israeli athletes, murder at 1972 Olympics, 16

J

Jet lag, 246–247
Jogging, 54, 66

K

K-jog, 43–44
Kaggestad, Johan, 162, 165
Kardong, Don, 34
Kick, 113–114
Kristiansen, Ingrid, 68, 108, 121 133n, 162, 187, 195–196, 197, 198

L

Lebow, Fred, 128
L'eggs Mini Marathon: 1979, 83, 186; 1983, 157; 1985, 78, 156, 185
Legs, heaviness in, 74, 116
Lewis, Carl, 79
Lie, Ingrid Ellingson, 215
Lifestyle, of runners, 59–65; balanced, 146–161; children and, 151–152; fitness obsession and, 146–147; perspective and, 153–157; planning time and, 148–149; relationships and, 150–151; stress management and, 157–161. *See also* Norway: lifestyle in
Lloyd, Chris Evert, 165

London Marathon, 1983, 127, 144–145
Lopes, Carlos, 96, 108, 149, 204
Lower back stretch, 231–232

M

Make-up, 201
Maracescu, Natalia, 37
Marathon races, 128–145; cutoff points
    for, 132; decision to run in, 147;
    dropping out of, 138–140; and
    fatigue, 138; fluid intake during, 137–
    138; number of runners finishing,
    130n; preparations for first, 134–137;
    reasons for running in, 132;
    recommended annual number of, 141;
    recovery from, 140–142; and respect
    for the distance, 133–134; starting
    problems in, 84–85; Waitz's
    performances in, 236–237; Waitz's
    training schedules for, 142–145
Massage, 218, 221, 222–223. *See also*
    Self-massage
Matpakke sandwich, 212
Media. *See* Press
Medical officials, 139
Melpomene Institute for Women's Health
    Research, 197
Menstruation, women runners and,
    189–192
Mental fatigue, postrace, 84
Mental powers, racing and, 120–127;
    and aggression, 125–126;
    concentration and, 123; and
    discipline, 124; mental toughness and,
    123; and pain, 126–127; and psycho-
    regulatory training, 223–224; and
    self-confidence, 124–125; and
    visualization, 121–122
Møller, Kai, 169
Moller, Lorraine, 34
Money: under-the-table, 33; racing and,
    32–34
Mood swings, 60–61
Motivation, mental powers and, 121
Muscle soreness, 61. *See also* Tying up

N

Naps, 160
Negative splits, 108
Nenow, Mark, 167
Nervousness, 79–80, 160
New York City Marathons, 93n;
    applications for, 79; disabled runners
    in, 48; fame and, 25–26; 1978, 7, 19,
    20–21, 128–131; 1980, 80, 161;
    1981, 137, 155–156; 1982, 23, 142–
    143; 1983, 84, 85, 114; 1984, 80–81,
    123, 145, 161; 1985, 30, 123, 133n;
    preparations for, 132; prize money in,
    33, 34; Waitz's victories in, 24, 25–26;
    women runners and, 184, 188
New York Times, The, 37
Norway: attitude toward famous people
    in, 26; fitness in, 41–46; K-jog
    program in, 43–44; lifestyle in, 41–
    46; Nazi occupation of, 9; sports in,
    42; typical diet in, 205–206. *See also*
    entries under "Norwegian"
Norwegian dessert crackers, 211
Norwegian Federation, 18
Norwegian Nutrition Council, 214
Norwegian Olympic Committee, 28, 40
Norwegian press, 17, 18–19
Norwegian Sports Federation, definition
    of sport, 41
Norwegian Track and Field Federation,
    32, 116
Nutrition, 63–64, 202–217; common
    sense rules from Norwegian Nutrition
    Council on, 214; cooking tips and,
    216–217; and eating out, 215–216; in
    Norway, 205–206; and Norwegian
    recipes, 208–213; prerun and prerace,
    77–78, 214–215; and restoration
    therapy, 224; in U.S. and Norway
    compared, 42–43; and Waitz's
    shopping list, 213

O

Olympic Games: marathons, 120, 130;
    1972, Munich, 16–17, 36; 1976,
    Montreal, 17–18; 1980, Moscow, 17;
    1984, Los Angeles, 17, 24, 126;
    politics and, 16–17; rumors about
    drugs at, 36
Oslo Breakfast Program, 43, 203
Overtraining, 115–117, 156; blood tests
    for determination of, 116–117; and
    marathons, 136; symptoms of, 74; and
    training diary, 167–168

P

Pacing, 107–108; and avoiding tying up,
    86; controversy over in mixed races,
    184–185; in marathons, 133; and
    surging, 113

Packing tips, 245–246
Pain, 126–127; and marathon racing,
  129–130. *See also* Injuries
Peaking, 108–110
Pedersen, Terje, 11–12
Perspective, racing and, 153–157
Petrova, Tonka, 37
Physical checkups, 53
Physical problems, racing and, 85–89.
  See also Injuries
Politics, Olympics and, 16–17
Porridge, Saturday night, 211
Posture, 235
Potato, baked, meal-in-one, 213
Pregnancy, women runners and, 192–
  199; exercise guidelines during, 198–
  199
President's Council on Physical Fitness
  and Sports, 41; Physical Fitness test,
  151–152
Press: and New York City Marathon, 24–
  25; and Weitz signing of International
  Olympics Committee petition, 187;
  and women athletes, 183. *See also*
  Norwegian press
Pressure, fame and, 27–28
Prize money. *See* Money
Product endorsements, 29–30
Psycho-regulatory training, 223–224
Puica, Maricica, 111

Q

Quality training, 71–73; for advanced
  runners, 97–101; double workouts
  and, 102–103; for marathons, 135

R

Racecourse, familiarity with, 78
Racewalking, 55
Racing, 75–94: for advanced runners,
  95–119; age and, 96; and aggression,
  125–126; for children, 152–153; and
  concentration, 123; and discipline,
  124; entry blank and, 78; familiarity
  with course, 78; gear preparation, 78;
  intangibles involved in, 92–94; kick
  and, 113–114; logistics, 77–79; male-
  female inequality in, 187–188;
  menstruation and, 190–191; mental
  power and, 120–127; mental
  rehearsal for, 79–82; nervousness
  and, 79–80; nutrition prior to, 214–

215; pacing and, 107–108; and pain,
  126–127; and peaking, 108–110;
  post-pregnancy, 197; and postrace
  recovery, 83–84; potential physical
  problems of, 84–85; preparation for,
  76–83; reasons for, 75–76;
  scheduling races, 89–92; and self-
  confidence, 124–125; spectators and,
  76; strategies, 111–112; and stress
  management, 157–161; surging and,
  113; tapering off training before, 76–
  77; toilet needs during, 88–89;
  training for, 97–101; traveling and,
  246–247; and visualization technique,
  121–122; Waitz's competitions and
  race analysis, 1971–78, 180–181. *See
  also* Marathon races
Racing gear, traveling with, 246
Reagan, Ronald, 24–25
Recipes, Norwegian, 208–213
Recovery: double workouts and, 103;
  from marathon races, 140–142;
  overtraining and, 115–116; postrace,
  83–84. *See also* Restoration therapy
Rest, 70–71; and marathon training,
  136; peaking and, 109–110
Resting pulse, determination of amount
  of training and, 73–74
Restoration therapy, 218–235; defined,
  220–221; exercises, 224–233; general
  tips, 235; and massage, 222–223; and
  nutrition, 224; and psycho-regulatory
  training, 223–224; recovery and
  performance and, 218–221; and self-
  massage, 234
Retirement, 39–40
"Rigging." *See* Tying up
Rodgers, Bill, 65
Roe, Allison, 34, 119, 133
Rudolph, Wilma, 121
Runners: age of, 47; attitudes toward
  fellow competitors, 156–157; body
  types of, 65; compared with joggers,
  66; diet and nutrition for, 202–217;
  disabled, 48; and drugs, 36–38; fluid
  intake of, 215; form for, 56; lifestyle
  of, 45; money and, 29–30; product
  endorsements and commercials by,
  29–31; schedule for, 62–63; secrets of
  success, 3; shoes for, 240–244; total
  fitness and, 48; training diary for,
  166–173; in U.S., 41–42. *See also*
  Advanced runners; Beginner runners;
  Intermediate runners' training
  program; Lifestyle; Racing; Women
  runners
"Runner's high," 59

Runner's World race, 20–21
Running Great with Grete Waitz (video), 30
Running shoes. *See* Shoes
Russian women runners, 17–18, 114; racing strategy, 111
Ryffel, Markus, 168

S

Salazar, Alberto, 68, 119, 133
Saleh, Ahmed, 133*n*
Samuelson, Joan Benoit, 65, 68, 81, 94, 108, 111, 112, 120, 126, 133*n*, 152, 165
Sandoval, Dr. Tony, 38
Sandwiches, matpakke, 212
Saturday night porridge, 211
Save the Children, 28
Seko, Toshihiko, 68
Self-confidence, 124–125
Self-massage, 234–235
Sevene, Bob, 108
Sex testing, 35–36
Shangold, Dr. Mona, 192
Shoes, 53, 87, 240–244; care of, 242; selection of, 240–241; trends in, 243–244; wear, 242
Short interval workouts, 114
Shorter, Frank, 130
Silver medal, attitude of Norwegian press toward, 18, 19
Simple boiled fish, 210
Skin care, 200–201
Slaney, Mary Decker, 65, 84, 156, 187
Sly, Wendy, 111, 157, 201
Smith, Geoff, 133
Smith, Joyce, 96
Spectators, effect on racers, 76
Speedwork. *See* Quality training
Split squat, 228–229
Spot reducing, 49
Starting, in mass race, 84–85
Static stretches, 225–228
Stationary biking, 196, 221
Steroids, 36, 38
Stomach and intestinal problems, 87–88
Straddle stretch, 227
Strengthening exercises, 63, 232–233
Stress management, 91, 157–161
Stretches. *See* Dynamic stretches; Static stretches
Strömme, Sigmund B., 116
Surging, 113
Swimming, 74, 104, 196, 221

T

"Talk test," 55*n*
Target heart rate, 53, 55
Team Xerox, 29
Ten-week beginning running program, 56–59
Time trials, 99–100
Toilet needs during races, 88–89
Tomato vegetable soup, homemade, 212
Training, 19; aids, 105; amenorrhea and, 190; balanced lifestyle and, 147–151; for children, 152; diary, 166–173; holidays from, 110; for marathons, 129, 131, 132, 135–136; Norwegian compared with U.S., 97; practicing kick in, 114; during pregnancy, 195, 196; rigors of, 39; tapering off before race, 76–77; on track, 102, 105, 107; traveling and, 247–248; Waitz's schedules for marathons, 142–145; Waitz's summary and analysis of, 1971–78, 174–180. *See also* Intermediate runners' training program; Quality training; Restoration therapy
Traveling to races, 78–79; defeats and, 109; stress and, 160
Treadmill tests, 72–73
Trunk twists, 231
Tying up, 85–87

U

Ulmasova, Svyetlana, 23–24
United States: attitude toward famous people in, 25–26; fitness in, 41–46, 146–147, 151–152; running boom in, 41–42; thinness obsession in, 200
Upper back stretch, 228

V

Vainio, Martti, 37–38
Vidar Sports Club, 12–13, 15
Viren, Lasse, 109
Visualization, 121–122
Vitamin megadoses, 215

W

Waitz, Grete: attitude toward breaking records, 21–22; attitude toward defeats, 144–146, 156–157; attitude toward drugs, 34–38; attitude toward fame, 25–28; attitude toward financial aspects of racing, 32–34; attitude toward marathons, 131; attitude toward retirement, 39–40; awards and rankings, 239–240; career highlights, 236–240; career from 1965 to 1978, 11–19; charity work, 28; competition, 1971–78, 180; cross-country titles, 237; daily diet, 207–208; decides to run on own, 18; and decision on having children, 192–194; defeats, 22, 23–24, 109; early sports of, 50–51; eating habits of, 43; and European Championships of 1978, 18–19; first New York City Marathon, 7, 128–131; first world record, 17; food shopping, 213; gives up teaching, 28–29; impact of world records on, 20–22; income, 29–30; injuries, 23, 69, 219; lifestyle, 45–46, 148–149; marathon performances, 236–237; and marriage, 222; meets *Dynasty* cast, 25; meets Reagan 24–25; obstacles to running career, 182–184; and overtraining, 115–117; personal records, 238–239; personality of, 5, 6–7, 8–10, 27; physical effects of running on, 189–192; pressures on, 18–19, 22–24; race analysis, 1971–78, 181; racing schedule, 90, 91–92; racing strategy, 111–112; reaction to drug use, 36–37; reasons for racing, 75–76; and restoration therapy, 218–221; road racing highlights, 239; running partners, 60; running shoes, 244; sample training week, 106; and sex testing, 35–36; and signing of petition to International Olympics Committee, 186–187; summary and analysis of career training, 174–180; track highlights, 238; training diary, 168–173; training methods, 19, 67–69; training schedules, 97–98, 142–145; travels, 24–25, 245; on writing book, 1–5. *See also* Andersen, Grete

for years before marriage
Waitz, Jack, 1, 2, 3, 4, 5, 6, 8–9, 10, 21–22, 32, 33, 39, 40, 60, 62, 74, 76, 80–81, 100, 110, 123, 127, 131, 137, 160, 194, 223; as agent for Grete Waitz, 30, 31; attitude toward Grete Waitz's career, 151; background, 9; coaching role, 17, 18, 23–24, 162, 164; and defeats, 23–24; lives with Grete Andersen, 17; marries Grete Andersen, 17; meets Grete Andersen, 15; role as sports psychologist, 224
Walkers Club of America, 55
Walking, 55, 74
Wall stretch, 225
Warm-ups, 55, 63, 82, 107
Water intake, 63, 64, 88. *See also* Fluid intake
Weather, racing and, 48, 90–91, 132, 137
Weight gloves, 105
Weight reduction, 16, 64–65, 202–203
Weight training, 104–105
Welch, Priscilla, 96
Whirlpools, 221
White sauce, 211
Women runners, 182–201; body image, 199–200; competition with men, 187–188; hair and skin care, 200–201; menstruation and, 189–192; obstacles and progress, 182–188; physical effects of sport on, 189–201; pregnancy and, 192–199
Workouts: double, 102–103; to practice kick, 114n; to practice surging, 113n
World Championships, Helsinki, 1983, 21–22, 35–36, 131, 143–144
World Cross Country Championships: 1978, 35; 1983, 113; 1984, 76
World Cup marathon, 1983, 94
World records, impact on Waitz, 20–22

X

XL-1 (drink), 29, 137–138, 207n